The Singing Bourgeois

Songs of the Victorian Drawing Room and Parlour

Derek B Scott

Open University Press
Milton Keynes · Philadelphia

for my mother, Jean

Open University Press
Open University Educational Enterprises Limited
12 Cofferidge Close
Stony Stratford
Milton Keynes MK11 1BY

and
242 Cherry Street
Philadelphia, PA 19106, USA

First Published 1989

British Library Cataloguing in Publication Data

Scott, Derek
    The singing bourgeois: songs of the
    Victorian drawing-room and parlour.—
    (Popular music in Britain).
    1. Popular songs in English, history
    I. Title   II. Series
    784'.0942

    ISBN 0-335-15291-0
    ISBN 0-335-15296-1 Pbk

Library of Congress Cataloging-in-Publication Data

Scott, Derek B.
    The singing bourgeois/Derek B. Scott.
        p.   cm.—(Popular music in Britain)
    Bibliography: p.
    Includes indexes.
    1. Popular music—England—To 1901. I. Title. II. Series.
ML3492.S4 1988
784.5'00942—dc19   88-19625   CIP   MN
    ISBN 0-335-15291-0   ISBN 0-335-15296-1 (pbk.)

Typeset by Rowland Phototypesetting Limited
Bury St Edmunds, Suffolk.
Printed in Great Britain by St Edmundsbury Press Limited
Bury St Edmunds, Suffolk.

Contents

Editorial Preface

What *is* British popular music? Does such a thing exist? What makes certain music and songs popular? And who made the musical cultures of these islands? What did Scots, Welsh, Irish and North American people have to do with the process? What part did people in the English regions play – the Geordies, Cockneys, Midlanders and all the rest? Where did the Empire fit in? How did European 'high' culture affect what most people played and sang? And how did all these factors vary in significance over time? In the end, just how much do we know about the history of musical culture on these tiny patches of land? The truth is that we know very little, and this realization led to this series.

The history of British people and culture has been dominated by capitalism for centuries; and capitalism helped to polarize people into classes not only economically, but culturally too. Music was never *simply* music: songs were never *simply* songs. Both were produced and used by particular people in particular historical periods for particular reasons, and we have recognized this in the way in which we have put this series together.

Every book in this series aims to exemplify and to foster inter-disciplinary research. Each volume studies not only 'texts' and performances, but institutions and technology as well, and the culture practices and sets of social relationships through which music and songs were produced, disseminated and consumed. Ideas, values, attitudes and what is generally referred to as ideology are taken into account, as are factors such as gender, age, geography and traditions. Nor is our series above the struggle. We do not pretend to have helped produce an objective record. We are, unrepentantly, on the side of the majority, and our main perspective is from 'below', even though the whole musical field needs to be in view. We hope that by clarifying the history of popular musical culture we can help clear the ground for a genuinely democratic musical culture of the future.

Dave Harker and Richard Middleton

Acknowledgements

Thanks to:

The series editors, Richard Middleton and Dave Harker, who offered constructive criticism, encouragement, and advice throughout my writing of this book. (If the reader perceives defects in my work, they more than likely result from my failure to act upon some of that advice.)

Sara Dodd, who listened, argued, and helped me to sort out my ideas.

Donald Campbell, who did his utmost to ensure that his beloved Gaelic language was correctly spelt by me.

Margaret Turner, who speedily and accurately prepared my final typescript.

The staff who assisted me at the British Library, the National Library of Scotland, Hull Central Library's Music Department, and the Brynmor Jones Library at the University of Hull.

Introduction

This is not the first book in the Open University Press's *Popular Music in Britain* series to challenge assumptions about a particular body of music. At issue, here, is the myth constructed around 'Victorian parlour song', a term almost always used as if it denoted a clear-cut genre characterized by stereotyped musical and literary features. In fact, there was a remarkable variety of musical forms and styles of song acceptable in the Victorian middle-class home. Some of these, indeed, were firmly established well before Victoria came to the throne, such as the 'refined' traditional air and the English operatic air – though nothing now seems to immediately evoke an atmosphere considered more quintessentially Victorian than 'The Last Rose of Summer' (from a volume of Moore's *Irish Melodies* published in 1813) or 'Home, Sweet Home!' (from Bishop's English opera *Clari* of 1823). Religious nonconformists were brazenly eclectic in commandeering whatever musical features could be made to function in their interests and favoured a strong, tuneful idiom which also frequently found its way into the parlour. Later, the music of the blackface minstrel show and the 'respectable' type of music-hall song were added to the drawing-room repertoire. The desire to categorize a particular portion of all this as 'Victorian parlour song' by reference to an arbitrary selection of musical and literary criteria has created a 'parlour song' consensus in its own way as misleading as the 'folksong' consensus attacked by Dave Harker.[1] It is to avoid such categorization that I call this book *The Singing Bourgeois*.

The 'parlour song' consensus, it should be stressed, is not something that has been as systematically constructed by key mediators in the same manner as the 'folksong' consensus but results rather from a sloppy use of terminology (for example, using the term 'parlour song' sociologically but actually trying to define it musicologically). There again, some writers use the term with the intention not of referring to the whole range of songs sung in the middle-class home, but of pinpointing those songs aimed directly at the domestic market. Yet, this is unhelpful because the real target of the sheet-music publication of almost all Victorian song is the middle-class home.

Even when some of the diverse ingredients of bourgeois song began to solidify under the influence of the Ballad Concerts promoted by the music publisher Boosey, it remains difficult to formulate an empirical definition of what constitutes the typical Boosey ballad. Here is an attempt from *The New Grove Dictionary of Music and Musicians*: 'The texts were sentimental verses about love, gardens and birds, the music simple strophic settings marked by easy melody, stereotyped accompaniments, and maudlin harmonic progressions.'[2] One of the three 'typical' examples chosen to illustrate this, Sullivan's 'The Lost Chord', is *not* about love, gardens, or birds; it is *not* a simple strophic setting; it is melodically awkward in parts rather than easy (see Chapter 7); and its piano accompaniment is unusual in having been contrived to suggest a church organ. Whether its harmony is maudlin or not is a question which needs to be considered in relation to 'presentist' value judgements discussed below. It is evident that a 'parlour song' or 'drawing-room ballad' is going to be more easily defined sociologically as a song designed or appropriated for bourgeois domestic consumption.

In the nineteenth century the description 'parlour song' is extremely rare, although 'drawing-room ballad' is often encountered (and with increasing frequency after the establishment of Boosey's Ballad Concerts in 1867). In the first half of the century the description 'popular song' was very common; like 'favourite' and 'celebrated' it was used by publishers to suggest widespread demand. A guarantee of quality followed, because a song could be popular in a commercial sense only by attracting sufficient numbers of musically literate bourgeois consumers. Naturally the bourgeoisie thought the songs they enjoyed were of unquestionable merit and took comfort in the knowledge that, if a song was described on its sheet music as 'popular', it automatically implied that it was regularly performed in 'respectable' homes.[3]

In the succeeding pages I choose to employ the term 'drawing-room ballad' rather than 'popular song' in order to avoid possible confusion about the class orientation of this material. I must stress, however, that I use it as a generic and not a specific term until we reach the 1870s; from then on there was, indeed, a move towards a standardization of songs which were accorded this label (there is more on this subject in Chapters 6 and 7). I would like to argue that used generically 'drawing-room ballad' helps to locate a cohesive body of song of a class-aligned nature. The tightly controlled, written-out structures of songs produced for the drawing room are singularly adaptive to bourgeois individualist ideology; the performer implicit in these structures is an interpretative servant of the songwriter. This is not to say that bourgeois songs cannot be appropriated by the working class, who – as will be seen in Chapter 9 – have the possibility of constructing new meanings in the way they 'consume' them. Conversely, the bourgeoisie are able to appropriate working-class musical practices and through the effort of mediation assimilate oppositional elements.

Apart from the easy judgements that have been made in categorizing bourgeois domestic song, our understanding of this music has been hampered by the contempt now heaped upon it from some quarters. The expression 'presentism' has been coined to describe a critical vision which implies that our present values are objective rather than historically conditioned. 'Informed' critics of the nineteenth century were equally convinced of their objectivity in describing Restoration comedy as the result of an embarrassing lapse of artistic standards. The status of an artistic genre is better regarded as 'whatever is valued by certain people in specific situations, according to particular criteria and in the light of given purposes.'[4] The modernist musicologist's scorn for bourgeois domestic song arises from its failure to meet the criteria of the Western 'art music' tradition, in which an assumption is made that art progresses under its own laws independently of the material basis of the society within which it is produced.[5] The movement of art is therefore interpreted as a succession of styles, each led and perfected by creative geniuses. Modernist theory accepts with equanimity the absence for centuries of 'important' female composition, and even that an entire country may be without any real music – before Smetana, for example, 'there had been no genuine Czech music.'[6] From this perspective, which still so often sets the terms of the debate, a figure as important to British musical life in the nineteenth century as Sullivan can be dismissed in half a sentence,[7] having failed to illustrate a purely musical-historical movement.

An alternative theoretical framework exists, in which the nineteenth-century bourgeois songwriters can be seen as inextricably bound to and providing a cultural response to the society of which they form a part. Song production can be located in terms of its function and use, its relationship to class dominance and hegemonic struggle. The bourgeois 'popular song' was the first product which showed how music might be profitably incorporated into a system of capitalist enterprise. It is in the production, promotion, and marketing of the sheet music to these songs (and the pianos to accompany them) that we witness the birth of the modern music industry. As already noted, for whatever apparent reason a song was originally written (say, for an English opera), it was possible for it to be tailored to the requirements of amateur music-making in the middle-class home.

Class is a problematic term which warrants a few words of explanation. Class is only discernible in a relationship: when I use the term 'middle class' or 'bourgeoisie' I refer in the eighteenth century to merchants, artisans, and shopkeepers; in the nineteenth century I refer to the capital half of the capital /labour relationship. It is important to remember that class is a process; the middle class is constantly changing and adapting. It can be argued that the term 'middle class' immediately hypostasizes this process. The description 'bourgeoisie' is preferred by many writers on the Victorian period to avoid the seeming contradiction of a dominant class being given a label which carries a suggestion of a fixed hierarchical position beneath the aristocracy.

Along with coercion, a class manifests its supremacy by exercising *hegemony*, a key political term employed by Gramsci in his *Prison Notebooks* to describe 'intellectual and moral leadership'.[8] The dominant culture in a society is hegemonic: it aims to win its position of ascendancy through consent rather than impose itself by force. Hegemony is a process of struggle which often calls for compromise: for example, in the later nineteenth century membership of a trade union was finally accorded respectability. The state apparatus is invaluable in establishing hegemony; the dominant culture is mediated through institutions such as schools, in, for instance, the choice of songs for teaching purposes (a topic touched on in Chapter 9). It might be thought that the diversity of ideology found in bourgeois songs (drinking v. temperance, belligerence v. compassion) argues strongly against the theory of hegemony. Gramsci, however, argues that bourgeois hegemony necessitates an alliance of fractions, a 'historical bloc'; it therefore follows that the dominant culture is not homogeneous but subject to (and able to tolerate) conflicting strands within the hegemonic alliance. Since the 'Glorious Revolution' of 1688 the middle class had held a share of power, but the middle class did not become the hegemonic class until the nineteenth century, after a long period of struggle marked by important victories in 1832 (the passing of the Reform Bill) and 1846 (Repeal of the Corn Laws). There should not, then, be any surprise to find the eighteenth-century middle class enjoying the satire in Gay's *The Beggar's Opera* directed at a government which was in part middle class. The power bloc which allows stable class rule is only achieved through struggle between various contending classes and fractions; only one class within the alliance may exercise hegemony, but the dominant culture (although in itself hegemonic) will contain evidence of the conflicts within that alliance. Notice that a key Victorian term *respectable* has a hegemonic function: it connotes adherence to a code of what is socially acceptable and thus seeks to impose a behavioural conformity which sanctions the existing social structures. The terms 'polite' and 'wholesome' are used in a similar fashion, to lay down the correctness of certain social values.

I should now explain what I mean by 'dominant culture', and clarify the standpoint from which I view the relationship of art to the society within which it is produced. One of the sources of Gramsci's theory of hegemony was a statement by Marx: 'The ideas of the ruling class are in every epoch the ruling ideas, i.e. the class which is the ruling *material* force of society is at the same time its ruling intellectual force.'[9] In feudal society paying homage to one's lord seemed natural, just as consumerism seems natural in a society based on generalized commodity production. A quotation from Marx's 'Preface' to his *Critique of Political Economy* sheds further light on the subject: 'It is not the consciousness of men that determines their existence but, on the contrary, their social existence determines their consciousness.'[10] A little earlier in the same work Marx introduces the notion of economic base and ideological superstructure, a model which gave rise to a type of Marxist theory now commonly referred to as 'vulgar Marxism', 'reflectionism', or 'economic determinism'. This asserted the primacy of the economic base and reduced the complex relationship between that and the world of ideas to one of rigid determinism. The seductiveness of reflectionist thinking can be illustrated by the argument that playing the piano was considered such an essential accomplishment for well-bred Victorian girls because the major commodities of the music industry were pianos and sheet music (and today musical literacy is no longer valued because records are a more important commodity than sheet music). An argument like this, of course, begs many questions, including why playing the piano was more important for girls than boys. Evidence that economic determinism was already gaining theoretical ground in the late nineteenth century is shown by Engels' desire to emphasize that the economic element is not the sole determining factor.[11] Recent Marxists have been at pains to stress the dialectic between social existence and social consciousness rather than fall back on the mechanical metaphor of base and superstructure.

The culturalists and structuralists of the 1970s, with their contending paradigms, were at least agreed in attributing *relative autonomy* to the artist (albeit for different reasons). Culturalists stressed that social existence, including cultural experience, influences and conditions consciousness rather than determines consciousness, allowing an active role for human agency. Structuralists under-lined the importance of differing pre-existing systems of signification present in each field of creativity – if ideological signs determine consciousness then it is always with the understanding that those signs mean different things to different social groups. My own approach is oriented towards culturalism in so far as I seek to examine these songs in relation to the class outlook of the Victorian bourgeoisie. The concept of the 'hegemonic bloc' I also find helpful in contribut-ing to an understanding and explanation of the internal conflicts within the bourgeoisie (who ought not to be viewed as monolithic). Overall I adopt what may be called the 'popular culture' perspective as opposed to the 'mass culture' perspective. The latter tends to focus on the depraving effects of the 'culture industry', whereas the hallmark of the 'popular culture' perspective is that meaning is made in the consumption – here is a space for relative autonomy and hegemonic negotiation. The 'popular culture' perspective does, of course, pose a challenge to the uncritical acceptance of 'high culture'. I should add, in conclud-ing this section, that there is no easy one-to-one relationship between art and social history: for example, it is possible to find melancholy songs in times of economic buoyancy (or when a war is going well) and optimistic or romantic songs in times of depression.

The historical specificity of this book now needs explaining. I start in the eighteenth century in discussing the foundations of bourgeois domestic song styles not because there is any kind of absolute beginning there, but because the performance of the politically combative *Beggar's Opera* seems a more significant cultural moment than, say, the publication of Yonge's *Musica Transalpina* (a collection illustrating the importance of bourgeois taste in the late sixteenth century). I close the survey around the year 1898 when the drawing-room ballad of the Boosey type was wilting in the face of the challenge from Tin Pan Alley as the United States of America moved to dominate the commercial music industry. That year, too, musical comedy from the United States was exciting interest after the sensational London première of Kerker's *The Belle of New York*. Furthermore, dissemination of music was soon to be transformed: the pianola had arrived in 1897 and the English Gramophone Company set up business the following year.

In the first chapter I have tried to locate the roots of that distinctive character which lends a homogeneity to nineteenth-century bourgeois song-types. There is some inevitable cramming in my attempt to condense within a single chapter everything in the eighteenth century which I thought relevant. Chapter 2 examines the early amateur music market, and Chapter 3 follows this up by concentrating on the opportunity taken by women, who were so crucial to this market, to write songs themselves. Chapter 4 considers the manner in which the ethnic cultures of Celts and Afro-Americans were subject to assimilation by the English and North American bourgeoisie (symptomatic of this was the creation of two new 'American' instruments, the five-string banjo and the 'concert D' uilleann pipes). Chapter 5 has a religious theme; it deals chronologically with the range of sacred music which became available and discusses the emergence of the 'sacred song' as a branch of the drawing-room repertoire. All these chapters are concerned mainly with pre-1870 developments.

After 1870 a period of rapid growth begins which sees the development of a more organized music industry, so Chapter 6 returns to the subject of the music market during these years and the changes being brought about by the increasing professionalization of music. Chapter 7 tries to demonstrate the extent of formula following during the post-1870 ballad boom. For that purpose it has been necessary to include detailed analyses in order to show how my conclusions have been obtained (a Glossary of Musical Terms is at the rear of the book). A problem I feel I have not resolved in this chapter is how to explain artistic distinction without romantic mystification. The next two chapters are on subjects which range over the entire period: Chapter 8 looks at bourgeois song in the context of the growth of English nationalism and the continuity/discontinuity debate concerning British imperialism; Chapter 9 deals in brief with bourgeois song and hegemony (a whole book could be written on the subject). At various points the reader is referred to additional relevant material via the footnotes. In the final chapter I give an account of the dilemma facing ballad composers as a result of the challenge from the United States and the simultaneous feeling of exhaustion which had overtaken the British ballad.

In the main, given fair representation of song types and influential composers, my selection of songs for the purpose of analysis has been directly related to their degree of commercial success, in the belief that the producer/consumer relationship is clearest where the mutual rewards are apparently highest. Nevertheless, failure is also important, since it helps to define the tolerances of the genre when pulled in the direction of either of the polar extremes of novelty or familiarity. In Chapter 7 I discuss a failure like Adams and Weatherly's *The Light of the World* because it shows that the application of a familiar formula does not guarantee success, thus offering further confirmation of the relative autonomy of the consumer.

The contemporary relevance of a study of nineteenth-century bourgeois domestic song extends beyond the insight it provides on the workings of the commercial music industry and on the continuing resonances of this music which may be felt in twentieth-century gospel and country music. To the nineteenth-century bourgeoisie it was never simply a question of how best to produce and consume a particular musical product, but how to put into practice the belief that music-making was of benefit to everyone's development as a human being. Any future society which thinks practical musicianship to be life enhancing will have to address the same question. There was a genuine, if ideologically motivated, attempt in the mid-nineteenth century to promote the *musica practica* that Barthes regards as having almost disappeared from high culture.[12] Of course, drawing-room ballads were never popular in any truly democratic sense; Victorian domestic music was class based and reinforced bourgeois ideology (particularly that of the family). All the same, there was a search for a kind of music which would permit maximum participation. In recent times punk rock may be seen as a determined though brief attempt to develop a proletarian democratic style derived from the 'garage band'.[13] Vastly different in almost every respect as the music of the Sex Pistols was from that of Stephen Foster, they each represented the ultimate simplicity and directness in their respective genres and thus helped to demonstrate the enormous potential for diversity of expression those qualities may contain.

1   *The Foundations of the Drawing-room Genre*

The multifaceted edifice of bourgeois 'popular song' was built upon foundations laid in the eighteenth century: the most important of these were the English opera, the collections of arrangements of 'traditional airs' and the Table Entertainments pioneered by Dibdin. The not insignificant part played by nonconformist hymns will be considered elsewhere in this book, as will the influence in mid-century of Afro-American music. Bourgeois song was obviously indebted to aristocratic musical practice and to the cosmopolitan musical character of eighteenth-century London. In the first half of the century rich merchants aped the manners of the upper class. An interest in the art patronized by the aristocracy was a proof of social distinction for the upwardly mobile. Hogarth satirized this behaviour and depicted in *Marriage à la Mode*, 4 (1745), a merchant's daughter who aspires to upper-class values by listening to a castrato singer and collecting 'decadent' art objects. The court remained the focal point of musical activity during the reign of George II, although the first regular series of public subscription concerts started in 1729 at Hickford's Room in James Street. The nobility inherited a music tradition almost completely bound to either the church liturgy or the court ceremonial, and in the early 1700s they supplemented it by importing Italian *opera seria*.

The flowering of opera in Naples, which occurred slightly later than in Venice, provided the model for imitation in Hanover, London, and Vienna. The most popular of all Italian operas in London, *Il Trionfo di Camilla, Regina de Volsci*, was originally written for Naples in 1696 by Giovanni Bononcini (1670–1747). It received 111 performances from 1706–28 but always either completely in English or in a mixture of English and Italian. It therefore came to be considered an English opera and had just concluded a successful run in the English Opera Season at Lincoln's Inn Fields Theatre before *The Beggar's Opera* opened there in 1728. The enormous success of the latter, a work pointedly intended to appeal to the middle class, demonstrated the potential size of the new audience for a composer who, like Handel, would be willing to make appropriate concessions. Bononcini abstained from pursuing this opportunity, being more inclined towards the private concerts of the aristocracy in Britain and Europe.

The work which established Italian opera in its native tongue in London was Handel's *Rinaldo* (1711). London was a cosmopolitan town, the home of many Italian musicians, Handel himself, as a German who acquired fame writing

Italian operas for the English, personally testifies to this cosmopolitan character. Aaron Hill, the director of the theatre in the Haymarket, had concocted a libretto from bits of Tasso and Ariosto and suggested Handel set it to music when he met him in London on his first visit to England. Handel agreed, so it was speedily translated into Italian by Giacomo Rossi.

Handel was successful in providing aristocratic entertainment but his real sympathies lay with the bourgeoisie. Although he received royal patronage, he never held an official court position and was often out of favour with certain members of the aristocracy whose resentment became overt when they organized a rival 'Opera of the Nobility' in 1734. During the 1700s Handel was increasingly aware of the possibility that a large commercial public might be catered for by a new art-form. The public reactions to *The Beggar's Opera* and Carey and Lampe's burlesque *The Dragon of Wantley* (1737) showed wide-spread scorn for *opera seria* which was damaging his box-office receipts. His solution was to blend the music of Italian opera, the German Passion, and the English choral tradition, to create an original and eventually highly successful hybrid, the English oratorio. In Italy the term meant, more or less, a concert performance of a sacred opera during Lent, when the Pope had decreed that opera houses were to be closed. Handel pleased the middle class by using English as the language of his oratorios, and the biblical subject matter was more to their taste than that of the opera. In a period of expanding empire it was easy to identify with God's chosen people and their heaven-sent victories. In the seventeenth and eighteenth centuries the major European countries were engaged in commercial wars for the control of overseas markets. Britain's sea-power was crucial, so it is no surprise to learn that the patriotic song 'Rule, Britannia!' dates from this time (1740). By the end of the Seven Years War (1763) Britain had outstripped her rivals in the building of a colonial empire and had secured both North America and India.

The traditional court composer's commemoration of a victory would be a work like Handel's 'Dettingen Te Deum', written to celebrate the fortunate outcome of the last great charge in British history led by the king himself, at the battle of Dettingen in 1743 (his horse having accidentally bolted in the direction of the enemy). Now, Handel also had an alternative means of response to national conflict and chose to celebrate the victory over the forces of feudalism at Culloden, in an oratorio, *Judas Maccabeus* (1746). Prince Charlie was the grandson of the dethroned monarch James II, and the focal point of pro-Stuart sympathy among the aristocracy. The true patriot was called upon to reject feudalism in the cause of establishing a middle-class democracy. It is ironic that an old song revitalized for the cause in the 1740s, 'God Save the King', probably originally referred to 'the king over the water' (still suggested by 'Send him victorious', and in an early version the epithet 'true-born'). Handel identified with the aims of middle-class liberals, having for ever turned his back on feudal Germany and become naturalized as English in 1726. *Judas Maccabeus* caught the bourgeois mood and was to be one of his most regularly performed pieces. The English are represented by the Israelites who are fighting a Roman aristocracy, and the Duke of Cumberland (alias 'the butcher') is undoubtedly intended for comparison with the divinely favoured eponymous hero.

It is worth while pondering the kind of freedom for which English soldiers were being asked to sacrifice their lives, if need be. The agrarian revolution had destroyed the ancient village communities, and the system of co-operative husbandry had been replaced by individual farming. Furthermore, the effect of the Enclosure Movement was to dispossess small tenants and cottagers in the interests of capitalist farmers. The result of political reformation meant that people were more and more bound together by self-interest rather than gaining freedom. The liberty being fought for was the freedom to sell one's own labour-power or hire that of others, depending on whether one owned or had been stripped of property. After the suppression of the '45 rebellion, the Highland chiefs were, in Dr Johnson's description, changed from 'patriarchal rulers' to 'rapacious landlords'.[1] In the later eighteenth century enforced clearances took place in the Highlands to make room for profitable sheep-farming.

The rightness of the Protestant religion is strongly hinted at in the Rev. Morell's libretto (despite the obvious anomaly that the Israelites worship a tribal deity), with the anti-papist slant of the cries of 'down with the polluted altars' and the recommendation to hurl 'priests and pageants' to 'the remotest corner of the world' in order to avoid deception by 'pious lies'. The enemy Rome also suggests Catholicism and its association with the Jacobite cause. Performers in oratorio, of course, were not under the same suspicion of popery as those in Italian opera.

The religious revival which took place in the later eighteenth century was important to the emerging industrial bourgeoisie. Methodism began to acquire respectability, and the middle class in industrial areas took advantage of the organizing experience to be gained from Methodist meetings which relied upon lay leadership and devolution of responsibility. Success in industry was also more likely to result from the sort of skills that were emphasized in Dissenting schools. The subject of nonconformism and its influence on bourgeois song is treated later.

Before the industrial revolution, middle-class town-dwellers were merchants, artisans, or shopkeepers. Social change was set in motion by the cotton industry, and the inventions of Arkwright and Crompton which, together with Watt's steam-engine, created the factory system. Because of steam power the British coal deposits were of immense significance, and scores of mines were opened. The mining of copper and iron was needed, too, for the production of the machinery itself. Arkwright was a typical example of the new industrial hero: he was a Preston barber in 1768, a mill owner in 1771, and thereafter he was continually adding to his accumulation of capital the royalties he received from machinery built to his patents (whether or not the invention he had patented was actually one of his own). When British industrial production figures began to climb, war was once more to prove a decisive factor in crushing foreign competition and securing captive markets (1793–1815).

A transformation in political and intellectual life is indicated by the birth of classical economics: Adam Smith attacked mercantilism and advocated free trade in Book IV of *The Wealth of Nations* (1776) and, according to Engels, 'reduced politics, parties, religion, in short everything to economic categories.'[2] In music the effects of bourgeois democratic ideas were seen in a deliberate popularization and simplification of style. Even a composer like Haydn, who had spent most of his life in employment at the Esterházy court, working within the traditions of aristocratic musical entertainment, reveals his republican sympathies by deliberately accommodating himself to this 'democratic' tendency in his London Symphonies of 1791–5 (e.g. the slow movement of the *Surprise Symphony*, No. 94). He also wrote twelve canzonets to English words, one of which, 'My Mother Bids Me Bind My Hair', became a firm favourite in the drawing-room repertoire. Haydn was much influenced by the music of Handel which he heard, and the kind of simple descriptive effects that can be traced from a work like Handel's *Israel in Egypt* to Haydn's *The Creation* were again a beloved feature of bourgeois song.

The middle class did not reach a position of political dominance overnight, but significant milestones were 1832, when the Reform Bill was passed, the boom in railway investment (essential for the development of capital-goods industries like iron and coal) which helped to shake off the 1842 depression, and the repeal of the Corn Laws in 1846. The importance of the Reform agitation was the new polarization of class antagonism between labourers and capitalists (rather than labourers and aristocracy) which followed. E. P. Thompson in *The Making of the English Working Class*[3] sees Chartism as the inevitable result, and so, incidentally, did Disraeli:

> In treating the House of the Third Estate as the House of the People, and not as the House of a privileged class, the Ministry and Parliament of 1831 virtually conceded the principal of Universal Suffrage . . . its immediate and inevitable result was Chartism.[4]

The importance of riding out the 1842 depression was that afterwards Britain was no longer dependent on one main industrialized sector, and the ensuing boom years were a contributing factor in setting English unrest apart from that on the continent in 1848. The importance of the repeal of the Corn Laws was that it gave a victory to the industrial bourgeoisie over the landed aristocracy, leaving the latter economically and politically weaker.

The English opera

The work which pointed most clearly to the cultural appetite of the growing urban middle class and set in motion major changes in operatic entertainment was *The Beggar's Opera* by John Gay (1685–1732). It was in every respect the antithesis of *opera seria*: instead of gods and heroes the characters were highwaymen and prostitutes; instead of broad spans of embellished melody the tunes were simple and direct; instead of a falsetto the protagonist was a tenor, a rarity in *opera seria*. Gay satirized the court and aristocratic entertainment at the same time as he carefully instilled into his work a moral purpose which, while designed to appeal to the taste of a middle-class audience, was calculated not to offend the aristocracy at large.

Ironically, Gay had really written a play rather than an opera and originally intended the songs to be sung entirely without accompaniment. When Colley Cibber refused him the opportunity of performances at Drury Lane, it was John Rich, at whose theatre in Lincoln's Inn Fields the piece was first seen in 1728, who persuaded Gay to allow his resident musical director Johann Pepusch to provide accompaniments. This alteration of Gay's plans did not work to the play's advantage throughout. The pace of Act 3: scene 13, for instance, where Macheath sits in the condemned cell drinking and singing snatches of ten different songs, is seriously impeded. In consequence of its being a last-minute decision, Pepusch's arrangements are fragmentary and sketchy, and because of this the unusual convention arose that all revivals of the work became musically 'updated'. Arne and then Bishop, who both produced later versions, were among the first to build a tradition which has lasted to the present day. Frederic Austin's 1920 arrangement of the score, which ran for over three years at the Lyric Theatre, Hammersmith, has been the most acclaimed revival so far this century. *The Beggar's Opera* also provided the stimulus for Brecht and Weill's revolutionary landmark in the history of modern musical theatre, *Die Dreigroschenoper*, written to commemorate the bicentenary of Gay's pioneering drama in 1928. This time, however, the shafts of political satire were aimed from the perspective of the proletariat rather than the bourgeoisie.

The source for the majority of Gay's tunes was the collection *Pills to Purge Melancholy*[5] by the bawdy Restoration poet Tom Durfey (or, spelt in the quasi-aristocratic manner he preferred, D'Urfey). This fact is clear because they are cited by the names they bear in this collection, even when they exist under different titles elsewhere. Most of the Scottish songs are from Thomson's *Orpheus Caledonius*,[6] to which Gay's patroness, the Duchess of Queensbury, subscribed. Many other songs are originally from theatrical productions, and among them are simple, tuneful pieces by Purcell, Eccles, Leveridge, and even Handel and Bononcini. They are sometimes not simple enough, however, as the incorrect version of Handel's march from *Rinaldo* demonstrates. No doubt the reason for this error was that it was notated from memory, either from its regular performance by the band of the Royal Horse Guards, or its previous parody as a tavern song, 'Let the Waiter Bring Clean Glasses'. Gay may have been entirely unaware that he had converted what in *Rinaldo* was a march of the Christians into a march of the highwaymen.

Allan Ramsay's *The Gentle Shepherd* (1725), which he described as a Scots pastoral comedy with songs to ballad airs, is often considered a forerunner of *The Beggar's Opera* and other ballad operas, as they came to be labelled. The truth is that, until the success of Gay's opera, it was a spoken play with just four songs. Only following an Edinburgh production of *The Beggar's Opera* did Ramsay augment its musical substance to twenty 'sangs'. Theophilus Cibber adapted this version for performance in London as *Patie and Peggy* (1730). The latter's father, Colley, who had shown initial lack of enthusiasm for Gay's piece, had already leapt onto the bandwagon with his own ballad opera, *Love in a Riddle* (1729). That same year in Dublin the major theatrical centre outside London, Charles Coffey produced *The Beggar's Wedding*.

The success of ballad operas depended on their librettists alone since it was they who selected the tunes to which they wished to write new or parodied words. It is not surprising to find prestigious literary figures such as Henry Fielding joining the growing numbers attracted to this genre. Fielding was also not averse to creating political controversy, as *The Welsh Opera* of 1731 shows. Here political satire is directed at both parties and even involves the Royal Family. In 1737 the government had had enough and passed the Licensing Act in response to continuing satirical attacks. From now on there were to be only two legitimate theatres in London, Covent Garden and Drury Lane, and all plays were subject to a well-regulated system of censorship. The limitation on theatre numbers lasted until 1843, but the strict enforcement of censorship begun by the Act lasted until 1968.

There were also completely original works, like Thomas Arne's *Thomas and Sally* (1760), composed to a libretto by Isaac Bickerstaffe. This has a small cast, lasts under an hour, and was performed at Covent Garden as an 'afterpiece' opera. Although described by Burney as having 'very little musical merit',[7] it was an immediate and lasting success. For the most part Arne writes the simple strophic settings (that is, the same tune for each verse) which dominate ballad opera. The melodic style, however, is more ornate than the ballad airs, indicating a return to the influence of the Italian aria which, because of its aristocratic ties, was felt to be more refined than the English song. Another Italian feature is the use of the declamatory musical style known as recitative instead of spoken dialogue. Arne also has a penchant for Scottish elements of a fashionable artificiality: the overture contains a 'Scotch Gavotte' which demonstrates this quality in its title and style.

The reason for the opera's appreciation must be attributed in part to the hero's chauvinism; he arrives on stage fresh 'From ploughing the ocean and threshing Mounsieur'[8] (Britain was in the midst of the Seven Years War). Thomas is a forerunner of the jolly Jack Tar who is later given enormous popularity by Dibdin. He constantly employs nautical metaphors and even interprets the squire's attempted rape of his beloved Sally as 'A pirate just about to board my prize!'[9] The moral of the piece is one that became a great favourite of the Victorian bourgeoisie, who never tired of recommending it to those who lacked fortune or position; it is summed up in Sally the milkmaid's remark, 'Virtue commands me – Be honest and poor'.[10] The emphasis throughout is on true-heartedness, thus contrasting markedly with the fickleness of the characters in *The Beggar's Opera*, an arrangement of which Arne had produced at Covent Garden the year before.

There is no space here[11] to discuss the stage entertainments of composers like Samuel Arnold (whose *Inkle and Yarico* (1787) concerned slavery in the West Indies and was contemporary with Wilberforce's agitation), James Hook, Thomas Linley, or Stephen Storace (whose *The Cherokee* was the first English opera based on the American Wild West). Charles Dibdin, although he too created some pieces in the ballad-opera vein, such as *The Waterman* (1774) and *The Seraglio* (1776), will be treated separately in connection with his more original entertainments.

The most 'popular' type of opera towards the close of the century was a light sentimental comedy which contained a mixture of original music, favourite tunes from other operas, and traditional airs. Musical director of Covent Garden at this time was William Shield (1748–1829), and those of his operas which were most admired were of the afterpiece variety rather than full length, and used traditional airs alongside freshly composed music. *Rosina* (1782) contained the tune now sung to the words 'Auld Lang Syne', and was, indeed, responsible for the spreading of this melody's popularity throughout Britain. The song 'The Plough Boy', with its attractive 'whistling' piccolo part, comes from *The Farmer* (1787), one of the many operas he wrote in partnership with the Irish dramatist John O'Keefe.

An authentic composition of Shield's which became a war horse of the Victorian drawing room was 'The Wolf', from his and O'Keefe's *The Castle of Andalusia* (1798).

> At the peaceful midnight hour,
> Every sense, and every pow'r
> Fetter'd lies in downy sleep;
> Then our careful watch we keep.
> While the wolf in nightly prowl,
> Bays the moon with hideous howl.
>
> Gates are barr'd – a vain resistance;
> Females shriek, but no assistance;
> Silence, or you meet your fate!
> Your keys, your jewels, cash and plate.
> Locks, bolts, and bars, soon fly asunder,
> Then to rifle, rob, and plunder.

It held a place throughout the nineteenth century as one of the half-dozen best-known bass songs. Shield's 'The Wolf' does much to encourage a cult for the low-pitched menacing song. Not that it is so very alarming: no one had heard the 'hideous howl' of a wolf in Britain for over half a century. It is specifically aimed at the wealthy: 'Silence, or you meet your fate!' might be taken by the average person as a threat of death, but the main emphasis is on the fear of losing possessions rather than one's life. The precious possessions whose possible loss chills the hearts of the drawing-room audience are the vanities of luxury – jewels, cash, and plate.

The reason needs to be explored why, at this stage of evolution of the English opera, a drawing-room classic should emerge. As noted above, the words relate to the fears of the wealthy bourgeois, but why did the song survive musically? A song such as 'The Wolf' presented itself as unaffected, realistic, while at the same time imaginative and polished. Yet, some of its features, for example, the excessive use of sequence (the repetition of a melodic phrase at a different pitch) borrowed from *opera seria*, would have sounded routine and old-fashioned in the nineteenth century. The principal explanation for its continued musical fascination would seem to be the possibilities it offered for a melodramatic rendition. The tempo moves from a gentle, rocking rhythm for the sleepy world, to a slightly quicker, atmospheric section for the prowling wolf, to a vigorous final section for the robbing and plundering. The stimulating effect of the increases in speed, which are coupled to similar increases in loudness, only wanted the addition of a dramatic flair on the part of the singer to be sure, in the language of the day, of creating astonishment in the listener.

The next operatic composer relevant to this survey, John Braham (1774–1854), one of the most celebrated tenors of the first half of the nineteenth century, contributed three perennial favourites to the drawing-room repertoire, the song 'The Anchor's Weigh'd', the duet 'All's Well', and the recitative and aria 'The Death of Nelson'. None of them display any willingness to venture beyond the simplest harmonies. 'The Anchor's Weigh'd' moved thousands to tears with its yearning pauses and its pathetic farewells uttered by the sailor lad parting from his true-love. 'All's Well' contained the drama of excited questioning between the voices but elsewhere they sing in the plainest sweetest-sounding harmony. This duet was the first to give wide popularity to the partnership of tenor and bass, a blend of voices chosen by Balfe in 1857 for perhaps the most famous of all drawing-room duets, his setting of Longfellow's 'Excelsior'. Braham's duet originally appeared in *The English Fleet in 1342*, an opera written for Covent Garden in 1803 in return for what was, by the standards of the time, the enormous sum of one thousand guineas.

Many Victorians expected the tenor aria 'The Death of Nelson', from the opera *The Americans* of 1811, to confer immortality on the name of Braham. Instead he acquired the anonymity which Auden said all great artists should aspire to, when, in 1931, the editor of *The Oxford Song Book*[12] included this by now traditional song with the composer given as unknown. This neglect was unkind, even if an old rumour was believed that Braham based his piece on a French sailors' song, for it would still have required extensive reworking in order to accommodate S. J. Arnold's lengthy stanzas. The Oxford version also omits the preceding atmospheric recitative 'O'er Nelson's Tomb' and rejects Brahams most imaginative music, the first fourteen bars of verse 3, in favour of a repeat of the equivalent bars in verses 1 and 2.[13]

RECIT. O'er Nelson's tomb, with silent grief oppress'd
Britannia mourns her hero now at rest;
But those bright laurels ne'er shall fade with years,
Whose leaves are water'd by a nation's tears.

ARIA 'Twas in Trafalgar's Bay
We saw the Frenchmen lay;
Each heart was bounding then:
We scorn'd the foreign yoke,
For our ships were British oak,
And hearts of oak our men!
Our Nelson mark'd them on the wave,
Three cheers our gallant seamen gave,
Nor thought of home or beauty;
Along the line this signal ran:
'England expects that every man
This day will do his duty!'

And now the cannons roar
Along th' affrighted shore –
Our Nelson led the way:
His ship the 'Vict'ry' named –
Long be that 'Vict'ry' famed,
For vict'ry crowned the day!
But dearly was that conquest bought,
Too well the gallant hero fought
For England, home, and beauty!
He cried, as 'midst the fire he ran:
'England shall find that every man
This day will do his duty!'

At last the fatal wound,
Which spread dismay around,
The hero's breast received:
'Heav'n fights upon our side!
The day's our own!' he cried.
'Now long enough I've lived!
In honour's cause my life was pass'd,
In honour's cause I fall at last,
For England, home, and beauty!'
Thus ending life as he began,
England confess'd that every man
That day had done his duty!

The singer is frequently interrupted by fanfare-like musical punctuations which are designed to arouse those whose emotions have not already been overtaken by patriotic sentiment.

The well-known words concerning England, home, and beauty, are set tranquilly and lyrically to obtain maximum dramatic contrast.

For Eng-land, home-and beau-ty,   For_ Eng-land, home-and beau-ty!

The tragic final verse begins with a conventional switch to the minor key to convey melancholy; and the receipt of the fatal wound is recorded loudly and sonorously in the depths of the accompaniment.

At   last   the   fa - tal   wound,   (Which)

The words attempt to engage the listener's sympathy by continual use of the possessive pronoun 'our': 'our ships', 'our men', 'our Nelson' (twice), 'Heav'n fights upon our side!' Ostensibly this is because it is sung by a participant in the battle of Trafalgar; yet notice the lines '*His* ship the "Vict'ry" named' (not *our* ship), and 'Three cheers *our* gallant seamen gave' (not *we* gallant seamen). It is clearly aimed at those who did no fighting and invites them to bask in the glory of victory, sharing the pride of being part of a nation which has produced such a hero as Nelson. Naval victories of previous years are conjured up by the quotation of words from the eighteenth-century patriotic song by Garrick and Boyce, 'Heart of Oak'. Nelson's famous call for Englishmen to do their duty could not fail to swell the patriotic breast of the industrial bourgeois faced with no more immediate danger than a decline in the rate of profit.

Braham's junior by twelve years, Sir Henry Rowley Bishop (1786–1855) was a composer of immense importance to early nineteenth-century theatre music. Over a dozen of his songs, taken in the main from stage productions, remained in the drawing-room repertoire for the rest of the century and beyond. Even in 1918 there were prestigious musicians who believed his songs had 'put on immortality'.[14] Bishop's only compositions at all familiar today are the song 'Home, Sweet Home!' and the dance 'The Dashing White Sergeant', taken from a song of that title composed to verses by General Burgoyne in 1826.

It was in one of his English operas (in reality, for the most part a spoken play) *Clari, or The Maid of Milan* (1823) that his famous song 'Home, Sweet Home!' was first heard, sung by Miss Maria Tree. It functioned in this domestic drama as an all-pervading melancholy tune which stamped its character on the entire piece. Yet, in 1829, Bishop decided something fresh was required to exploit the success of his song and put on a drama called, not surprisingly, *Home, Sweet Home!*

The tune of the verse exists in a Goulding and Dalmaine publication of 1821, *Melodies of Various Nations*, edited by Bishop. Here, also, are several other airs by Bishop masquerading under such descriptions as 'Portuguese' or 'Hindostanee'. His air labelled 'Sicilian' had words by the fashionable poet Thomas Haynes Bayly: 'To the Home of My Childhood in Sorrow I Came'. Bishop later deposed on oath in court that he had composed the tune himself, being unable to locate a genuine Sicilian air. The words of the second version, which now includes a refrain, are by John Howard Payne, an American actor and dramatist, who ironically never had a settled home. Widespread as the song's fame was in the late 1820s, its celebrity and cultural importance increased towards the end of Bishop's life when it became a favourite of the 'Swedish Nightingale', Jenny Lind. Bishop, however, seems to have felt greater financial satisfaction than musical pride in its success.

Jacqueline Bratton, in *The Victorian Popular Ballad*,[15] quite rightly points out that it is an 'assemblage of talismanic words', but she is misled by its emotional associations in describing it as a 'wailing, tear-laden tune'. One has only to listen to a tune like Tucker's 'Sweet Genevieve', which aptly suits that description, to realize how very plain Bishop's melody is by contrast. Even so, it has an Italianate quality in its simplicity, more reminiscent of an aria such as Handel's 'Verdi Prati' (from *Alcina*, 1735) than an English air. A typical operatic feature is the musical decoration around the significant words 'There's no place like Home!' (completely ironed out in many late Victorian editions). The accompaniment is a variant of an eighteenth-century cliché known as the Alberti bass. Another cliché is the trilling accompaniment to 'The birds singing gaily', although its naïve simplicity almost disarms criticism. Harmonically the song also demonstrates the same artlessness: it consists of no more than four different chords throughout. The melody, except for two of its moments of brief ornamentation, uses only the notes of the major scale and is of narrow range. Each line of the verse and refrain comes to rest on either the first or the third degree of the scale. Bishop constantly requires a hushed vocal tone and asks for the voice to be slightly raised just once, for the penultimate 'There's no place like Home'.

HOME, SWEET HOME!

John Howard Payne   Sir Henry Rowley Bishop

world,   is not met with   else -where.   Home!   Home!___

sweet, sweet   Home! There's no ___ place like   Home! there's no place like ___

Home!

An Ex - ile from Home, splendour   daz - zles in   vain,___   Oh!

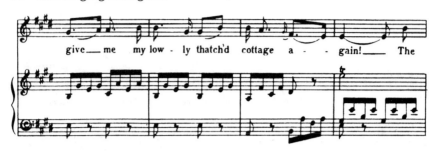

give＿me my low - ly thatch'd cottage a - - gain!＿ The

birds sing-ing gai-ly that came at my call,＿ Give me them with the

peace of mind dear - er ＿ than all.   Home!   Home!＿

Largo

sweet, sweet Home! There's no＿place like Home! there's no place like Home!

Note that 'home' is always begun with a capital letter, as if to emphasize its hallowed quality. The words had universal appeal, for, no matter what or where one's home was, it could be argued that that there was no place like it. If a person no longer possessed a home it evoked nostalgia or recalled the Christian promise of a heavenly home in the hereafter. To the working class the home was increasingly the retreat from the exhaustion, tedium, and alienation of their labour. The many paintings which adopt the title of this song depict a multiplicity of homes, from a wealthy young middle-class couple with a baby to a dog lying content in his kennel. Its universality of appeal and the simplicity and ready comprehensibility of its musical language equipped it for a hegemonic role: the journalist and poet Dr Charles Mackay maintained that it had done 'more than statesmanship or legislation to keep alive in the hearts of the people the virtues that flourish at the fireside'.[16] Even a group of Zulus, members of the only tribe in South Africa to resist the might of British imperialism, were reported to have been melted by a performance of this song by the celebrated Marie Albani in Kimberly.

Superficially, the song seems to be addressed to the person living in a lowly home; in reality it is aimed at the new urban wealthy, in whom it awakens tender reassurances that the change in their fortunes has not entailed a change in the simplicity of their hearts. The song provides them with a nostalgic yearning for the simple life which is a fantasy of rustic bliss (trotting out of the cottage to call to the gaily singing birds) rather than a picture of the actual poverty and squalor endured by most occupants of humble country cottages. The emphasis on 'home' implies that a spiritual, if not material, contentment is available to everyone – peace of mind is 'dearer than all'. Listeners are assured that they would not be seduced by the glittering splendour of a palace because it would not be home.

Its Italian manner gives it polite sophistication but, unlike some of Bishop's output, it does not display an affectedly Italian style (his song 'Tell Me My Heart', for example, makes use of the characteristic turns of musical phrase designed for the common weak endings of Italian words for the setting of strong one-syllable English words). Careful attention is paid to the accenting of words (a care not shown by editors of later editions): the music is not merely repeated for verse two; rhythmic differences are notated with some subtlety. For instance, Bishop marks that the word 'dearer' is to be sung at a quicker pace than the words 'met with' which occur at the corresponding position in verse 1.

Bishop is nowadays known solely for the simplest of his songs in spite of his enormous efforts to please his contemporary audience and singers. He was willing to furnish them with music in any vein which was profitable. If this meant cashing in on the success of others, so be it. ''Tis When To Sleep', from *The Maniac* (1810), is a most flattering imitation of Shield's best-seller, 'The Wolf'. For virtuoso singers he was ready to compose display pieces which would guarantee them rapturous applause. A few of these, such as 'Lo, Here the Gentle Lark', remained in the repertoire of operatic divas like Amelita Galli-Curci this century. His rewards were not just financial (most of these gains were quickly spent): he was one of the first professors of music at the University of Edinburgh (where Senate jealousy restricted the time allowed for music lectures to a maximum of two per year); he was the first musician to receive a knighthood; and he replaced Dr Crotch as professor of music at the University of Oxford towards the end of his life, becoming a doctor of music himself.

Bishop's work consolidated the new blend of drama and music which had developed in the eighteenth century, and he ensured the English opera's survival as a rival to the Italian variety. The biggest problem facing English opera was that it had won no real status as an art-form because of the scorn of the aristocracy. There was still a noticeable class division in the audience for opera: the aristocracy, on one side, showed contempt for the English opera, while the middle class, on the other, felt suspicious of the foreign variety (particularly on moral and religious grounds). The division is observable in the fact that between 1792–1843 the King's Theatre in the Haymarket (which became Her Majesty's on the accession of Queen Victoria) was the only London theatre licensed to perform opera in Italian. The middle class differed in their attitude to opera in a factional way among themselves; some respected the taste of the aristocracy and sought to emulate it, while others, notably the largely nonconformist industrial bourgeoisie, were inclined to reject all opera as decadent. For aristocratic taste the Italian language was considered the perfect medium for singing; the lack of diphthongs meant pure vowel sounds, which in turn meant steadier pitch and evenness of tone. The artistic status of Balfe's *The Bohemian Girl* was considerably raised when it was given at Her Majesty's in Italian translation as *La Zingara*. It was rare for any opera to be presented in English at this theatre, and during the years 1810–40 Mozart, Bellini, Donizetti, and Rossini were the most frequently performed composers.

Although Italian opera began to gain ground among the middle class thanks to the charm of Rossini, it should be stressed that this wider audience was for Italian opera in English. Rossini's music first won over the Covent Garden audience in 1829, when Robin Lacy used music from *Semiramide* for an operatic adaptation of Scott's *Ivanhoe*, giving the work the fashionable title *The Maid of Judah*. Virginal heroines are frequently found in opera titles at this time, perhaps as a guarantee of the moral wholesomeness of the drama. Once Rossini's music had been accepted at Covent Garden, there was bound to be a certain amount of influence on the theatre's other stage entertainments because the same singers were used in all the repertoire. When Alfred Bunn became lessee of both Covent Garden and Drury Lane in 1833, the influence was spread further as a result of the meanness of Bunn's contracts which committed his singers to performances at both his theatres (sometimes on the same evening).

Bunn was one among many who believed that a fusion of elements between English and Italian opera could produce a national variety of grand opera which would be universally admired and consequently prove immensely profitable. Bunn made determined efforts to establish an English operatic tradition; together with Edward Fitzball (originally of the unadorned surname Ball), and occasionally working in partnership with him, he dominated the writing of libretti. In 1835 he staged Balfe's first success, *The Siege of Rochelle* (libretto by Fitzball), which ran for three months at Drury Lane. The next year, scenting a windfall, he overcame his customary parsimony and offered the celebrated Madame

Malibran the unprecedented salary of £125 a week in order to persuade her to sing the title role in another Balfe opera, *The Maid of Artois*, a setting of Bunn's own libretto. Alas, neither he nor Balfe were to make their fortune with this work, partly because they failed to recognize the exact nature of the artistic compromises which had to be made if an English opera was to achieve success. The unavoidable conflict of artistic principles which composers and librettists faced but seldom satisfactorily resolved will become evident below. Bunn often translated and adapted what he thought to be suitably romantic libretti from operas which had been successful on the continent. *The Daughter of St Mark* (music by Balfe), for example, is based on a French libretto by J-H. V. de St Georges, *La Reine de Chypre*, set to music by Halévy three years earlier, in 1841. Plagiarism was by no means confined to Bunn in England; Lachner's *Catharina Cornaro* (Munich, 1841) and Donizetti's *Catarina Cornaro* (Naples, 1844) are both musical settings of versions of the same original French libretto.

A survey of English opera in nineteenth-century Britain is only relevant here in so far as it acts as one of the storehouses of drawing-room song.[17] It will suffice to give brief descriptions of the character and output of the most successful composers working in this field, and to single out Balfe as a representative figure for closer scrutiny. The dream of many composers was of being the first to sow the seed of a strong English operatic tradition. The conditions for growth were made unfavourable, however, by the presence of two conflicting demands: one of these was dictated by the drama and the other by the middle-class audience. The latter tended to judge English operas by the resources they offered for use in the drawing room; a perfect opera from this point of view was a chain of 'favourite airs'. Obviously, this limited the dramatic interaction between characters because of the resulting restriction imposed upon ensemble passages (Mozart's rapid and eventful *Marriage of Figaro*, for example, is full of ensembles).

While Bunn was trying to establish English opera at his theatres, the Lyceum reopened its doors as the English Opera House. In a bid to stimulate interest, it began its first season with a grand opera, *Nourjahad*, composed by Edward James Loder (1813–65) and based on a play by Arnold, the theatre's manager. The real success, however, came with the next production, *The Mountain Sylph* by John Barnett (1802–90). Barnett showed his artistic aspirations in opting for recitative instead of spoken dialogue, which gave *The Mountain Sylph* the distinction of being the first through-composed English opera since Arne's *Artaxerxes*. In spite of that, it ran for three months initially and remained in favour for the rest of the century; indeed, Gilbert and Sullivan's *Iolanthe* consciously satirizes it. Nevertheless, the English Opera House was not financially viable and Barnett himself later failed in two attempts to set up a permanent venue for English opera. When he left for Cheltenham in 1841 to devote his career to the teaching of singing, he took with him the conviction that there was a conspiracy to crush English opera on the part of concert promoters.

Loder also decided to leave for the provinces, though he too had enjoyed a notable success with a fairy-tale romantic opera, *The Night Dancers*. He obtained the post of musical director at the Theatre Royal, Manchester, in 1851. If he had hopes of greater success for English opera in the liberal climate there, he was mistaken. His last important opera, *Raymond and Agnes* (libretto by Fitzball),[18] failed because the music was too difficult for a provincial theatre to cope with in 1855. Loder had a limited success in the drawing room, but his music clearly shows that he is torn by conflicting interests: sometimes he writes in the style of the English 'traditional' air, as in his two popular settings of H. F. Chorley, 'The Brave Old Oak' and 'The Three Ages of Love'; at other times he demonstrates his dramatic skills and his indebtedness to the Italian romantic operatic aria, as in 'The Diver'.

The Irish composer William Vincent Wallace (1812–65) was regarded with a mixture of disapproval and admiration as a wild rover. The son of a bandmaster, he became, perhaps surprisingly, not a wind player but an outstanding violinist and pianist. He was much involved with the rich musical life of Dublin as a young man; then, at the age of twenty-three he emigrated with his wife to Tasmania. A few years later, heavily in debt, he deserted his wife and child and fled to South America. Here, and afterwards in North America, he built considerable fame as a performer. He also began concocting stories about his past – his service in punitive expeditions against the Maoris, his rescue by a chief's daughter, and all manner of well-received apocrypha. When he finally came to London in 1845, Fitzball, who nourished the idea of being a wild man himself, was impatient for his consent to the request that he compose the music to *Maritana*. If an operatic heroine was not a fairy or a maid then she would more than likely be, as Maritana is, a gypsy. Fitzball no doubt assumed that this would suit Wallace's temperament, and he was proved right when Wallace completed the score the same year. The opera had a successful run only exceeded in the nineteenth century by Balfe's *The Bohemian Girl* (another gypsy). In *Maritana* he had managed to maintain the delicate balance between the demands of stage drama and home music-making. It has favourite airs in plenty ('Yes! Let Me Like a Soldier Fall', 'Alas! Those Chimes So Sweetly Stealing', 'There Is a Flower', 'Scenes That Are Brightest', etc.), but also contains some well-thought-out concerted sections (such as the finale to Act II).

Michael William Balfe (1808–70), another Irish composer, was the person who seemed most likely to establish a proud future for English opera in view of the acclaim he received for *The Siege of Rochelle*, *The Maid of Artois*, and greatest of all for *The Bohemian Girl*, which was first presented at Drury Lane in 1843 and went on to become the most frequently performed opera after *The Beggar's Opera*. Balfe's experience as a professional singer (like Braham he had toured widely as a young man) obviously stood him in good stead as a composer for the voice. He was not concerned, however, with trying to thrill the opera audience with the virtuosity of vocal displays by characters on stage; musical fireworks might win admiration for the singer but they would hamper sales of the song. Balfe learned this lesson when, flushed with success, he ambitiously followed *The Bohemian Girl* with a 'grand opera seria' *The Daughter of St Mark*, making few concessions to the amateur market. It effectively demonstrated to him the financial penalty of a failure in the drawing room. He concentrated his skill afterwards into writing simple, affecting melodies. As a result, more operatic airs by Balfe found their way into the drawing room than those of any other composer. Because of the close links Balfe and Bishop enjoyed with the fashionable area of Covent Garden, they were both able to command higher sums for their songs than the majority of composers. Balfe in particular was prepared to engage in hard bargaining over this lucrative source of income.

The best-known number from *The Bohemian Girl* was, and still is, the soprano air 'The Dream'.[19]

> I dreamt that I dwelt in marble halls,
> With vassals and serfs at my side,
> And of all those assembled within those walls
> That I was the hope and the pride.
> I had riches too great to count – could boast
> Of a high ancestral name;
> But I also dreamt, which pleas'd me most,
> That you lov'd me still the same.
>
> I dreamt that suitors sought my hand,
> That knights upon bended knee,
> And with vows no maiden heart could withstand,
> They pledg'd their faith to me,
> And I dreamt that one of that noble host
> Came forth my hand to claim;
> But I also dreamt, which charm'd me most,
> That you lov'd me still the same.

'The Dream' is a perfect example of the detachable English operatic air: it relies in no way upon any knowledge of its function in Act II nor, indeed, is any understanding of the opera's plot necessary to make sense of the words. It therefore has the advantage of appealing to those of the middle class who felt uncomfortable about attending opera performances and who chose to avoid the risk of being infected by the theatre's not altogether scrupulous consideration of moral proprieties (on top of which, it was often a pick-up place for prostitutes). The title, *The Bohemian Girl,* suggests that unsavoury characters may be represented on stage. Bohemianism could also extend, in a more alarming manner, to the subversive status of a counter-culture, particularly among rebellious creative artists. In opera bohemianism is little else than simple escapism; the gypsies are no more of the real world than the fairies. In the case of 'The Dream', not only are words and music part of a self-contained unit which makes sense outside of its original operatic context, but mood and message comply with the requirements for consumption in the intimacy of the drawing room. The mood is nostalgic, the vein of melancholy Bunn tapped most successfully. Memory provides Bunn with the theme of this air, as in many of his other well-known lyrics, such as 'The Light of Other Days', 'The Heart Bow'd Down' ('mem'ry is the only friend'), 'When Other Lips' ('you'll remember me'). 'The Dream' is Arline's subconscious memory of her childhood.

Its message out of context is clear: the love of a good man is more important than the possession of marble halls, the services of vassals, or the payment of homage by knights. The contemporary bourgeois listener is thus given room to consider the bygone accoutrements of feudal power in a harmlessly romantic light and led to ponder instead upon the wider mysteries of the power of love and the strength of individual character. Balfe attempts to evoke a mood by eschewing the overtly dramatic technique of 'word-painting' seen in the songs which have been previously analysed. The mood is one of exhilaration: it is conveyed by the giddy waltzlike momentum and the breathless repetition of the words about being loved. Balfe creates the effect of breathlessness by allowing scarcely any time for the singer to inhale before each of the last two musical phrases in both verses.

True to his usual form, Balfe is cavalier in his word setting. He specifies an off-beat rhythmic effect in the middle of many of the bars but is unconcerned that, because of this, accents fall on unimportant words such as 'at' and 'of', or on unstressed syllables as in 'assem*bled*'. Worse still, he rides roughshod over the enjambment in lines 5–6, breaking up the continuity of meaning by writing a separate musical phrase for each line. See the musical example on page 21.

   Balfe does the same thing with even more devastating effect in Thaddeus' Act III air 'The Fair Land of Poland' when he brings a positive conclusion to a musical phrase at the end of line 2 of the following:

rich-es too   great   to   count— could boast   Of a   high   an -

> When the fair land of Poland was plough'd by the hoof
> Of the ruthless invader, when might
> With steel to the bosom and flame to the roof,
> Completed her triumph o'er right:

Enjambment is not a device which lends itself readily to convincing musical treatment so Balfe prefers to ignore it.

Influence of the Italian opera composers on the style of Balfe's melodies and accompaniments is evident, although the contention that there is an all-pervasive imitation of Rossini would be an exaggeration. The trio in *The Daughter of St Mark*, for instance, bears an unmistakable family resemblance to the quartet in Beethoven's *Fidelio*. A typical Rossini-like feature employed by Balfe is the repetition of a musical phrase which seems to be on the point of concluding a melodic sentence. Earlier examples, however, are easily found in Mozart.[20] Balfe appropriated enough Italian features to appear progressive and fashionable, but he knew full well that Bellini, Donizetti, and Rossini were rarely heard in the drawing room. Rosina's aria 'Una voce poco fa' from Act II of Rossini's *The Barber of Seville* may have been a great favourite with opera audiences, who could appreciate the rapid runs and elaborate decorations woven around what was a simple and appealing melodic skeleton, but it demanded a virtuoso soprano technique which ruled it out for amateur performance. Balfe was careful to introduce only slight decoration in his airs, after noting that the loudly applauded virtuoso numbers he had written for celebrated singers like Malibran did more for their performers' reputations than for his own pocket. He enjoyed using the Italian procedure of following a succession of two-bar phrases with an extended and decorated closing phrase. Again, this had been done by Mozart,[21] had been taken up by Rossini,[22] and is found later with greater frequency in Donizetti[23] and Bellini.[24] Balfe uses this procedure, in preference to a straightforward repetition of his final phrase, in many of his most 'popular' airs, such as 'The Heart Bow'd Down', 'When Other Lips', 'The Light of Other Days', 'In This Old Chair' and 'The Peace of the Valley'. The beautiful cavatina 'The Power of Love', from *Satanella*, has its short structure elongated by a whole series of Italianate phrase extensions, motivic repetitions, and word-painting; at the same time it retains a limpid charm typical of Balfe. It is this melodic attractiveness that allows him to succeed with a setting of Longfellow's 'The Arrow and the Song' very much arioso in style (a half-way house between recitative and aria) where others would have been dull.

Balfe's banality lies in his accompaniments: they seldom contain any melodic interest and are generally no more than repeated broken-chord patterns. It cannot be argued that he is deliberately catering for the parlour pianist, since solo piano interludes in his songs require a higher level of skill. Nevertheless, he avoids obvious clichés; an examination of the accompaniment to 'The Light of Other Days' will reveal his efforts to avoid a commonplace Alberti bass.

There was a late success for an English opera at Covent Garden in 1862 (*The Lily of Killarney* by Sir Julius Benedict), but otherwise interest had flagged. The dream of the national opera house still haunted Victorian composers, however, and the last attempt to make it a reality came with the building of the Royal English Opera House which opened in 1891 with Sullivan's *succès d'estime Ivanhoe* (libretto by J. Sturgis, after Scott). English opera was an unpredictable art-form; it always seemed ready to blossom and was always found to be blighted. A parallel might be drawn with the twentieth-century musical and the constant high hopes which have been entertained for its potential as an elevated artistic genre. The same demand for the detachability of certain songs is there; the only difference is that these demands are now born of the desire to market best-selling records instead of sheet music.

The cultivation of refined 'folk' airs

Two things need to be made clear at the outset: no one in the eighteenth and early nineteenth centuries spoke about 'folk tunes'; they talked, instead, of old airs and minstrelsy, and the main interest was in Celtic airs, particularly those of the two countries in which major rebellions had been recently suppressed. Scotland is the first to make an impact on the English with its 'national airs'. The reason could be traced back to the homesick Scots at the Anglo-Scots court produced by the Union of Crowns in 1603. The Scottish songs which directly helped to shape nineteenth-century bourgeois taste were, however, of more recent date, being associated with the name of Robbie Burns.

Interest in Scotland had increased in the eighteenth century following the Act of Union, 1707; until then England and Scotland had one ruler but were two states with two governments. It has already been pointed out that Gay selected tunes from the first published collection of Scottish songs, William Thomson's *Orpheus Caledonius* of 1725. One of the attractions of this collection was Thomson's claim that seven of the airs were composed by Queen Mary Stuart's Italian secretary, David Rizzio. James Oswald went so far as to include airs of his own in *The Caledonian Pocket Companion*, stating that they were also by Rizzio. There is, in fact, no evidence to suggest that Rizzio ever composed anything. The fifteen small volumes of Oswald's publication appeared 1745–65 and were aimed to satisfy not just the market for songs but also the demand for music suited to the fashionable flute.

Allan Ramsay (previously mentioned in connection with his ballad opera, *The Gentle Shepherd*) felt the need to preserve Scottish culture. His *Tea-Table Miscellany* (1723) contains words to Scottish airs which are named but not notated. Ramsay's preservation process involved the words in a great deal of literary improvement and moral purification, an exercise which was to become standard practice. Thomson took, without consent, thirty-eight of Ramsay's songs for his *Orpheus Caledonius*. As Burns did later, Ramsay portrays a peasant Scotland: his popular song 'The Yellow-Hair'd Laddie', depicting a love-sick girl milking her ewes, was something an urban society found quaint and appealing. It was Ramsay's 'Auld Lang Syne' which was later added to by Burns (although Burns did not expect the words to be put to Shield's tune).

Interest in Scotland was given a boost by James Macpherson's alleged translations of ancient Gaelic poetry transmitted to him orally. The verse was supposed to be the work of Ossian, a third-century bard. The collected works appeared in 1765. By reading Macpherson, Thomas Percy was stimulated to collect his unreliable and 'improved' *Reliques of Ancient Poetry*. Dr Johnson, who never once credited the myth of Ossian, excited further interest in Scotland when he embarked upon his Hebridean tour in 1773.

Set against the fascination with Scottish culture is the fact that after the 1745 rebellion the Act of Proscription was passed, forbidding any wearing of Highland dress under threat of imprisonment without bail for six months (for a first offence) or transportation for seven years (for a second offence). This did not simply demand a change of fashion but a change of wardrobe necessitating a complete alteration of the weavers' looms which were set up for the weaving of the traditional sets. In some areas the poor were reduced to wearing sack cloth. The implied proscription of the *piob mhor*, the Highland war-pipe, may have done incalculable damage to *ceol mor*, the most unique and highly developed form of Celtic music. Those pipers who turned to the fiddle are responsible for today's distinctive West of Scotland fiddle style. There was no interest, either, in the living culture of Gaelic laments such as 'The Lament for William Chisholm', composed by his widow after his death at Culloden.

Another song undoubtedly inspired by Culloden was Jean Elliot's 'The Flowers of the Forest'. However, the words (set to an old air first notated in the Skene MS, *c*.1615) are ostensibly about the battle of Flodden Field in 1513 when, in two hours of fighting, ten thousand Scots were killed and James IV was hacked to pieces. Maurice Disher claims that 'The Flowers of the Forest' was 'so deeply felt as to solemnize national mourning still'[25] and scorns the later version by Alicia Rutherford (Mrs Cockburn). He seems unaware that the pipe lament played at Scottish funerals to this day is, in fact, based on the 'improved' version of the tune by this middle-class Edinburgh lady.

By the time Pitt was recruiting from the Highlands for the conquest of Canada (1759), a ban on tartan could be lifted and songs could be permitted which celebrated Jacobite victories. 'Johnnie Cope' by Adam Skirven, which first appeared in a volume of Oswald's *Companion*, mocks the general who fled at the battle of Prestonpans, 1745. Many have no doubt assumed that the use of this tune for reveille by the present-day Scots Guards is designed to exasperate the English with a reminder of their defeat. Ironically, Sir John Cope was serving in that regiment 1710–12 before it was brought south to London by Queen Anne (to remain out of Scotland for two hundred years).

Relations with Scotland were further healed by the restoration of many forfeited estates in 1784. It was three years later that James Johnson began publishing *The Scots Musical Museum* which ran to six volumes. This work provided the cultural moment for an aesthetic reappraisal of Scottish songs: from now on the emphasis would not be on contrasting the artistic pretension of the Italian operatic aria with the simple 'folk' air, but on annexing the latter to the realm of high art. The key figure involved with the collection was the poet Robert Burns (1759–96), and the significance of this moment in Scottish culture was retrospectively acknowledged by the adoption of Burns' 'Scots Wha Hae' as the Scottish national anthem. He had published only a single volume of verse when he began contributing to the *Museum*. Burns was heavily involved in volumes 2 to 5 and did not hesitate to 'improve', add to, and rewrite any songs he found. He also contributed to George Thomson's *Select Collection of Original Scottish Airs* (the first volume of six being published in 1793). Although Burns had failed to rise in rank in his regular employment as an excise officer because of his republican sympathies, he consistently refused payment for his songs until nine days before his death when he requested help with the payment of a haberdasher's bill. A sense of the cultural importance of compiling a museum of Scottish song and preserving the Lallans dialect was sufficient motivation.

Johnson's *Museum* had presented the songs in the simplest of musical arrangements (a bass part with figured directions for harmony) by Stephen Clarke. George Thomson was more ambitious. As a cultivated member of the tasteful Edinburgh Musical Society and a clerical officer with the Board of Trustees for the Encouragement of Art and Manufactures in Scotland, he hit upon the idea of publishing Scottish airs in arrangements by Europe's leading composers.

Indicating the general change taking place in aesthetic attitude, the publisher William Napier had the identical idea at the very same time. The two great rivals in London in 1791 were Haydn and Pleyel, so it is no surprise to find Napier engaging the former and Thomson the latter. Ignace Pleyel's cello and piano accompaniments were too elaborate for the amateur market Thomson had in mind, so he changed to Leopold Kozeluch for his second volume. Kozeluch's arrangements did nothing to boost sales so he switched to Haydn. Haydn was then seduced away by another publisher, William Whyte, who offered to double Thomson's rate of one guinea per song if he would provide arrangements for his own two-volume *Collection of Scottish Airs* (1804–7). Haydn was apologetic; he was suffering financially from the effects of inflation which was crippling Vienna as a result of the war. Thomson seemed doomed to make little money on his project, yet he still insisted on the best-quality paper and binding and, as he saw it, the best-quality arrangements. He was not a professional publisher in the mould of Napier and Whyte; his motivation, like that of Burns, was patriotic sentiment.

Thomson's dream was to produce 'a work that will ever remain the standard of Scotish [sic] Music'.[26]

The publisher William Power saw a potential market for Irish songs 'improved' in a similar manner. The United Irishmen's revolt had been suppressed and the Act of Union in 1800 had prompted a drift of the Anglo-Irish aristocracy towards London. Power approached Tom Moore (1770–1852) who in 1807 had fallen out of favour with his patron, the Prince of Wales. Moore had already achieved acclaim for his drinking songs and the opera *The Gipsey Prince* (music by Michael Kelly, 1801). The products of this encounter, the *Irish Melodies*, were to prove a veritable corner-stone of bourgeois 'popular song' and provide Moore with a lucrative source of income, since he negotiated terms which gave him one hundred guineas per song. Between 1808 and 1834 they were issued serially in ten volumes, plus supplement. As happened with Burns, the cultural significance of Moore was later endorsed by the adoption of one of his songs as a national anthem: 'Let Erin Remember' remained Ireland's anthem until separation in 1921. These anthems illustrate classic hegemonic compromise: some acknowledgement of autonomy is demanded by Scotland and Ireland, yet their independence is recognized only in the context of a romantic and shadowy past. Of more recent date, the Welsh national anthem, 'Hen Wlad fy Nhadau' ('Land of My Fathers'), conforms to the same pattern, and here the possession of an ancient independent language becomes a symbol of the country's relative autonomy.

One of Moore's main sources for Irish tunes was Edward Bunting's *A General Collection of Ancient Irish Music*, the first volume of which had appeared in 1796. Bunting, a prominent Belfast musician, was inspired to begin his collection by the Belfast Harp Festival of 1792. In spite of considerable financial inducements, only eleven players arrived (one being Welsh), a symptom of the decline of the bardic tradition which had followed the rise of the Anglo-Irish gentry. Bunting's collection contained distortions dictated by contemporary taste: there were new English words, piano accompaniments, and, of course, the use of a 'classical' musical notation which 'corrected' what in terms of its own grammatical system were regarded as barbarisms, while being able only to approximate (when it was not simply ignored) the richness of traditional melodic ornamentation.

Moore chose to use no Irish dialect, but sometimes a novel English metre resulted from his fitting words to a Gaelic melody:

> At the mid-hour of night when stars are weeping, I fly
> To the lone vale we lov'd, when life shone warm in thine eye;

In the example above, an old Irish metre is used, called *ambrániocht*.[27] Not all the melodies Moore chose, however, were Irish in the first place: 'Believe Me If All Those Endearing Young Charms' was written to a tune already familiar to the words 'My Lodging Is on the Cold Ground', and 'As Slow Our Ship' uses the tune 'Brighton Camp', already popular in the eighteenth century as 'The Girl I Left Behind Me'.

The main sources for the words of Moore's historical songs included established works such as *Walker's Historical Memoirs of Irish Bards* and Warner's *History of Ireland*, as well as the most recent transactions of the Gaelic Society of Dublin. 'Avenging and Bright', the song written to the Gaelic air 'Cruchàn na Fèine', is drawn from a translation of *Deidre* by O'Flanagan, a leading researcher in the Gaelic Society. Some of Moore's metaphors are taken from ancient Irish poetry, for example, a 'chain of silence' or the 'sun-burst' of an unfurled banner. The *Irish Melodies* were in large part responsible for a new romantic view of Ireland and often contained nothing more than melancholy nostalgia (like 'The Meeting of the Waters'), occasionally not involving Ireland at all (like 'Love's Young Dream'). Nevertheless, nostalgia for the days of Ireland's liberty could leave a subversive quality just beneath the surface of some songs. Take the last lines of 'The Valley Lay Smiling Before Me', set, tactfully, in the remote period of Henry II:

> But onward! the green banner rearing,
> Go, flesh ev'ry sword to the hilt;
> On *our* side is VIRTUE and ERIN,
> On *theirs* is the SAXON and GUILT.

The words could as easily apply to the raising of the green banner at the battle of Vinegar Hill, 1798. For similar reasons it is no surprise to find 'The Minstrel Boy' reappropriated as an Irish song of resistance. Moore left Ireland to study law in London in 1799 but had been a friend of Robert Emmet, who led the unsuccessful Dublin Rising of 1803. Emmet was executed after being captured on a visit to his girlfriend Sarah Curran, who reputedly died thereafter of a broken heart. Moore makes oblique reference to these events in 'She Is Far from the Land'.

Sir John Stevenson, the vicar-choral of Christ Church Cathedral, Dublin, provided the accompaniments to Moore's *Irish Melodies*. It was a shrewd decision to steer clear of the Viennese style which was so ill suited to the collections of Scottish airs. Stevenson's sympathies lay with the Italian style. This was not entirely inappropriate since Celtic music had been coming to terms with Italian music for many years. In Scotland, over three hundred years before, James IV had emulated the life-style of an Italian Renaissance prince. In Ireland the 'last of the bards', Turlough Carolan (1670–1738), showed the unmistakable influence of those Italian contemporaries whose music was heard in Dublin (Corelli, Vivaldi, Germiniani) in his own harp music. Stevenson was familiar with at least some of Carolan's music: he adapted Carolan's wide-ranging air 'The Fairy Queen' for four voices in order that Moore could set words to it. The task of fitting words to this melody is considerable and shows the extent of Moore's skill. Stevenson's accompaniments rarely favour strong rhythmic patterns ('The Minstrel Boy' is an exception); he prefers to write rippling harp-like figuration. The simple, unfussy quality, in which, perhaps, rhythmic languor plays a necessary role, earns the arrangements the epithet 'chaste' from a mid-Victorian editor, who goes on to say in respect of the words: 'Little need be said of the merits of the work, the sentiments and narrative of the songs being such as will ever recommend them to the universal praise and sympathies of mankind.'[28] In further support of Moore's healthy universality of appeal, Holman Hunt depicts in *The Awakening Conscience* (1854) a fallen woman beginning to realize the error of her ways after hearing her lover play a few bars of 'Oft in the Stilly Night' (one of Moore's *National Melodies*).

The most well-known of the *Irish Melodies* was 'The Last Rose of Summer'.[29] The tune was taken from Alfred Milliken's *The Groves of Blarney* of the eighteenth century, in turn thought to be based on a seventeenth-century Irish harp tune. The Irish harp certainly could not have played 'The Last Rose of Summer' in its present melodic shape, since once tuned it was fixed in pitch and therefore unable to cope with the sharpened note in the phrase 'no rosebud is nigh'. The accompaniment throughout is harp-like, although the chords are spread from low note to high in classical manner rather than high to low in the old Irish manner. Stevenson writes an accompaniment in triplets (three notes performed in the time of two) even though there is nothing particular in the tune to justify this approach. The rhythmic effect of triplets was soon to become a common device employed to generate gentle musical tension, evoking a mood of sweet melancholy. The melody itself is decorated with notes which momentarily clash, then resolve on to the accompanying harmonies, as occurs at the word 'of' in ''Tis the last rose of summer'.

These dissonances also create the musical tension necessary for evocation of the desired mood. Sometimes the dissonance is crude and unconsidered, as on the final syllable of 'rosebud'.

Three of the four musical phrases reach their highest point in their respective first bars and are then dominated by a falling motion; it is easy to hear them as emotional musical parallels to the drooping of the dead 'lovely companions' and the heaving of 'sigh for sigh'.

'Tis the last rose of summer,
Left blooming alone;
All her lovely companions
Are faded and gone.
No flow'r of her kindred,
No rosebud is nigh.
To reflect back her blushes,
Or give sigh for sigh.

I'll not leave thee, thou lone one,
To pine on the stem;
Since the lovely are sleeping,
Go, sleep thou with them;
Thus kindly I scatter
Thy leaves on the bed,
Where thy mates of the garden
Lie scentless and dead.

So soon may I follow,
When friendships decay,
And from love's shining circle
The gems drop away!
When true hearts lie wither'd,
And fond ones are flown,
Oh! who would inhabit
This bleak world alone?

Moore's verses are typical of his output in seeking to conjure up a sense of loss; there is usually no remedy offered beyond the melancholy pleasure of indulging the feeling for its own sake, but in the circumstances described above he advocates floral euthanasia. The imagined loss of love and friendship was a cosy emotion to wallow in while encircled by family intimacy in the drawing room; in fact, it could only reinforce the pleasure of family ties in the comfortable knowledge that one did not inhabit this bleak world alone. It thus promoted the important 'Victorian values' of friendship and family.

While Moore was producing his *Irish Melodies*, George Thomson had managed to interest Beethoven in arranging airs. At first Beethoven arranged Irish songs because Thomson was temporarily out of stock of Scottish songs (even so, Beethoven's *25 Irish Songs* of 1814 include such unlikely examples of Hibernian minstrelsy as 'The Massacre of Glencoe'). Thomson had also taken an interest in Welsh airs, publishing three volumes of *A Select Collection of Original Welsh Airs* between 1809 and 1817 (Beethoven furnished twenty-six arrangements for the last volume). Moore's success soon found an echo in Thomson's publications: five tunes arranged by Beethoven in 1816 had already been used by Moore. Thomson has the poet William Smyth provide words of no possible ambiguity for 'The Soldier' (his version of 'The Minstrel Boy'): it is full of a military bravado befitting the calls of 'honour', 'country', and 'duty' during the close of the Napoleonic war.

> 'Tis you, 'tis I, that may meet the ball;
> And me it better pleases
> In battle, brave, with the brave to fall,
> Than to die of dull diseases;

Thomson had several other poets working for him, including Sir Walter Scott, and also relied upon verses written by Burns. Beethoven, to his frustration, was often denied the text; Thomson feared that he would have the songs published on the continent and that they would then work their way from there into Britain. To Thomson's surprise, however, Beethoven's arrangements lacked the commercial success of Stevenson's. Thomson thought, in view of Beethoven's greater stature as a composer, that it was the comparative difficulty of his arrangements which was to blame. Beethoven responded tetchily to a reprimand on these lines, saying Thomson should have given him a better understanding of 'le goût de votre pays et le peu de facilité de vos executeurs'[30] (your country's taste and your players' lack of expertise). A comparison between a Stevenson and a Beethoven arrangement of the same tune would indicate that the problem was not merely ease of execution. The song 'By the Side of the Shannon' (no. 8 of Beethoven's *12 Songs of Various Nationality*) employs the same melody, 'Paddy's Resource', as that used for the alternative version of Moore's 'When Daylight Was Yet Sleeping'. Comparing nothing more than the melody's accompaniment, it is indeed evident that Beethoven demands more playing skill, but he also does two things which Stevenson does not: he duplicates the melody on the piano, and he provides musical punctuations within the phrase structure of the song rather than confining the accompaniment's independence to before and after the verses. Doubling a melody in the accompaniment is a common practice of Beethoven's, featuring in his songs of all kinds; but this sort of support for the singer was beginning to seem unnecessary and old-fashioned.

When — day-light was yet sleeping un- der the billow, And stars in the heavens still lin- ger- ing shone,—

(Stevenson's arrangement)

By the side of the Shan-non was laid a young lov-er .. "I hate this dull ri-ver" he fret-ful-ly cried,—

(Beethoven's arrangement)

Beethoven's Viennese style and his own strong musical character are more jarring than the anonymously Italianate Stevenson. Neither of them sees much attraction in the modal nature of some of the airs they handle: Beethoven's second version of 'Highland Harry' (No. 6 of *12 Scottish Songs*) shows him modernizing the tune by making continual use of the sophisticated chord of the dominant ninth rather than treating it as the 'antiquated' dorian mode. The modes were the old system of scales ousted by the 'invention' of keys in the seventeenth century. Beethoven must have made a conscious decision to bring the modal airs up to date by supplying contemporary harmony; his familiarity with modal practice is demonstrated by the slow movement of his String Quartet Op. 132. When Stevenson was confronted with modes (as in 'Avenging and Bright' and 'Lesbia Hath a Beaming Eye'), he reacted as Beethoven did and squeezed them into the nearest equivalent modern key; no doubt he regarded this as a form of musical refinement.

Like Stevenson, Beethoven arranged some of the airs for more than one voice but preferred a high voice to carry the melody even in a solo setting, whereas Stevenson favoured the middle-voice range which made his arrangements more accommodating to the untrained voices of amateurs. Stevenson's accompaniments were for piano only; Beethoven added parts for violin and cello. The added string parts were not popular, so Thomson urged a reluctant Beethoven to consider the fashionable flute instead of the violin. The request helps to locate the position of Thomson's project in Scottish cultural life; it illustrates the distance between the musical interests pursued by Thomson's middle-class patrons and the indigenous style of Scottish fiddling, promoted by the landed aristocracy, which was in its heyday. Beethoven only succumbed to the pressure to write for flute in his purely instrumental op. 105 and op. 107. In some ways these piano and flute variations represent Beethoven's most successful treatment of the airs he received: op. 107, no. 8, for example, shows an imaginative working in his distinctive late style.

Thomson engaged other composers, such as Hummel, Weber, and even Bishop (who had been the arranger for the three volumes of Moore's *National Airs*), yet in the end his publications met with limited success. In 1855 he sold off his entire stock cheaply to a music dealer. He must have noted with bitter irony how Tom Moore's 'Those Evening Bells', set to a melody attributed to Beethoven, had become a drawing-room favourite.

Burns and Moore had pointed the way ahead to the Scottish and Irish ballads of the Victorian period and to a refined pseudo-folksong. In the years immediately after Burns' death, Sir Walter Scott (1771–1832) was collecting for his *Minstrelsy of the Scottish Border* (three volumes, 1802–3), assisted by Joseph Ritson (1752–1803) and James Hogg (1770–1835). The latter, the son of an Ettrick farmer and often styled 'the Ettrick shepherd', made a determined effort to assume the mantle of Burns in his *Jacobite Relics of Scotland* (two volumes, 1819–20). The true successor to Burns, who produced a wealth of enduring Scottish songs, was Lady Carolina Nairne (1766–1845). She was named Carolina after Prince Charles Stuart, and became 'Lady' Nairne only after the revival of the Jacobite peerage in 1824 (one of the relaxing measures which followed Scott's invitation to George IV to visit Scotland two years earlier). Many of her songs appeared anonymously in *The Scottish Minstrel* (1821–4). A collected edition, acknowledging her authorship, was published posthumously in 1846 as *Lays from Strathearn* (musical arrangements by Finlay Dun). Her songs are an innocuous blend of romantic and sentimental Jacobitism (as seen in 'The Hundred Pipers' and 'Will Ye No Come Back Again?').

As was the case with operatic airs, nostalgia was the favourite mood of the 'national airs'; the urban bourgeoisie felt no interest in the contemporary reels and jigs of figures of such central importance to Scottish fiddling as Niel Gow (1727–1807) at Blair Castle or William Marshall (1748–1833) at Gordon Castle. Rev. J. Riddle of Oxford, for one, was far more interested in further dignifying Lady Nairne's verse by translating it into ancient Greek. The second volume of Hogg's *Jacobite Relics* does contain verses written to 'Flora MacDonald's Lament', a violin tune by Niel Gow Jun. (1795–1825); and Lady Nairne supplied words to a tune by Nathaniel Gow (1763–1831), one of a series in which the fiddler intended to illustrate the street-cries of Edinburgh. In 'Caller Herrin'' he attempted to portray the cry of the Newhaven fishwives set against the pealing of the bells of St Andrews, George Street.

From the desire to dignify a Celtic air to the wish to imitate one, or decorate a song with Celtic features, was a small move. Imitation Scottish song was not a new thing; James Hook's ''Twas Within a Mile o' Edinburgh Town' is a well-known eighteenth-century example of pseudo-Scottish song. Products like Mrs Gibson's setting of Byron's 'Lochnagar' and Rev. William Leeves' setting of Lady Lindsay's 'Auld Robin Gray', however, signal a new departure which will be discussed in Chapter 4.

The respectable entertainer

Moore was an early example of a new kind of respectable entertainer who sang self-accompanied at the piano songs of impeccable moral sentiment. The first person to achieve public celebrity as a respectable entertainer was Charles Dibdin (1745–1814). As a young man, in between singing in the chorus at Covent Garden and working for a music publisher, Dibdin had shown himself to be possessed of versatile talent. At the age of nineteen he wrote both the words and music of a pastoral opera, *The Shepherd's Artifice*, and also took the leading role himself at its first performance. He developed a flair for comic opera in the pasticcio/ballad-opera manner, collaborating for a while with Bickerstaffe. Some of his most imaginative work was done at this time, particularly in the writing of dramatic ensembles, but it was with his Table Entertainments that he made the greatest impact on the direction of bourgeois 'popular song'. The editor of the first complete collection of Dibdin's songs says of these Entertainments,

> These were produced by him when in the maturity and vigour of his powers, and in the full tide of his popularity; and it is on them that he seems to have put forth the utmost strength of his genius.[31]

Dibdin had run into debt with a project to run a venue combining opera and equestrian displays and had decided to emigrate to India. When adverse winds drove the ship into Torbay, he gave an impromptu musical entertainment combining songs and patter. Its success made him abruptly change his departure plans and, meeting similar enthusiasm at performances given in various country towns, he thought he would try the idea in London. He opened at Hutchins' Auction-Room, Covent Garden, with the appropriately titled *The Whim of the Moment*, in 1788. Alas, the size and enthusiasm of the audience were both disappointing, but a song concerning a sailor with a touching faith in Providence, 'Poor Jack', became immensely popular. Its use of vernacular speech, nautical metaphor (mainly of the 'shiver me timbers' variety) and sailors' jargon, provided a prototype for many more Dibdin songs. Dibdin made a second attempt, and his next Entertainment, *The Oddities*, gave him the acclaim and financial reward he was seeking. He now moved to a room opposite the Beaufort Buildings in the Strand, naming it Sans Souci; here, he brought out another new Entertainment called *Private Theatricals*. His success multiplied, enabling him to purchase a small theatre in Leicester Place in 1796, which he also named Sans Souci.

Dibdin's appeal as an entertainer lay largely in his talent for character roles; he relied on mimicry of accent and manner rather than dress. His fun was at the expense of rustics, Jews, Negroes, and foreigners in general, at a time when such activity carried no trace of moral reprehensibility. He himself asserted that it was 'sacredly incumbent' upon him 'in no instance to outrage propriety or wound morality'.[32] His piano sounded unique: the instrument was adapted to incorporate chamber organ, bells, side drum, gong, and tambourine. The percussion was operated by mechanical contrivances. Sailor songs were to prove the most popular part of his output; although not one of them suggested any of the discontent in the Navy concerning bad provisions, low pay, harsh discipline, or the resentment of the pressed men. In June 1803 he was awarded a government pension which was kept on when the ministry changed and Pitt became First Lord of the Treasury. However, in 1806, the year by which all the famous naval battles had been fought, Lord Grenville decided that the pension should cease.

An offended Dibdin brought out a pamphlet in 1807, *The Public Undeceived*; in it he claims to state the material facts relative to his 'trifling pension'. He says that its discontinuation is an insult to his public service, dating from as far back as 1793, 'when I had my theatre in the Strand, opposite to which lectures were given, which broached those violent democratic opinions that all good subjects held in detestation.'[33] He maintained that, despite insinuations to the contrary, he acted without government bribes. Nevertheless, it does seem that the annuity was originally given partly in return for the production of war-songs: Dibdin admits, 'war-songs could be of no object to me, for they were sure to be pirated'[34] and so he was not disposed to produce them without financial inducement. He also had an arrangement whereby he was to receive any profits from musical publications brought out 'at the instance of Government'.[35] The settlement of £200 per annum disappointed his expectations and he reproachfully points out in his pamphlet that he would have been a rich man if he had continued touring and entertaining instead of serving the government.

In 1793, the year to which Dibdin traced back his record of public service, he included a new song in *The Quizzes* (his latest Table Entertainment) entitled 'Ninety-Three'. It was added in January, just before the beheading of the French Royal Family. The song was intended to check the spread of revolutionary opinions in Britain.

> Some praise a new freedom, imported from France;
> Is Liberty taught, then, like teaching to dance?
> They teach freedom to Britons! our own right divine!
> A rushlight may as well teach the sun how to shine.
> In fam'd ninety-three
> We'll convince them we're free; –
> Free from ev'ry licentiousness faction can bring,
> Free with heart and voice to sing – God save the King!

It revolves around a definition of the word liberty, making tendentious contrasts between French and English varieties in what was to become a familiar propaganda ploy. After the naval mutinies in the Channel Fleet at Spithead and the North Sea Squadron at the Nore, Dibdin's anger became more impassioned: 'The Invasion', in his 1798 Entertainment *The King and Queen*, referred to the threatened invasion by Napoleon and whipped up patriotic fervour against the 'mad liberty scheme'. His official government backing, on the resumption of war, in 1803, bore first fruit in *Britons, Strike Home!* In this he had the assistance of a military band in promoting enthusiasm against the French. It contained many war-songs, for example, 'The Call of Honour', 'The British Heroes', and 'Soldiers and Sailors'. It also included 'Erin Go Bra', a song designed to flatter and appease the Irish (after the recent rebellion):

> Shake off disaffection, to duty be true,
> And cherish your natural friend.

Dibdin's most celebrated song was from his early Entertainment, *The Oddities*, of 1789, and was originally called 'Poor Tom, or The Sailor's Epitaph'; in the nineteenth century it was always known as 'Tom Bowling'.[36]

> Here, a sheer hulk,[37] lies poor Tom Bowling,
> The darling of our crew;
> No more he'll hear the tempest howling,
> For death has broach'd him to.
> His form was of the manliest beauty,
> His heart was kind and soft,
> Faithful below he did his duty,
> And now he's gone aloft.
>
> Tom never from his word departed,
> His virtues were so rare,
> His friends were many, and true hearted,
> His Poll was kind and fair;
> And then he'd sing so blithe and jolly,
> Ah many's the time and oft!
> But mirth is turn'd to melancholy,
> For Tom is gone aloft.
>
> Yet shall Poor Tom find pleasant weather,
> When he who all commands
> Shall give, to call life's crew together,
> The word to pipe all hands.
> Thus death who Kings and Tars dispatches,
> In vain Tom's life has doff'd,
> For, though his body's under hatches,
> His soul is gone aloft.

The tune has less in common with the elegant style associated with the recently deceased figures of Bach and Abel than with a robust 'traditional' English air; an obvious exception is the phrase which bears the repeated final line of each stanza. See the musical example on page 35. This phrase is the only point at which any attempt is made musically to illustrate the words: the rising motion offers symbolic confirmation that this is the direction in which Tom's soul has gone. Of course, in a strophic (same tune for each verse) setting there is little room for word-painting. Dibdin favours straightforward strophic treatment in his Table Entertainment songs, though some, like 'Poor Jack' and 'The Anchorsmiths', are more sophisticated in phrase structure than 'Tom Bowling'. Dibdin's typically

And now he's gone a-loft, _____ And now_ he's_ gone_ a-loft!

humorous use of nautical metaphors has a wry effect, owing to the melancholy subject matter: the song has widely been held to be an epitaph to his elder brother Tom, the Captain of an Indiaman, who was struck by lightning at sea when Charles was a boy. The picture of the kind, honest, jolly sailor, whom death visits with the same impartiality as it may do a king, is stock Dibdin. The situation on board ship is a microcosm of the Christian's life on earth: the Commander in the sky will one day order the whistle to be sounded to summon up his crew (a novel departure from the more orthodox last trumpet). To the middle class his songs seemed to express 'natural sentiments in plain language' even if they could not help but be aware that the features of the sailor's character had been 'elevated, refined, and united with a delicacy of sentiment and firmness of principle' beyond what were met with in the realities of life.[38] Dibdin undoubtedly had a sense of moral purpose which helped to keep his music alive in parlours and drawing rooms long after he had himself 'gone aloft'. In his autobiography he firmly advocated a didactic approach to song-writing: 'The song, written to please, may be so managed as to instruct.'[39]

He gave up his Entertainments in 1805 but had to resume professional activity at the age of sixty-three when his pension was halted by Grenville's administration. His career ended in bankruptcy, and a relief fund was initiated by a Mr Oakley of Tavistock Place. Mr Oakley was not apparently a personal friend; Dibdin had been unable to remain on good terms with anyone and eventually died a lonely man in Camden Town. He had deserted his first mistress, leaving her with two children, Charles and Thomas, who both grew up to write for the stage. He was outraged when they took his surname and he seems to have entirely neglected them: his son Thomas's *Reminiscences* barely touch upon him. Thomas actually outdid his father's patriotic popularism with 'The Tight Little Island', his own song written at the time of the threatened Napoleonic invasion.

Charles Dibdin preferred to give public entertainments on his own premises; the poet Thomas Haynes Bayly (1797–1839), however, like Tom Moore, was a darling of the salons. Bayly, too, favoured the kind of delicacy and wilting melancholy found in many of the *Irish Melodies* rather than Dibdin's melodic vigour. Bayly has already been mentioned in connection with the prototype of

'Home, Sweet Home!' in the first volume of *Melodies of Various Nations*. Bishop was a frequent collaborator with Bayly and set over 130 of his lyrics. The most popular of these settings were the autobiographical 'Oh! No! We Never Mention Her' (referring to Bayly's failed first courtship) and 'The Mistletoe Bough'. The latter was a gruesome tale of a young bride who accidentally locked herself in a disused oak chest and was not found until years later. A deal of speculation surrounded the origin of the story; houses at Bramshill and Malsanger, and Marwell Old Hall contended for its true location. Bayly's motto at the head of his poem (which does not appear in the published music) makes it clear, however, that his source was the story of Ginevra in Rogers' *Italy*. The fascination with 'The Mistletoe Bough' was such that it spawned a play of the same title, produced at the Garrick, Whitechapel, in 1834.

Bayly was the son of a Bath solicitor and spent a lot of his own life in Bath, having first turned down the idea of entering the law and then the church as a profession. The majority of his songs belong to the 1820s, when he gave entertainments in the fashionable drawing rooms of Bath, partly, of course, to promote sales. Ambition to become a dramatist brought him to London in 1829. Unfortunately, a few years later, he ran into financial problems with his coal-mining investments. Further financial difficulties soon followed as the result of the fraudulent dealings of the agent looking after his wife's property in Ireland.[40] He found it necessary to move to Paris with his family. Returning to England after three years, he relied almost entirely on his writing and it was not long before overwork took its toll. He died in Cheltenham where he had gone to take the spa water for his health.

Bayly sometimes selected airs for his own verses, as Moore had done. All the airs of his *Songs of the Boudoir* of 1830 (which contained the great favourite 'We Met') were selected by Bayly and arranged by T. H. Severn. He also composed tunes himself, as was the case with 'I'd Be a Butterfly', a drawing-room favourite for half a century. The first verse is given below.

> I'd be a butterfly born in a bower,
> Where roses and lilies and violets meet;
> Roving for ever from flower to flower,
> And kissing all buds that are pretty and sweet!
> I'd never languish for wealth, or for power,
> I'd never sigh to see slaves at my feet,
> I'd be a butterfly born in a bower,
> Kissing all buds that are pretty and sweet.

His wife provided the first accompaniment to this song; the words were supposed to have been written on impulse as he watched a butterfly fluttering about in the summer-house of Lord Ashtown's villa at Chessell on the Southampton River. The summer-house was later redecorated and named Butterfly Bower in honour of the occasion. Bayly was a friend of Moore and flatters him with an obvious echo of the sentiments of 'The Last Rose of Summer' in his third stanza:

> Surely 'tis better, when summer is over,
> To die when all fair things are fading away:

Bayly was certainly an entomophile; he produced a whole volume of verse entitled *The Loves of the Butterflies*, set to music by George Alexander Lee (1802–52). Another 'popular song' written and composed by Bayly himself was 'Fly Away, Pretty Moth!' Indeed, he was soon known as 'Butterfly' Bayly, a description which suited his dandified manner.

The message of the song is that being a humble butterfly and leading a life of irresponsible hedonism is preferable to the misery of being rich and powerful. The hedonistic tone of the song later caused Bayly some concern and he chose to modify his philosophic outlook in 'Be a Butterfly Then!' He had been goaded by 'The Bee and the Butterfly', written by R. Morland and composed by G. W. Reeve in answer to Bayly's song, wherein they conclusively demonstrated that the busy, useful bee 'with a house and a home' was indisputably the butterfly's moral superior. Answers to songs, as well as parodies of songs, were becoming tremendously fashionable. Bayly was so irritated with the innumerable parodies of 'I'd Be a Butterfly' (such as 'I'd Be a Nightingale' and 'I'd Be a Rifleman') he retorted with his own parody, beginning:

> I'd be a Parody, made by a ninny,
> On some little song with a popular tune,
> Not worth a halfpenny, sold for a guinea,
> And sung in the Strand by the light of the moon . . .

Bayly's songs were much parodied; a few examples are given below.

Original title	*Parody*
'The Soldier's Tear'	'The Policeman's Tear'
(music by Lee)	(Shirley Brooks)
'She Wore a Wreath of Roses'	'He Wore a Pair of Mittens'
(music by J. P. Knight)	(W. H. Guest)
'We Met – 'Twas in a Crowd'	'We Met – 'Twas in a Mob'
(music selected by Bayly)	(Thomas Hood)

Answers, which usually employ a fresh tune and take issue with the original song, are also plentiful. More flattering to Bayly were the translations of his verse into foreign tongues, not always a living language either: Archdeacon Wrangham was so enamoured of Bayly's lyrics that he published a volume of translations into rhyming Latin verse ('I'd Be a Butterfly' became 'Ah! Sim Papilio').

The musical form of a Bayly song is usually shorter, simpler, and more regular than Dibdin's strophic settings; again, the *Irish Melodies* make a better comparison: they seem to have served as a model for the sort of music Bayly composed and selected as well as for that which his musical collaborators found most appropriate to provide. Their melodic compass is generally small, which undoubtedly recommended them to amateur singers of limited technique. This is the reason that a Bayly song like 'Long, Long Ago' will still be found today in an elementary instrumental tutor. It was Bayly's verse, however, which really earned him the admiration of his contemporaries. Pecksniff Hall wrote: 'The songs of Mr Bayly have obtained a popularity almost without precedent in our time. With the exception of Moore, no living writer has been so eagerly sought after by musical composers . . .'[41]

The trio of Burns, Moore, and Bayly represented a peak of achievement by songwriters who were first and foremost poets. As has been pointed out already, Moore and Bayly performed as respectable entertainers in the drawing rooms of the landed gentry and the upper echelons of the bourgeoisie, whereas Dibdin had provided an entertainment for the paying public on his own premises. Dibdin, nevertheless, firmly aligned himself with bourgeois values. Allowing for the effects of social change on these values, the same may be said of a quite different personality, who in many ways was Dibdin's successor, Henry Russell (1812–1900). He was not an immediate successor, of course; Dibdin had died when Russell was a baby. During Russell's childhood and early manhood the bourgeoisie were struggling to become the dominant fraction of the power bloc, spurred on by a new disaffected middle-class group who had been thrown up by the events of the industrial revolution. The element of evangelical humanitarianism in Russell's character places him in conflict with the *laissez-faire* philosophy which maintained that people driven by self-interest to create wealth forwarded the general good. Ironically, social reformers at this time were often paternalistic Tories practising their code of *noblesse oblige*: the Factory Acts of 1833 and 1847 and the Public Health Act of 1848 were all passed in the face of opposition from *laissez-faire* dogmatists. Sometimes, as in Yorkshire, there was what amounted almost to a coalition between Radicals and Tories. Russell's song, 'The Happy Days of Childhood' (poetry by George Pendrill), would have appealed more to Lord Shaftesbury than to a textile-factory owner.

Russell established the norm for respectable entertainers: he selected verse or collaborated with poets he admired and sang his compositions, accompanying himself at the piano. Like Dibdin, he had been involved with the theatre as a young man. Having had a good voice as a boy, he had studied in Italy under Bellini when his voice broke, and had become chorus master at Her Majesty's on his return. Disillusioned with the prospects of making his living in England, he decided to emigrate to Canada. After the experience of a storm in Toronto, he quickly moved to Rochester, New York, and became a teacher at the Rochester Academy of Music, and organist and choir master at the First Presbyterian Church. His New York début as a singer was in 1836, and during that year he toured with the composer Wallace. The next year he embarked upon his career as a solo entertainer. His songs about the New World, added to his popularity and influence in the United States, led to his being considered an American composer. He did, in fact, write many of his well-known songs there; but the two periods of his life spent in the United States total less than ten years, only half the time that he spent as an active entertainer in Britain.

Russell, together with his long-standing friend Charles Mackay (later, editor of the *Illustrated London News*), was a fervent champion of the New World. They collaborated on emigration songs such as 'To the West' and 'Far, Far upon the Sea', as well as a vocal and pictorial entertainment, *The Far West or, The Emigrant's Progress from the Old World to the New*. Their song 'Cheer, Boys! Cheer!' became the anthem of optimism for those leaving Britain's shores; it was even sung by the

Guards as they departed for the Crimea. Russell claimed his songs induced the starving to seek prosperity by emigrating. He also claimed that slavery was 'one of the evils I helped to abolish through the medium of some of my songs'.[42] Certainly he adopted a strong anti-slavery stance: this is clear in his entertainment *Negro Life in Freedom and in Slavery* (words by Angus B. Reach) which includes the song 'The Slave Sale'. Russell's anti-slavery sentiment is of the Harriet Beecher Stowe variety (although it pre-dates *Uncle Tom's Cabin*); yet he is not content with condemnation: his *gran scena* 'The Slave Ship' contains a call for action,

> Let every man arise to save,
> From scourge and chain, the Negro slave!

Russell's *gran scenas* are especially charged with moral purpose; it was in this form, taken from the operatic set piece for anguished prima donna, that he could bring the full panoply of melodramatic devices to the service of his own enthusiasm. His *scena* 'The Gambler's Wife' depicts a mother and child desolately waiting as the clock strikes each hour from one to four o'clock in the morning, at which point the gambling father returns to a domestic tragedy. This *scena* must have influenced Henry Clay Work's famous song on a similar theme, 'Come Home, Father!' Russell's *gran scena* 'The Maniac' may easily appear today as a tasteless example of horror for entertainment's sake and at the expense of the mentally ill: such is obviously Edward Lee's opinion in *Music of the People*.[43] Russell insisted, however, that it was composed with the specific intention of 'exposing that great social evil – the private lunatic asylum'[44] where people were unlikely to be declared sane while they proved profitable inmates. The eponymous character in 'The Maniac' is driven mad by the asylum itself. The piece stands as an indictment to the blanket application of the principle of *laissez-faire*.

Russell also specialized in composing a simpler form of dramatic narrative song, and he was always delighted at his ability to command the intense involvement of his audience with these. There are several anecdotes in his autobiography which tell how people caught up in the mood of the song would shout questions to him on stage. For example, after singing 'Carlo, the Newfoundland Dog' (a dog who, in the song, jumps overboard to rescue a young boy) a gentleman in the audience asked,

> 'Excuse me, sir, . . . Was that dog yourn?'
> 'No, it was not,' I replied.
> 'Did he save the child?'
> 'He did.'[45]

On another occasion, after singing his celebrated ballad 'Woodman, Spare That Tree!', the following exchange took place:

> 'Was the tree spared, sir?'
> 'It was,' I said.
> 'Thank God for that.'[46]

Russell made his English début in March 1842 at the Hanover Square Rooms but was soon to hear his tunes on barrel organs and hurdy-gurdies all over town.

He noted that his kind of entertainment was then 'practically a new idea in England'[47] but acknowledged Dibdin as a forerunner. With a work such as *The Far West*, he was able to escape the Lord Chamberlain's proscription of plays during Lent, since it was a sung entertainment. Russell took advantage of this situation to the full in 1851, when he mounted a Lenten Entertainment at the Olympic Theatre.

Russell's social conscience took him to Dublin, where he gave two entertainments for the exclusive benefit of evicted tenants during the Irish famine. His success here encouraged him to make a tour of Ireland (places visited included Cork, Waterford, Limerick, Wexford, Drogheda, Newry, and Belfast) and he eventually raised almost £7000.

Many of Russell's songs remained favourites all century, particularly 'The Old Sexton', 'Woodman, Spare That Tree!', 'Cheer, Boys! Cheer!', and 'The Old Arm Chair'. The song which outlived every other, however, was 'A Life on the Ocean Wave' (words by an American, E. Sargent, based on verses by S. J. Arnold).[48] Its longevity has been aided in our own time by its having been adopted in 1889 as the official march of the Royal Marines. The first verse runs as follows:

> A life on the ocean wave,
> A home on the rolling deep!
> Where the scatter'd waters rave,
> And the winds their revels keep!
> Like an eagle caged I pine
> On this dull unchanging shore,
> Oh! give me the flashing brine,
> The spray and the tempest's roar!
> A life on the ocean wave, etc.

The song has the same pioneering spirit as another Russell favourite, 'I'm Afloat!' It shows an adventurous, optimistic nature, in contrast to his other common mood of sentimental nostalgia; this emotional dichotomy is found with great frequency among the nineteenth-century bourgeoisie. Whatever the mood of his songs, however, they are generally stamped with several of the following hallmarks: a limited vocal range; a partiality for major keys; a contrasting key area for the middle of the song; a pause with, perhaps, a short cadenza (a vocal flourish) before the main tune reprise; and a fragmentation of the tune at the end. 'A Life on the Ocean Wave' contains all these features. The fragmented ending is less common in his pathetic ballads but does appear on occasion as, for example, in 'The Old Sexton' (incidentally, a rare example of his use of a minor key). Though normally of no great length, Russell's melodies are skilfully crafted within a musical idiom that has now achieved such autonomy as a distinctive style there is little point in tracing 'art music' influences.

Russell could be singled out as the composer mainly responsible for popularizing the maudlin, over sentimental song, the 'promoter of the moist eye'. He was enormously fond of the word 'old' in these ballads; indeed, 'The Old Arm Chair' was a setting of Eliza Cook's 'The Favourite Chair' and it was Russell who requested that the title be changed. It is hard to realize now that Russell felt there was no sentimental excess in any of his songs: he believed their healthy moral tone prevented that happening.

> the moral tone of a song depends upon the moral tone of the individual who writes it: by which, I mean, a healthy song comes from a healthy man and likewise produces healthy effects, whereas sickening sentiment is born of a sickening mind and generally produces sickening effects.[49]

Unfortunately, Russell's stricture runs into difficulties if applied to his celebrated predecessor, Dibdin. Dibdin's first editor commented that his music was never 'contaminated by anything gross or licentious . . . but alas for the infirmity of human nature! Dibdin may be added to the numerous illustrations of the maxim, that the character of an author is not to be gathered from his works'.[50]

Access to music

The final section of this chapter will look briefly at some varieties of entertainment not previously covered and examine the sources of access to music for the urban middle class. A typical middle-class venue at which Henry Russell may have appeared would be a Song and Supper room. No women were allowed here, but many Russell songs, like 'A Life on the Ocean Wave', are implicitly addressed to a male audience anyway. The Song and Supper rooms provided entertainment while patrons ate and drank. They began to emerge in the 1820s as an expansion of the kind of access to music formerly provided in taverns and coffee houses. Among the most famous were the Coal Hole, Evans's (Covent Garden), the Cyder Cellars, and the Wrekin, which all flourished in the 1830s and 40s. Some of the early music-hall artists, for instance, Charles Sloman and Sam Cowell, served their apprenticeship in these rooms; the entertainment was liable to switch from respectable glee singing to bawdy songs once midnight had sounded.

As indoor provision for entertainment increased, so outdoor provision began to contract: the pleasure garden was not the important scene of musical activity it had been in the eighteenth century. Then, the same musicians would often be heard in the pleasure gardens as had been heard in the theatre or concert hall. The pleasure garden therefore gave access to the kind of music performed at subscription concerts, such as the Bach–Abel Concerts (1765–82), which were beyond the pocket of the petit bourgeois. In the second half of the eighteenth century there were nearly two dozen pleasure gardens and tea gardens providing musical entertainment. Marylebone and Vauxhall were the oldest, having both opened in the seventeenth century. In the early 1770s the future for music seemed brightest at Marylebone, recently bought by the composer Samuel Arnold (with his wife's money) and employing as organist and composer the prolific James Hook (1746–1827). Sadly, Arnold was forced to sell, owing to the criminal activities of an employee, and the gardens did not long survive his departure. Meanwhile Hook had moved to become composer and organist at Vauxhall, a post which he held for nearly fifty years. He was required to provide songs and cantatas and to perform an organ concerto every night of the season. As the garden season was in the summer, it made them a particularly middle-class locale, since the aristocracy had returned to their country residences at this time of the year. Music was not the only thing provided in pleasure gardens: there were firework displays, side shows, and cold suppers served in alcoves. They were favourite places for courting couples, which explains the popularity of love songs. Hook's Vauxhall songs range from the coy 'No, No, No, It Must Not Be' to the flirtatious 'Take Me, Take Me, Some of You'. Usually, song-writers have the tact to avoid giving embarrassment, by introducing lovers in the traditional and inoffensive shape of nymphs and shepherds. Many songs take advantage of the outdoor setting, either imitating birdsong, like Hook's 'The Blackbird', or capturing the romantic evening mood. Love songs were always to remain popular at Vauxhall: two well-known later examples are C. E. Horn's 'Cherry Ripe' of 1825, and Bishop's 'The Bloom Is on the Rye', which was the big success of the 1833 season. No one, however, was to equal the creative energy Hook dedicated to the pleasure garden; in songs alone his output exceeded two thousand, many of them being published in the annual *Vauxhall Songs* collection. His elegant style, which is indebted to the *style galant* of Bach and Abel, can be perceived in his still familiar song 'The Lass of Richmond Hill.'

Ranelagh had provided an outlet for Welsh music in 1746, when the blind harpist, John Parry, appeared there. He was joint editor, with Evan Williams, of the first collections of Welsh melodies; predictably, these were subjected to the usual 'improvement' according to the fashionable taste of the day. Performances of traditional ballads at Ranelagh may have suggested to Dibdin the idea of giving some of his new strophic narrative songs the title 'ballads': one of the earliest examples of this application of that term was in the publication *The Ballads sung by Mr Dibdin at Ranelagh Gardens*, which appeared about the year 1770.

Sadler's Wells was originally a small pleasure garden, consisting of a medicinal spring and nearby music house. In response to the growing urban population, the spring was discarded and a theatre built on the site to cater, instead, for the middle class's thirst for musical entertainment. Music in the theatre has been dealt with in much detail already; but there were many varieties of music theatre, a diversity which resulted from the restrictions on spoken drama. After the Licensing Act of 1737, the only theatres allowed to present performances of spoken plays were Drury Lane, which until the late eighteenth century held less than two thousand people, and Covent Garden, which held just over that figure. The Little Theatre in the Haymarket managed to obtain a patent in 1766 to enable it to open for plays in summer, when Drury Lane and Covent Garden were theoretically closed. This meant that, like the pleasure gardens, it relied on a middle-class clientele, since the landed gentry were in the country.

Audiences were alerted to what was on at the theatre by newspaper advertisements or by announcements given out either vocally or in handbills at a theatre they were attending. Not all the middle class were sufficiently independent to be able to spend whole evenings in the theatre: lower middle-class shopkeepers, for instance, did not finish work until at least eight o'clock, so they had to make do with the afterpiece, a short work like Arne's *Thomas and Sally* which filled up the evening's entertainment (except in those rare cases when the mainpiece was a very lengthy work such as *The Beggar's Opera*). Entrance to see the afterpiece was at half price. In 1763 Covent Garden attempted to end this concession and thereby provoked the worst theatre riot of the eighteenth century; it cost them £2000 worth of damage. As for the relative expense of seats within the theatre, the galleries were cheaper than the pit (the modern-day stalls), while the boxes cost most of all. The upper boxes were frequented by prostitutes; houses of ill repute were usually conveniently situated near theatres. Indeed the word 'actress' was a common euphemism for prostitute. It was the reason that the growing numbers of industrial bourgeoisie, with their religious nonconformism and new-found respectability, shunned and despised the theatre, however much they might admire individual theatre songs.

When Charles Dibdin the younger took over at Sadler's Wells at the turn of the nineteenth century, he introduced the novelty of aquadramas, like *The Siege of Gibraltar*. His major crowd-pullers, however, were the pantomimes starring the clown Joe Grimaldi. English pantomime had developed out of attempts to popularize the court masque. Most eighteenth-century pantomimes had mythological or grotesque plots involving characters from the traditional Italian *commedia dell'arte*. The earliest contained no dialogue, but included songs, dances, and miming during instrumental interludes known as the Comic Tunes. John Rich, who was fond of playing the character of Harlequin himself, had popularized pantomimes at his Lincoln's Inn Fields Theatre. Machinery, trick scenery, and all manner of gadgetry helped attract audiences, but in the opinion of people like Colley Cibber and Henry Fielding the pantomime was a fatuous and inferior art-form. Drury Lane found it financially attractive to present pantomime afterpieces, but to follow a Shakespeare play with a pantomime would have been condemned as vulgar. The modern pantomime can be seen emerging in Linley's *Robinson Crusoe* (1781) and Shield's *Aladdin* (1788). The character of the clown was of little significance until Grimaldi arrived on the scene (the clown's original function was to serve Columbine's father, Pantaloon).

The comic scoffing tone of pantomime gave it a kinship with burlesque: it is probably no coincidence that Planché's first pantomime, *Rodolph the Wolf*, was performed at the Olympic Pavilion in the same year (1818) that his first burlesque, *Amoroso, King of Little Britain*, was performed at Drury Lane. The burlesque can be traced back to Elizabethan theatre, but begins to be a distinctive genre after the Reformation. A seminal work was *The Rehearsal* (1671) by the Duke of Buckingham, which made fun of both dramatic tragedy and contemporary attempts to bring opera to the English stage. Arne's *The Opera of Operas* (1733), based on Fielding's *The Tragedy of Tragedies*, established the character of eighteenth-century burlesque. Henry Carey's *The Dragon of Wantley* (music by Lampe), written in 1737, was the most successful of these: it mocked the castrato Farinelli and Handel's latest opera, *Giustino*, which contained a dragon. Burlesques continued to be popular in the nineteenth century and proved a major influence behind the Gilbert and Sullivan operettas: Gilbert produced his first burlesque, *Dulcamara*, five years before he began to collaborate with Sullivan.

Taverns and tea or coffee houses offered another important source of access to music. Before Hook's employment in the pleasure gardens, he played the organ to entertain customers taking tea at the White Conduit House in Clerkenwell.

Taverns were more likely to be the scene of active participation in music-making. The Anacreontic Society, which was made up of aristocrats and wealthy bourgeoisie, held their meetings at the Crown and Anchor in the Strand. The constitutional hymn of this society, 'To Anacreon in Heaven' (composed by J. S. Smith), was given new words and adopted in 1931 as the United States' national anthem, 'The Star-Spangled Banner'. The Concentores Sodales (friends of harmony) met from 1798 onwards at the Buffalo Tavern in Bloomsbury. Lower middle-class music lovers would meet at an alehouse, such as the Twelve Bells in Bride Lane. The Madrigal Society was founded there in 1741.

The taste of the eighteenth-century mercantile middle class was generally theatrical and secular; music in the church was in decline. More interesting than the musical life of St Paul's was that of Robert Smith's house in the churchyard. Here the Glee Club began to meet in 1783. It was for this club Samuel Webbe composed 'Glorious Apollo', which from 1790 was always sung at the start of their meetings. Glees were not always specifically written as glees,[51] but, just as an operatic air could be angled towards the drawing room, a musical ensemble in a stage entertainment could be aimed at future use in a glee group. Taking Bishop as an example, the following table gives the titles of several of his most admired glees and the works in which they first appeared.

'The Winds Whistle Cold' 'The Chough and Crow' }	*Guy Mannering* 1816 (opera)
'Mynheer Vandunck'	*The Law of Java* 1822 (musical drama)
'Hark, 'Tis the Indian Drum'	*Cortez, or The Conquest of* *Mexico* 1823 (historical play)

In addition to the sources of access to music discussed above, the eighteenth century saw a growth in the number of musical publications. Periodicals stimulated interest in music and, as printing technology progressed, sheet music became cheaper and more accessible to an expanding amateur market. The early relationship between the nineteenth-century music industry and amateur music-making in the home will be explored in the next chapter.

2 The Growth of the Market for Domestic Music

After the Napoleonic Wars, Britain was involved in no major hostilities abroad for a lengthy period. Furthermore, the kind of internal dissent which met with vicious suppression at Peterloo in 1819 was contained, if not removed, by the passing of the Reform Bill in 1832 and, later, by the repeal of the Corn Laws in 1846. These two parliamentary moves helped stave off a British counterpart to the continental revolutions of 1848. During this time the industrial and mercantile bourgeoisie became increasingly prosperous as a result of soaring industrial production and booming foreign trade. The first plateau of economic expansion was marked with a Great Exhibition at the Crystal Palace in 1851. It is these years of growing middle-class affluence and its related cultural effects which will be considered in this chapter. The prime Victorian virtues of thrift, self-help, independence, and character, which found their eloquent champion in Samuel Smiles, all serve middle-class economic interests by stressing the importance of individual rather than collective action.

The first musical fruit of middle-class prosperity appeared in the form of a piano. It was the acquisition of pianos in large numbers which was to vastly extend the market for drawing-room ballads, and to standardize the genre as a song with piano accompaniment (rather than, say, harp). In the early part of the nineteenth century it was taken for granted that a song published with piano accompaniment was intended for home music-making, or 'at home' functions such as soirées, since songs at public concerts were normally performed with an orchestral accompaniment until the 1840s. The tradition of publishing music heard at concerts in versions aimed at amateurs stretched back into the previous century: then the passion for the German flute among gentleman amateurs had lain behind such remarkable publications as Handel's complete *Messiah* arranged for flute. The piano seemed to attract the middle class from its earliest arrival in England: Charles Dibdin introduced it at Covent Garden in 1767, and Drury Lane gained an official pianist in 1770. By way of contrast, the piano did not replace the harpsichord in the King's Band for another twenty-five years. In the 1830s there was a great variety of pianos available (grands, squares, upright grands, upright squares, cabinet pianos, table pianos, giraffe pianos, lyre pianos), but the design that won the day was Robert Wornum's cottage piano. Its small size was not created at the expense of tone quality, and its pleasant shape made it a satisfying piece of furniture. Wornum had been working on his cottage design since 1811. The action on an upright piano is unavoidably more complex than the grand, where the strings lie in the horizontal plane, and he continued to make improvements in the late 1830s: for example, his 'tape-check' action, which formed the basis of the upright action used in pianos today. Further improvements were made to upright design in the 1840s, and henceforth the softer-toned square piano began to lose favour. The grand piano, however, continued to be the first choice for the concert platform; the upright was considered a domestic instrument.

Cottage pianos may have been comparatively cheap compared with grands, but they were still very much luxury goods: Wornum's cottage pianos sold for between 42 and 75 guineas in 1838, while a Broadwood's price list of 1840 puts the cost from 44 to 80 guineas (their grands cost 90–125 guineas, and their squares 38–85 guineas).[1] These prices have to be measured against average middle-class incomes of £100–500 a year.[2] Although there was a growing market for pianos, as the number of urban middle class rapidly increased, piano making had remained a skilled trade, relying on few, if any, pre-manufactured parts. The preferred description 'piano maker' rather than 'piano manufacturer' itself suggests the pre-Industrial Revolution, labour-intensive method of production. There was no way such a complex instrument could be made cheaply under these circumstances. The main piano-making firm in England, Broadwood, developed an intricate system of divided labour in the hope of increasing their speed and efficiency, but that goal does not seem to have been achieved.[3] At mid-century there were around two hundred piano makers listed in London directories, many of them tiny businesses producing only two dozen or so instruments a year. The demand for pianos was greatest in London and accounts for its being the centre of piano making. The few piano makers operating outside London were, with one or two exceptions in the far north, small firms. Pianos reached the provinces via the railway network, after being sold to local dealers. The railway had revolutionized transport in the early Victorian period: by 1855 there were 8000 miles of track, and trains were no longer thought of as unusual. Dealers could not exist solely on selling pianos, since the trade was seasonal. Christmas and Spring were the best times for sales (the latter because of its popularity for weddings); for the rest of the year they needed to rely on music sales and their expertise in tuning.

The cost of pianos began to fall after mid-century; moreover, plenty of second-hand pianos were finding their way on to the market. D'Almaine & Co., who advertised uprights priced between 25 and 40 guineas in 1856, announced a sale in *The Graphic* of 22 January 1887 in which a new piano could be bought for just 12 guineas, and, what is more, on 'easy terms'. In the same column the London Music Publishing Company Ltd, boasting itself the originator of the 10-guinea piano, advertises 'PIANOFORTES, High Class, for the Million'. A little lower down, Kirkman and Son state that second-hand grands and cottages are 'always in stock'. Nevertheless, many cheap pianos were shoddy and unsatisfactory. An anonymous booklet, *The Guard*, which circulated in the mid-1850s, suggested that a twenty-year-old piano was often better than a new one because in those days 'music had not dawned upon the million, consequently only first rate, high priced instruments were manufactured.'[4] England and France had led

An advertisement for piano fortes, dated 1856.
Note the inclusion of a 'professional testimonial' in an attempt to boost sales.

D'Almaine & Co. announce a sale in 'The Graphic', 22 January 1887.

the industry in the early days, transport difficulties having handicapped the Viennese; but British manufacturers suffered badly from German competition from the 1880s onwards. Conservatism and mistrust of new technology was to blame: for example, over-strung pianos and metal frames were innovations of the late 1830s, yet Broadwood did not make their first over-strung piano until 1897, and metal frames were long and incorrectly held to give inferior tone to wood.

The piano became the pre-eminent bourgeois instrument for a variety of reasons. At first, it was a luxury instrument; therefore, its possession indicated worldly success. It was, as already remarked, a pleasing piece of furniture, gleaming in its mahogany or rosewood case. A fondness for excessive ornament emphasized this purely visual appeal; indeed, the decorative parts of pianos were the first to be mass produced: in the second decade of the nineteenth century Broadwood bought cast-brass moulding by the foot and stamped brass ornaments by the dozen. The extremes to which this decorative interest could stretch may be seen in the Victoria and Albert Museum, London, where there is a satinwood piano decorated with Gothic ornament, inlaid and gilded, with three silk panels at the front (probably the design of Charles Bevan). The piano had established itself as a luxury item of furniture in the 1830s, as the *Westminster Review* noted:

> With a little allowable flattery of the truth, the Book-case, in an inventory of the goods belonging to any well-ordered English house, might be designated as one of its necessary articles of furniture – not as one of its luxuries: the place of popularity among the latter being claimed by the Pianoforte.[5]

Sometimes imaginative modifications were made to improve its function as furniture; the Rev. Haweis, writing in 1871, offers the following advice on caring for a piano: 'Do not load the top of it with books; and if it is a cottage, don't turn the bottom – as I have known some people do – into a cupboard for wine and desert.'[6]

The piano was an instrument ideally suited to the parlour or drawing room in terms of its sound, unlike, for example, the trombone. Smiles, discussing domestic music-making in 1852, says of the piano,

> Ah! that's the instrument for the house and the home. Would that every household could have one! But pianos are still dear, perhaps because the demand of 'the million' for them has not yet set in.[7]

Furthermore, a rudimentary technique on a piano was more likely to win family approval than would an elementary skill on certain other instruments. Smiles warns of the violin, 'it is long, indeed, before any one, however perseverant, can acquire such dexterity on the violin as to give pleasure to a home-audience'.[8] Moreover, string instruments were thought of as a male preserve for most of the century. A crinoline served as an effective barrier to the cello and its unladylike playing position between the knees. Its small relation, the violin, was thought no more suitable for women, however, even in the hands of the virtuosic Paravicini. The latter, who toured in the early part of the century, won recognition and admiration for her technical brilliance, but her choice of instrument was deplored on the grounds that it was 'not suited to a female, a fact universally admitted, and which no skill or address can get over.'[9]

Of course, men were free to play violins and cellos in the parlour, but it was women who dominated home music-making, a fact acknowledged by *Macmillan's Magazine*: 'our young ladies . . . are the principle interpreters of our domestic music'.[10] A man tended to choose an instrument, such as a flute or clarinet, which would mean his calling upon the support of a woman to provide an accompaniment when he played. A woman chose self-contained instruments, like the harp, guitar, or piano, which could supply their own harmony. The obligation of ministering to the male was thus as much a part of domestic music-making as of a woman's other domestic duties. The harp and guitar began to decline in popularity towards the mid-century, since the piano coped far more readily with the ever increasing chromaticism which spelt progress for bourgeois music, and which filtered through from concert hall to drawing room.

Though piano pieces, duets, and occasional concerted pieces were played, domestic music-making was largely vocal. The preference for vocal music was explained in scornful terms by the Rev. Haweis in his *Music and Morals* of 1871 (an influential text arguing for the wholesome effects of 'good' music):

> It is thought almost as rude to interrupt a lady when she is speaking as to talk aloud when she sings. Accordingly the advantages of being able to sing in society are obvious. The lady can at any moment fasten the attention of the room on herself. If a girl has a voice, the piano is too soon suppressed in favour of it . . . It is true she usually accompanies herself; that is, she dabbles about on the keys, . . . but the room listens, and the room applauds. The maiden is happy; and mamma thinks she requires no more singing lessons.[11]

The cessation of singing lessons was no doubt eagerly welcomed by papa too, since half-a-guinea a lesson was not an unusual remuneration for 'professors of singing' at mid-century. The ability of a singer to command greater attention than an instrumentalist persisted throughout the century. E. Lake painted the following description of 'at home' functions in 1891:

> Here in London, we first ask an artist to perform, then ensues the pause of curiosity – the silence of expectation, but directly the music *begins*, then, if it be vocal we have the maddening murmur, whilst if it ventures to be instrumental, then . . . the row is deafening.[12]

Haweis considered drawing-room music to be little more than a manifestation of superficial and vain amateurishness. He regretted that piano playing had become a mere accomplishment for young ladies and that the piano occupied the same place in a girl's education as Latin grammar did in a boy's. Eliza Cook had also protested in her journal at the enforced musical training for girls, nearly twenty years before Haweis' book appeared:

> No one can love music more than ourselves, but we have a holy horror of the general domestic exhibitions of playing and singing. We cannot imagine why *every* girl should be expected to shine in an art which requires a peculiar combination of faculties, taste, and feeling.[13]

Cook found that her remarks led to her being involved in some 'serious domestic remonstrances', but, unabashed, in the next volume of her journal she wrote a satirical description of a soirée at Fullblown Villa, Notting Hill, the home of Mrs Perennial Peony. It is a humorous and probably all too accurate picture of domestic musical life among the wealthy middle class.

> There are three remarkably fine young feminine Peonys in the family, and all have received a 'first-rate education' – that is, upwards of two hundred a year has been expended on each of them. Music is the mania that pervades the establishment, – it is the petted exotic of their hotbed of accomplishments.[14]

All the daughters are described as having a genius for singing, but each plays a different instrument (this is 1852). Miss Peony plays the harp:

> she labours away at the poor strings, and vexes the ears of all around her with 'difficult compositions', alike interminable and tiresome. She has unfortunately acquired such alarming celerity of execution, that a runaway locomotive is the nighest approach to it.[15]

Miss Cora plays the piano, priding herself on her sentiment of expression,

> but her notion of expression is bounded by a consecutive number of hard bangs, and as uniform a consecutive number of weak touches that can scarcely be heard. Her head is accustomed to work with wondrous energy over the 'forte' passages, and her eyes are duly upturned to the ceiling at every interval of 'pianissimo' effect.[16]

Miss Lavinia, who plays guitar, is probably the least endurable,

> for, unfortunately, she 'takes no note of time', and leaves her hearers to do so only from its 'loss'.[17]

Cook concludes, 'music assumes the character of a rabid epidemic' in this family, and 'a serious infliction is endured' by all who sit out their musical soirées. A conflict persisted throughout the nineteenth century between the high hopes of people like Smiles, quoted earlier, and the reality of domestic music-making. When the middle class began to take an avid practical interest in music in the 1830s, it was welcomed by writers on music as showing 'signs of a disposition to restore music to its proper place, by cultivating it intellectually, and not sensually'.[18] And even in the 1870s, when the true nature of this 'intellectual' cultivation of music had been revealed, the Rev. Haweis is still torn between his contempt for drawing-room music and his over-riding belief in the morally wholesome effects of music:

> That domestic and long-suffering instrument, the cottage piano, has probably done more to sweeten existence and bring peace and happiness to families in general, and to young women in particular, than all the homilies on the domestic virtues ever yet penned.[19]

The problem was that Haweis desperately wanted domestic music to be taken seriously; but while music-making in the home was thought of as, in the main, a woman's pastime, it could never receive serious attention. In the same decade as Haweis's *Music and Morals*, a writer in *Macmillan's Magazine* points out, 'In England no disgrace is attached to ignorance of music and everything connected therewith.'[20] This is in spite of the fact that a piano was by then to be found in every respectable middle-class home, and that cheap concerts had become available: fifteen years earlier the same magazine had commented approvingly on the availability in London of so much good music which could be heard 'at a cheap rate', claiming 'Times are changed for the better.'[21]

One of the earliest effects of the widespread desire to play the piano was seen in the emergence of publications catering to the demand for progressive lessons in piano technique, such as Ferdinand Pelzer's *A Practical Guide to Modern Pianoforte Playing*, published in London in 1842. The biggest effect of the demand for music in middle-class homes, however, was on the technology of the music-printing industry. Alternatives were soon being sought to the costly process of engraving music. Lithography seemed to be the most promising of these; it had been invented in 1796 by Aloys Senefelder, who had patented the rights in Bavaria and joined up with a music seller. The first English examples, at the turn of the century, were called 'polyautography'. Between 1806 and 1807 Vollweiler printed a small amount of music lithographically in London, but then returned to Germany. Ackerman, an ex-saddler made good in the printing trade, established a lithographic press and pioneered the 'popular annual' (beginning with *Forget-Me-Not* in 1825). In 1837 Engelman took out a patent for chromolithography; the first English examples belong to the early 1840s. Mezzotint engraving existed before lithography but was a sophisticated process. *The Queen's Boudoir*, a musical annual published by Nelson & Jeffreys, took to colour lithography in 1841, and so too did D'Almaine's *The Musical Bijou*. Examples of music printing by lithographic process were exhibited at the Great Exhibition. Augener began by publishing lithographic editions only when the firm was founded in 1853. Nevertheless, the engraved plate was still the favourite medium for music printing well into the 1860s. Lithography lacked the clear edges of engraving, so tended to be used for pictorial title-pages rather than for the music itself. There was also a problem with the heavy stones and their storage, not to mention the heavy duty imposed by the government on their importation; later in the century, however, zinc and aluminium plates replaced the lithographic stone.

Some publishers looked elsewhere for the printing technology of the future and reconsidered printing from music type, a process Dr Arnold had patented back in 1784. The music supplements to *The Harmonicon*, 1823–33, were printed typographically. *The Harmonicon* is important because, as a reasonably cheap periodical, it provided the middle class with access to those songs which, in turn, formed the roots of the drawing-room ballad: the various strands of the latter genre are here gathered together in one collection. Almost all the key figures discussed in Chapter 1 are represented: for example, Bayly, Bishop, Braham, Dibdin, and Shield. It only lacked a selection of Moore's *Irish Melodies*, although five of these had circulated in a previous periodical, Walker's *Hibernian Magazine*, in 1810. The disadvantage of using movable types was that they were expensive, took a long time to compose and were then unusable for anything else until the edition for which they had been set up was discontinued. They were at their most advantageous when running off thousands of copies rather than hundreds. To attract large numbers of buyers, the product had to be aimed at the middle-class market. *The Musical Library* (1834–37) declared:

before this work appeared, the exhorbitant sum demanded for engraved music amounted to a prohibition of its free circulation among the middle classes; at a time too when the most enlightened statesmen saw distinctly the policy of promoting the cultivation of the art in almost every class of society.[22]

Like *The Harmonicon*, *The Musical Library* was printed by William Clowes. He claimed to have purchased a secret process of printing music, invented by Duverger of Paris; he had, however, obtained punches and matrices from Germany in order to cast new musical type for *The Harmonicon*. Another series printed by Clowes was *Sacred Minstrelsy* (1834–35), but his most lasting influence was on the firm of Novello. Shortly after the first issue of *The Musical Times* in 1844, Novello went into printing as well as publishing and took over, with some modification, the same system of musical type used by Clowes. Novello had pioneered the concept of 'Cheap Music' from the day the firm was established in 1811 and made further reductions in prices in 1849. By 1854 a vocal score of *Messiah* could be purchased for 4s., the price which in some cases was paid for a single drawing-room ballad. Of course, Novello could rely on many thousands of sales,[23] and had no royalty arrangements to make with singers in return for their promoting the work, nor any financial obligation to the composer; the only restriction on its cheapness other than production costs was the excise duty payable on paper. Not surprisingly Vincent Novello's son Alfred was a tireless campaigner against what he called a 'tax on knowledge', the payment of 3d. on every pound of paper. It was finally lifted in 1861. Novello and Company Ltd targeted the choral market, concentrating on sacred music and 'standard works'. The octavo edition, which is the present norm for choral works, has its origin in the size of *The Musical Times*; previously, folio editions had been the norm. One Novello edition to be found in every drawing room was of Mendelssohn's *Songs Without Words*. Being a collection of piano pieces by a living composer, it was not the musical terrain usually associated with Novello; the explanation for this departure was that the firm had managed to buy the British copyright outright in 1837.

Musical type was rarely used for drawing-room ballads, except for 'cheap' collections. The modern ballad was not expected to be cheap; expense was linked in the mind to notions of quality. Even the best type-printed octavo editions came in for criticism such as that made by W. H. Cummings later in the century:

> let us speak of the best type printed music. Here we find good paper, well-formed lines and notes, but all so minute and crowded that it requires a serious effort to identify and grasp the picture which has to be conveyed to the brain through the eye. The notes are small, but the words are smaller; and when you come to a recitative – in which, of course, the words form the more important element – you will find, for the sake of saving a little space, that the type setter has used a smaller letter than usual.[24]

Musical typography remained the most common medium for hymn books and psalters (where there was a lot of text), and for printing short extracts of music in educational literature; the advantage was that the music type could be set at the same time as the text type. On the other hand, the plate, punched (for noteheads) and engraved, was the most flexible medium available; it could cope with anything from piano music to full orchestra, and with equal ease.

Lithography proved to be invaluable for the packaging of music, as a means of lending additional desirability to the commodity on offer. A. H. King coins the term 'pictorial' for title-pages which are 'intended to give a visual representation of the music'.[25] A few pictorial title-pages were printed lithographically by Hawkes-Smith around 1821–22, but engraved title-pages were the norm until the 1830s. At this time, a full page given over to the title was uncommon: the pictorial element would most likely be a vignette, the music beginning immediately beneath. The first person to exploit to the full the eye-catching qualities of lithography in the context of the market for domestic music was the enterprising Louis Jullien, celebrated dance composer, conductor, publisher, and popularizer of the 'cheap concert'. During 1844–45 he had a series of polkas and quadrilles printed with enticing coloured title-pages, and, later, a series of coloured albums. In the 1840s and 50s, arrangements of operatic airs, particularly as dances, were favourite candidates for the pictorial title-page, but in the 60s attention shifted to music-hall songs. The most distinguished colour lithographer working in this field was Alfred Concanen (1835–86). The appetite for pictorial title-pages for drawing-room ballads was soon surfeited; critics scornful of them can be found in the early 1850s:

> The rage for pictorial ballads has, of course, given an impetus to purchasers, which must prove highly beneficial to all concerned. The composer becomes a kind of lacquey to the artist, and they are thus enabled to turn out of hand a very saleable sort of commodity – the picture itself being well worth the money, and the song illustrating the illustration in such a manner as almost to bring tears into the eyes of the susceptible.[26]

In the 1860s a coloured pictorial title-page came to be considered too showy and vulgar for the drawing-room ballad, and was associated with songs which lacked seriousness; where seriousness was not in doubt – as in religious ballads – it lasted longest. However, there is no doubt that music-hall songs, gaily adorned with colour lithographs, were bought by many a wealthy bourgeois: Jane Traies has shown how the pictorial covers were often slanted away from an accurate representation of the song-text towards an interpretation which would allow an up-market appeal to the drawing room.[27] Black-and-white lithographs were not thought to vulgarize a ballad as much as colour: admired precedents had been set, such as the lithographed song-title for the publication of Bayly's 'I'd Be a Butterfly' in 1827. Ballads in the catalogue of the *Musical Bouquet* (published originally by Bingley and Strange), 1846?–89, only ever had black-and-white illustrations, if they were illustrated at all. In fact, the decorative title-page, rather than the pictorial title-page, was more common for music which was regarded as serious or of high quality; its design relied on imaginative use of different type founts. An American invention of 1838 enabled type to be made automatically at 100 letters a minute, in marked contrast to the painstaking hand-made method using moulds, which yielded 400 letters an hour. The consequence was a dramatic fall in the price of type, enabling printers to stock up

Typical example of pictorial title-page for a drawing-room ballad (in this case, a duet). Black-and-white lithograph, c. 1865.

with a lot of unusual varieties of type founts from which attractive covers could be created.

Once a suitably appealing and tasteful commodity had been produced, an efficient means of dissemination was required. Since most of the music printing in nineteenth-century Britain took place in London, the market was restricted until

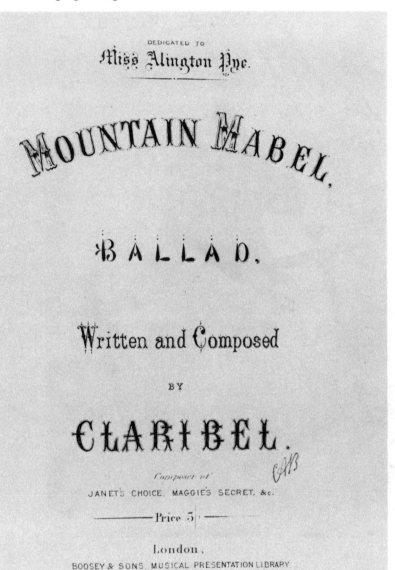

Typical example of a decorative title-page using a variety of type founts (1864). Note, in particular, the highly unusual founts used for the word 'ballad' and the pseudonym 'Claribel'.

the country had been opened up by the networks of road and rail. Once this had been achieved, and pianos and ballads were travelling side-by-side along those networks, the only problem was how the consumer was going to choose which ballads to purchase. Notices were given in women's journals of elegant soirées where professional singers could be heard; ideas for songs to sing at home could be picked up there. Ballads were also reviewed in the press outside London: for example, the following comments on songs by Miss Lindsay were made by Scottish journals in the 1850s:[28]

> So simple that singers of very moderate attainments will find little difficulty in singing it at first sight.
>
> (*Aberdeen Journal*, reviewing 'Speak Gently')

> It is easy, graceful, and pleasing. Her compositions are for the quiet family circle – the domestic concert – the home circle.
>
> (*Glasgow Times*, reviewing 'Jacob')

In the case of ballads published by Robert Cocks & Co., who proclaimed themselves 'Music publishers to her most gracious majesty Queen Victoria, his royal highness the Prince of Wales, and his imperial majesty the Emperor Napoleon III', one might assume that buying them meant singing the same songs as royalty. Wedgwood was also aware of snob value when he issued his Queensware set, which exploited the desire of the middle class to eat their dinner from the same plates as the Queen of England. A recipe listing the essential ingredients which go to make a 'popular' ballad is given in an advertisement printed on the back cover of one of Cocks' publications:

> What a lyrical composition intended to be popular ought to be – it has no unnecessary difficulties, and lies within a moderate range – being thus available for all who sing to amuse themselves or their friends, as well as of those who sing for the public.[29]

The same sort of opinion is obviously held by a reviewer of John Abel's setting of Felicia Hemans' poem 'The Better Land' (published by Chappell in 1844):

> The fault we should find with the composition is not that it has too little learning, but too much. It has great originality and beauty, but not the originality and beauty of simplicity . . . The accompaniment is of difficult execution, and with its innumerable accidentals not very easily read . . . A great part of the composition is in G flat, which might have been written in the more familiar key of F natural.[30]

It was not just the musical side of a ballad which had to be tailored to the technique of the domestic musician; it was equally important that the song had easily singable words. This points to one of the main reasons Walter Scott was not able to rival Burns' popularity as a songwriter. In certain cases the tunes Scott selected were, and still are, well-known; but it is more common to hear the tune announced by Scott's title and then played instrumentally rather than sung. 'Blue Bonnets', for example, can easily sound garbled as a result of what may be a well-intentioned attempt on Scott's part to capture the effect of bagpipe embellishments known as 'doublings' (marked * below).

March, march,   Et-trick and Te-viot da-le! Why, my lads, dinna ye march for-ward in or - der?

Scott seems unappreciative of the handicapping effect of dipthongs on an amateur singer's crispness of rhythm and accuracy of intonation; witness the bracketed bars below from 'Pibroch of Donuil Dhuibh' (the Gaelic words, incidentally, are not diphthongs):

Pibroch of Do - nuil Dhui, Pi-broch of   Do   -   nuil, Wake thy wild voice a- new, Summon clan Con - cuil;

On the subject of words, it is a pity so many drawing-room ballads are concerned with dreams; it is a difficult word to sing with a classically trilled 'r' without disrupting the kind of smooth flowing melody to which it is almost always set. Here is a typical example, the beginning of the refrain of Cowen's 'It Was a Dream':

It   was   a   dream,   It   was   a   dream,

It was common practice to build a collection of ballads suited to one's individual taste and technique and have them privately stitched together and leather bound. This practice declined in the 1890s when ballads could only be guaranteed to be in vogue for one concert season, rather than for years. Various reasons can be put forward for what amounted to a lack of serious musical effort in the drawing rooms of the majority of middle-class establishments: it may be said that music was simply thought of as a diverting and wholesome entertainment; for some it was merely regarded as a means of displaying their respectability (concern for spiritual improvement) and status (ownership of a piano); for others it was a woman's subject, and therefore, almost by definition, lacked seriousness. At the same time, there can be no doubt that there were those among the middle class who genuinely loved music, while resisting the application and discipline demanded by the art. Perhaps another reason for lack of concentrated effort lay in the physical conditions of the room itself. Such is the opinion expressed by Alexander Wood in *The Physics of Music*: 'the Victorian drawing room, with its heavy curtains and carpet and its upholstered furniture, had a very short time of reverberation, was acoustically "dead", and never encouraged musical effort'.[31] Furthermore, the effect of a hot drawing room on the strings of a harp or guitar would have been to create frustrating tuning problems. The piano, however, did not suffer to the same extent; this is another reason, added to those given earlier in the chapter, why it rose to pre-eminence.

Finally, a few words must be appended concerning the situation in America, since the ballad market linked Britain and America from its earliest days. Besides the steady flow of London publications across the Atlantic, there were the pirated copies of British ballads printed by American publishers who were taking advantage of the absence of international copyright. Music publishing started in the east, in Boston, New York, Philadelphia, and Baltimore; it then expanded westward during the years before the Civil War. Makers of musical instruments kept pace with these developments, so that the two businesses 'fed each other in a kind of symbiotic cycle'.[32] The opening up of the country by railroad was as important in America as in Britain.

Pianos were in great demand, but the square was preferred to the upright in American parlours. Alpheus Babcock had constructed a square piano with an iron frame in 1825, and it was this invention which lay behind the successful series of square pianos made by Jonas Chickering in Boston from 1840 onwards. An alternative keyboard instrument to the piano was the melodeon, a small reed organ with single bellows.[33] The melodeon was available in the early nineteenth century but became more widely so when Abraham Prescott set up in Concord, Massachusetts, in 1836. Small portable varieties were made which could be played on the lap and pumped by the elbow. The instrument is often confused with the harmonium, a reed organ developed from the *orgue expressif* and patented in Paris in 1842 by Alexandre Debain. Further confusion arises between the harmonium and the American organ: put simply, the European harmonium has reeds sounded by compressed air, while the American organ's reeds are sounded by suction. Perhaps the melodeon's suction bellows were the inspiration behind the cottage organs produced by the firm of Estey & Co., which set up in Brattleboro, Vermont, in 1856. Suction seemed to give a more balanced sound, and they were able to export great numbers to Britain, where little making of reed organs took place. There were 247 firms making these instruments in America in the second half of the nineteenth century. Though Julius and Paul Schiedmayer began mass-producing harmoniums in Germany in 1853, it was the American organ (often incorrectly called the harmonium) which caught on in Britain. What the cottage piano did for the concert grand, the cottage organ did for the 'king of instruments' – it domesticated it. Moreover, it became a serious rival to the piano in lower middle-class homes during the later century, because it was cheaper and it stayed in tune. The wealthy middle class acquired both instruments (examples of ballads written for both instruments are discussed later).

In America, as in Britain, the flute and violin were favourite instruments for male amateurs. The guitar sustained its popularity among the American middle class longer than it did among their British counterparts. Even in the late 1850s, this fact prevented the American ballad from becoming standardized as a song with keyboard accompaniment: many of Stephen Foster's songs, for example, were published in alternative versions for voice and guitar. The success of Foster further illustrates the similarity between the British and American markets for domestic music. His music, in the words of H. Wiley Hitchcock,

> was aimed at the home – at the typical American parlor, with its little square piano or reed organ, its horsehair-stuffed sofa, its kerosene lanterns and candlelight. Simple enough for amateurs to perform, the music of these songs was pitched at a modest level of artistic sophistication. The language of the texts was generally one step removed from ordinary American speech, with a slightly rarefied atmosphere of cultivated gentility.[34]

The appearance of several of his songs in an anthology of the 1850s entitled *Household Melodies* lends further emphasis to their domestic qualities.

3   *The Rise of the Woman Ballad Composer*

Bourgeois domestic music branched out in three new directions in the 1840s and 50s: songs by (or partly by) women were added to those by 'respectable' entertainers like Bayly and Russell; songs from the blackface minstrel shows were added to those taken from the English opera; and a new kind of sacred song supplemented the hymns sung on Sundays. These three developments are covered in the next three chapters. Women songwriters are treated first because they attracted a peak of attention in the 1860s (when they were being marketed as something of a novelty), whereas the minstrels were still going strong in the 1880s, and the sacred song proved to be one of the most durable forms of drawing-room ballad. There is another reason, too, for placing women composers after a chapter on the early amateur music market: a composer like Maria Lindsay can be seen to be consciously tailoring her music to amateur domestic rather than professional public performance. Moreover, her songs contain features common in amateur composition, such as incessant two-bar phrasing, and the simple melodic framework which is adapted to the differing demands (especially those pertaining to metre and stress) of individual verses.

Before discussing the rise of the woman composer, it would be valuable to examine briefly the social position of the middle-class woman in the nineteenth century. The Victorian 'perfect lady' was innocent and chaste before marriage and a devoted wife and caring mother after marriage. Her education took place within the family, and the range of subjects she could study was limited by the fear of making her opinionated and therefore less submissive to her future husband's views. Literary, artistic, and musical skills were thought appropriate to female study. The mechanics of the subjection of women were to be found in the ideologies of purity, chastity, and the family. Female sexuality was repressed by the ideology of purity and found sublimation in religion, motherhood, and the spiritual side of love. Middle-class men had to achieve financial security before marriage and so tended to marry late; the ideology of chastity served to remove the threat to family values of illegitimate children. The virginity of middle-class women was, ironically, protected by the large numbers of prostitutes available. In tacit acknowledgment of this, the state brought forward no serious legislation against prostitution until the necessity arose of preventing the spread of venereal disease among the armed forces (prompting the Contagious Disease Acts of 1865–69). The ideology of the family ensured that the primary role of women was breeding children; as a consequence, there developed a whole range of beliefs about gender behaviour which made women of all classes victims of sexism.

A middle-class woman's roles, then, were all family roles: she began as daughter and progressed in turn to being a wife and mother. Each role had its duties and obligations, thoroughly documented in Sarah Ellis's books, *The Mothers of England* (1843), *The Wives of England* (1844) and *The Daughters of England* (1845). A woman's status depended on her father's economic position before marriage and her husband's thereafter. Prospective husbands were influenced by the former of these conditions:

> They say, 'She's pretty, but, alas!'
> With hand extended, thus they flout:
> 'She has no cash!' and by they pass: –
> Ye gods! what are the men about?
>
> (from 'Not Married Yet', words unattributed, music by Henry Russell)

For a middle-class woman, being a caring mother did not imply that she devoted her time to looking after children; they would be put into the charge of nannies and governesses. There would be little work to do about the house, since that was attended to by servants. Charity work for the local church was common among those who wished to be active, but it was not admired if it became too zealous. If a middle-class woman failed to marry, it was usually a disaster: the best that might be hoped for was to become 'auntie' in a brother's house, or a governess. Unmarried working-class women supported themselves by going into factories, shops, domestic service, or becoming seamstresses. Elderly unmarried women of either class rarely received sympathetic treatment. The severest opprobrium, however, was reserved for the 'fallen woman', for example, an adulteress or prostitute; she posed the most outrageous threat to family values. When Holman Hunt, in *The Awakening Conscience* (1854), painted a fallen woman whose conscience is stirred by the divine power of music, many were appalled at what they considered to be Holman Hunt's poor taste. Even the possibility of redemption for such creatures was resented.

Questions concerning the rights of women were regarded during the Napoleonic Wars as akin to Jacobinism, though a minority kept alive the thoughts of people like Mary Wollstonecraft. The issue was revived after the war in radical publications and was reaffirmed by Shelley's circle. The most radical women were workers in the northern textile districts, where demand for their labour had effected a change in their economic status.[1] The debate about the rights of women was dominated in the 1860s by the arguments of Mill and Ruskin. Mill furnished a rational analysis of the subjection of women and called for emancipation. Ruskin countered with the ideology of chivalry: a woman has virtues unobtainable by men and can therefore 'rule' a man's conscience. Victorian chivalry was a hegemonic compromise which maintained patriarchal control and contained nineteenth-century feminism by emphasizing difference rather than inferiority.

In the 1880s the 'new woman' emerged, demanding an end to double standards in sexual morality and asking to be given an active participatory role in society. The *Westminster Review* noted with an air of revelation in 1884, 'wifehood and motherhood are incidental parts, which may or may not enter into the life of each woman'.[2] During this decade enormous demonstrations were being held in cities and large towns by the women's suffrage movement. Many Tories were in favour of extending the franchise to women 'inhabitant occupiers' in the hope that property-owning women would swing the political pendulum to the right (a woman living with her husband was not legally an inhabitant occupier). The Movement for the Higher Education of Women also began in the 1880s. The 'new woman' of this period is satirized in Gilbert and Sullivan's *Princess Ida* (1884). Gilbert's attitude to feminism may be dismissive, but his attitude to women is never simple. He is often accused, for example, of cruelty towards his elderly, unmarried female characters, an accusation which could be a largely male reaction born of self-serving male protectiveness (in the way Ruskin's chivalry was self-serving). Jane Stedman makes an alternative claim that in Gilbert's hands 'the middle-aged comic spinster took on an energy and independence which dramatists before and after him gave only to the high-spirited heroines'.[3]

For women to take to musical composition in any numbers, three conditions needed to be satisfied: they had to have the opportunity to develop the relevant musical skills, the opportunity to have their music performed, and examples of successful women composers to help them achieve. Middle-class women had leisure time they could spend on music. The economic stability of their position, which safeguarded a life of genteel idleness by enabling them to delegate chores to servants, had already encouraged them to indulge in more private forms of creative activity, such as writing novels. The *Westminster Review*, raising its eyebrows in 1856, said,

> We had imagined that destitute women turned novelists, as they turned govern-
> esses, because they had no other 'ladylike' means of getting their bread . . . But no!
> . . . It is clear that they write in elegant boudoirs, with violet-coloured ink and a
> ruby pen.[4]

Enthusiasm for writing verse had been scornfully referred to some years earlier, in a song called 'The Clever Woman', composed by the celebrated burlesque composer, Jonathan Blewitt, with words by the Hon. Grantley Fitzhardinge Berkeley:

> She gets some rich victim to pay for her pleasures,
> And learned revisers are waiting the same,
> To alter her prose and to finish her measures,
> And give to her poetry all but their name.

Leisure time for women to compose was not sufficient in itself, since, unlike prose or verse, music exists only as sound. Therefore, there was an additional requirement to have the composition heard. There were many problems to overcome, however, in order to obtain access to the male-dominated musical profession. A typical example of a composer stifled by the lack of this second kind of opportunity was Alice Mary Smith (1839–84). The daughter of a London lace merchant, she showed great aptitude for music, and her father arranged for her to study with Sterndale Bennett and G. A. Macfarren. She attracted interested attention when the Musical Society of London included a performance of a string quartet by her in 1861. She was accorded exceptional honours: she was elected as Female Professional Associate of the Philharmonic Society in 1867 (the year she married a QC who supported her musical activity); and she became an Honorary Member of the Royal Academy of Music in 1884. Her output included such large-scale works as symphonies, cantatas, and a clarinet concerto. Yet, in spite of her honours and achievements, no publisher was interested in anything other than her songs and piano music. Thus, whereas Bennett's and Macfarren's orchestral works were rushed into print and available for performances far and wide, Smith stagnated with her manuscript copies in London. The only far-reaching admiration she acquired was for her well-constructed duet 'Maying' (words from *The Saint's Tragedy*, by Kingsley), published in 1870. Where women were prepared to serve clearly identifiable economic interests, publication was possible; 'Maying' was tailored to the ballad market and proved such a success that the copyright sold for £663 the year before Smith died.[5] Because publishers were unwilling to take risks with orchestral works by women, and because women had restricted access to tuition in compositional skills (they were rarely taught orchestration, for example), the ballad was an obvious choice for their creative efforts. These facts need to be weighed when considering the sexual stereotyping of musical forms; but they also point to contradictions in 'essentialist' arguments that female cultural activity has a character of its own independent of social and economic circumstances. This extends from forms to moods: as soon as one finds something one may consider typically masculine, like imperialist bombast, one finds a woman who is equal to anything men can do (for example, Frances Allitsen).

Women learned music as an accomplishment, not as a profession. Mill remarked, in *The Subjection of Women*, that since women were taught music only for the purpose of executing it, not composing it, it was logical that in respect of composition (and composition alone) men were superior to women. Music often took pride of place among the range of leisure activities (such as sewing, sketching, and reading) which were available to middle-class girls. Lessons in singing were favoured because they yielded 'the showiest of all a young woman's accomplishments'.[6] Training in the science of music rather than just the execution of music only began to move within more general reach of women when Conservatoires and Academies of Music started to offer scientific grounding in music to boys as well as girls in the 1870s. In spring 1870 Sullivan delivered a course of lectures at South Kensington Museum in connection with a scheme entitled 'Instruction in Science and Art for Women'. Nevertheless, the constant charge of the 1880s was that women lacked an inventive faculty, the proof being that although they were almost all taught music, there was a dearth of female composers. The *Englishwoman's Review* argued in reply to such criticism,

> . . . the mechanical and superficial acquirement, which consumed so many hours of every girl's school-life, was not only unadapted to bring out the higher faculties, but possibly tended to stupefy them.[7]

In 1888, the year the above was written, women were continuing to prove themselves: a comic opera, *Carina*, by Julia Wolf was greeted with enthusiasm at the Opera Comique in London; a woman won first prize in counterpoint at the Paris Conservatoire; and women were coming to the fore in Germany and Italy. Women were fighting for the right to take university degrees in music. As early as 1856, Elizabeth Stirling had passed the 'exercise' for the Mus. Bac. at Oxford but was refused the degree. She was for over twenty years the organist at St Andrew's, Undershaft, a post she won in open competition. In 1878 Cambridge allowed women to take their music examinations and, if successful, receive a certificate which stated that they had passed but 'for various reasons' the degree could not be conferred upon them (Cambridge first awarded degrees in music to women in 1927). In 1885 Oxford allowed women to go part of the way towards a degree in music but were not to confer degrees in music upon women until 1921. The first music graduate of Victoria University (now the University of Manchester) was, however, a woman! She was Marian Millar who, in 1894, became the first woman to obtain a degree in music in England. It may be wondered why universities in the 1880s took women students at all, when they felt unable to award them degrees. Perhaps it is significant that each woman paid around £80 a year in fees, not including the cost of her private tuition. By the end of the century there was wider acknowledgement of the creative musical potential of women. The chairman, winding up a discussion on 'Woman as a Musician' at the annual conference of the Incorporated Society of Musicians (Grand Hotel, Scarborough, 2 January 1900), said he 'quite believed the part that women had played in the past had not been because they had not the genius, but because that genius had not been stimulated by their early training'.[8] Within a few years Ethel Smyth would be hailed as the first woman composer to establish herself on an equal footing with men, particularly after the performance of her opera *The Wreckers* in Germany in 1906.

Prior to the twentieth century, women composers were rarely given a place in history, though they were steadily growing in numbers from the seventeenth century onwards, when such notable figures as Barbara Strozzi (1619–44?), Mary Harvey (1629–1704) and Elizabeth-Claude Jacquet de La Guerre (1664?–1727) were active. Thus, there was no 'Great Tradition' and there were no obvious role models for nineteenth-century women. Women usually made a reputation as performers, since this served 'the linked economic and erotic interests of dominant culture'.[9] The most glamorized performer being the singer, it is interesting to note that the vocal arts alone have a 'Great Tradition' of women which overshadows that of men. Ambitious Victorian sopranos not only had the stimulus of the sensational London appearances made by Jenny Lind (the 'Swedish Nightingale') in 1847 and 1848–49 to help them achieve, but also the knowledge that home-grown sopranos like Elizabeth Linley and Nancy Storace had acquired international reputations in the previous century.

Women first entered the ballad market through the door of literature. Women writers had been establishing themselves as novelists, like Jane Austen (1775–1817), or dramatists, like Elizabeth Inchbald (1756–1821), or poets, like Felicia Hemans (1794–1835). The latter, née Browne, was the daughter of a Liverpool merchant. She demonstrated a precocious talent for poetry, writing verse in Byronic vein at first, but always with due regard to moral propriety. Her poems won a respected place in middle-class homes, where it was felt that 'mothers may safely place them in the hands of their children, certain that nothing but moral good can be obtained from them'.[10] Her importance to the history of the drawing-room ballad lies in her having written the words to a collection of songs entitled *Peninsular Melodies*, published by Goulding & D'Almaine, London. Following Britain's liberating efforts in the Peninsular War, there was a vogue for Spanish melody which lasted into the mid-1850s. Apart from Spanish subject matter, everything about Hemans' verse was contemporary and English; and this sets her apart, as a model to English women lyricists, from earlier women who had written song-texts in dialect like Susanna Blamire (who will be discussed in the next chapter). Sometimes, even the subject matter of a Hemans *Peninsular Melody* is not obviously Spanish (for example, 'Mother, O! Sing Me to Rest'). Therefore, following the success of these songs, it was a small step for composers of ballads to want to set her shorter poems to music. Indeed, one of the most famous of drawing-room ballads is a late Victorian setting of her poem 'The Better Land' by Cowen, a poem which had already acquired popularity as a song earlier in the century in an unattributed setting published by Z. T. Purday.

Another precocious female talent, Eliza Cook (1818–89), the daughter of a Southwark tradesman, followed in Hemans' footsteps. Like the latter, 'No vicious thought intrudes itself into her writings',[11] and she, too, acquired great popularity among the middle class: '. . . her poems hit the taste of that class, while a certain musical flow of the rhythm attracted the attention of the composers of the day, and many were set to music by Glover and other popular song writers.'[12] In her early career, her poems were frequently set to music by Henry Russell. Her reputation was at its height in the early 1850s, when *Eliza Cook's Journal*, a periodical she founded in 1849, was a favourite among women who sought modest social and political reform. The absence of fashion-plates and gossip vouched for its serious nature. The moral fervour of Cook's poetry may have dated towards the end of her life, but she had proved well before then that women could rival men in providing verse for drawing-room ballads. She did, occasionally, write both words and music herself, as in 'Dead Leaves' (1852).

The importance of Hemans and Cook is seen in Davidson's *Universal Melodist*, the first large collection of 'popular, standard, and original songs'. The first volume of 1853 contains 800 songs, dominated 90 per cent by men. The female side is most strongly represented by Cook, Hemans, and a selection of Mary Leman Rede's new texts to Moore's *Irish Melodies*. Women composers are very thin on the ground, although their numbers doubled in the second volume, published in 1854. Nevertheless, women composers barely account for 5 per cent of the entire collection of 1630 songs.

Another figure important to the gradual emergence of women into the ballad market makes her appearance in volume one of the above collection; her name is Caroline Norton (1808–77). She is shown there following Hemans' example, supplying texts to two Peninsular melodies; but in the same year as that volume she had an outstanding success with a 'Spanish' ballad composed and written by herself. 'Juanita', published by Chappell, became the first ballad by a woman composer to achieve massive sales.[13] Perhaps the Peninsular melody the market had been waiting for was just what 'Juanita' provided, a decidedly English ballad with an exotic hint of Spain in both words and music. A pseudo-Spanish musical turn decorates the name Juanita, and the postlude contains an imitation of the 'hammered-on' notes common in guitar music; otherwise, the refrain bears a striking resemblance to Handel's 'Lascia ch'io pianga', from *Rinaldo*. Caroline Norton was a granddaughter of the playwright Sheridan. She had to endure a long and stormy relationship when she married the Tory MP for Guildford, the Hon. George Norton; it included a sensational trial when, in an attempt to be rid of Caroline and to damage the Whig government, he brought a prosecution against the Prime Minister, Lord Melbourne, for 'criminal conversation' with his wife. Although the case was thrown out of court, her reputation never fully recovered: 'Through its revelations, and more especially through the advance publicity and speculation, Caroline had lost the indefinable aura of spotless inviolability at that time prized above all things for a woman.'[14] Moreover, the Hon. George Norton was not averse, it seems, to beating his wife, causing her to seek frequent refuge with her mother, even though she was then denied access to her children. These adversities may have acted as a spur to her creative activities, if only for the money she was able to earn and the relative independence that money bought. In this connection it is surely no coincidence that Hemans was separated from her husband and that Eliza Cook never married. However, as a result of George Norton's hiding her children, Caroline's career was diverted from the arts to writing pamphlets and becoming the prime mover behind the Infant Custody Bill (passed in 1839).

Reunited with her children, she lived as an independent writer until, in 1853, George was inspired to sue her for debt, thus laying legal claim to any money she earned from writing or songs; 1853, it will be remembered, was the year of *Juanita*. Caroline was again diverted into writing and agitating in support of the Divorce Bill and the Married Women's Property Bill. Some of her songs clearly reflect her own concerns, for example, 'The Mother's Lament' (1840). Others reflect them obliquely: 'The Arab's Farewell to His Favourite Steed' (music by John Blockley, published *c*. 1865) dwells upon the painful theme of separation and perhaps transfers some of the grief she felt at parting from her children to the Arab parting from his beloved horse.

Caroline Norton's importance to the history of the drawing-room ballad, however, is that she set an example for other women to emulate in producing a small body of contemporary songs of which she was both author and composer. In so doing, she not only paved the way for Claribel but also improved the status of women solely interested in composing the music for 'popular songs', something carried further by Maria Lindsay. In the second half of the 1850s, Miss M. Lindsay, as she chose to be known (sometimes giving her married name, Mrs J. Worthington Bliss, in parentheses), established herself as the first commercially successful woman composer. Her publisher, Robert Cocks & Co., signed her up on an exclusive contract; in the 1860s she was second only to Franz Abt as the most popular composer in their song catalogue. She was still popular enough in 1900 for Wickins and Co. to publish an *Album of Miss M. Lindsay's Songs*.

It is difficult to see now why her songs became such favourites: her accompaniments rarely venture beyond banal figurations of rocking or broken chords, and her melodic lines are undistinguished. It may be argued that her appeal lay in setting to music of an unobtrusive quality the verse of the most admired contemporary poets, such as Tennyson and Longfellow. It is obvious, too, from the preceding chapter, that a major attraction of her songs was their simplicity and consequent suitability for domestic music-making. Her songs also won approval for being of a high moral order. Her first best-seller, composed in 1854, admirably exemplified this trait: it was a setting of Longfellow's 'Excelsior', the subject of which is the striving after higher things, and the nobility attending even failure in that quest. The song is a lightly varied strophic treatment of seven stanzas, containing some clumsy accentuation (musical accents contradicting verbal accents), and accompanied by broken-chord patterns of a monotonous and predictable regularity.

Balfe's later duet version of 'Excelsior' is distinguished by his ability to evoke a variety of moods, his inventiveness in setting the oft repeated title word, his sense of what is musically dramatic, and his skill in constructing a broad musical shape which increases the suspense of the narrative by avoiding the static circular feel of a strophic setting.

Lindsay occasionally makes a gesture of sympathy with the verse she is setting: for example, in 'Home They Brought Her Warrior Dead' (composed to Tennyson's verse in 1858), she responds to the wife's weeping with an urgent rhythmic agitation of her usual banal figuration. See the musical example on page 68.

Lindsay's songs leave most of the questions of interpretation of the mood of the poem and its drama to the individual singer. The emotional intensity of her songs depends heavily on the expressive power of the singer's voice. Sometimes her melodies are a basic skeleton of notes which can be fleshed out in different ways to suit different lines of the poem. 'The Bridge' (words by Longfellow), published in 1856, demonstrates this approach. At other times, she writes a clear-cut tune, as

in 'Far Away' (1868), the most popular of her later songs (a two-part arrangement being published as late as 1911 by J. Curwen & Sons).

Another woman ballad composer who began to make her reputation in the 1850s was Dolores, or Elizabeth Dickson (1819–78). She, like Lindsay, began by setting Longfellow poems in 1854; she achieved a modest success with 'The Bridge', published in that year by Charles Jefferys (London). Dolores also tends to rely on various permutations of broken-chord patterns for her accompaniments. In her case, however, they are often unpredictable in shape and rhythm. Her song 'The Land of Long Ago' offers a good example.

This example dates from 1873, but her setting of Tennyson's 'The Brook', published in 1857, shows the same individuality with its delicate use of grace notes to suggest the rippling water.

Even when lapsing into conventional figuration, Dolores can save the day with an appealing melody, as she does in 'Wings'. This was published in 1861 but remained very popular throughout the whole decade, as is shown by the fact that three different piano arrangements of the song found their way on to the market.

The person who did most to convince people that women could compose ballads which would bear close comparison with anything similar by men was Virginia Gabriel (1825–77). She was born in Banstead, Surrey, the daughter of a major-general. She studied piano with the distinguished teachers Pixis, Döhler, and Thalberg. This was not so unusual, since professional women pianists were now becoming accepted (mainly thanks to Lucy Anderson and Clara Schumann); but Gabriel also contrived to gain a proper grounding in composition from Molique and Mercadante. All the same, she soon encountered the same obstacles to success as those mentioned earlier in relation to Alice Smith. Her operetta *Widows Bewitched* ran for several weeks, performed by the Bijou Operetta Company at St George's Hall in 1867, but no wide-ranging interest

BOOSEY & CO.'S LIST OF POPULAR SONGS.

MADAME SHERRINGTON'S SONGS.

		s. d.			s. d.
SOMEBODY	G. A. MACFARREN	4 0	SECRETS	CLARIBEL	4 0
CLOCHETTE	J. L. MOLLOY	4 0	GOLDEN GLEAMED THE RIVER	J. L. MOLLOY	4 0
COME BACK TO ERIN	CLARIBEL	4 0	RINGING THE FLOWER BELLS	J. L. MOLLOY	4 0
THE POOR BLIND BOY	J. LEMMENS	4 0	THE PORTRAIT	Mdme. SHERRINGTON	3 0

MDLLE. LIEBHART'S SONGS.

		s. d.			s. d.
THE SURPRISE	V. GABRIEL	4 0	LOVE'S MORNING	G. B. ALLEN	4 0
LITTLE BIRD SO SWEETLY SINGING	G. B. ALLEN	4 0	THE PRISONER AND THE LINNET	V. GABRIEL	4 0
MY HEART'S REPLY	C. J. HARGITT	4 0	WE'D BETTER BIDE A WEE	CLARIBEL	4 0
KIRTLE RED	J. L. HATTON	3 0	A MAY SONG	BENEDICT	4 0

MADAME SAINTON-DOLBY'S SONGS.

		s. d.			s. d.
RECOLLECTION	SAINTON-DOLBY	3 0	SILVER CHIMES	CLARIBEL	4 0
OH SWEET AND FAIR!	ARTHUR S. SULLIVAN	4 0	MY OWN TRUE LOVE TO MY		
GELERT'S GRAVE (LLEWELYN)	JOHN THOMAS	4 0	DYING DAY	J. L. MOLLOY	4 0
THE LOVE TEST	CLARIBEL	4 0	WILL HE COME?	ARTHUR S. SULLIVAN	4 0
SOMEBODY'S DARLING	GABRIEL	4 0	BYE-AND-BYE	GABRIEL	4 0
HE DOESN'T LOVE ME	LOUISA GRAY	4 0	WHEN THE PALE, PALE MOON	GABRIEL	4 0
ONLY AT HOME	GABRIEL	4 0	MAGGIE'S SECRET	CLARIBEL	4 0
OUT ON THE ROCKS	SAINTON-DOLBY	4 0	JANET'S CHOICE	CLARIBEL	4 0
STRANGERS YET	CLARIBEL	4 0	I CANNOT SING THE OLD SONGS	CLARIBEL	4 0
CLEAR AND COOL	BLUMENTHAL	4 0	THE SKIPPER AND HIS BOY	GABRIEL	4 0
WALTER'S WOOING	CLARIBEL	4 0	THE CHILDREN'S KINGDOM	BLUMENTHAL	4 0

SONGS BY "CLARIBEL."

	s. d.		s. d.
WHAT NEED HAVE I THE TRUTH TO TELL?		DREAMLAND. Sung by Mdme. PAREPA	4 0
(Robin's reply to "Wont you tell me why?")	4 0	FIVE O'CLOCK IN THE MORNING	4 0
FRIENDS FOR EVER	3 0	I REMEMBER IT. Sung by Miss POOLE	3 0
WHEREVER THOU ART WOULD SEEM ERIN TO ME	3 0	JANET'S BRIDAL. Sung by Mdme. PAREPA	3 0
THE PASSING BELL. Illustrated	3 0	JANET'S CHOICE. Sung by Mdme. SAINTON-DOLBY	3 0
TELL IT NOT	3 0	LITTLE BIRD, LITTLE BIRD ON THE GREEN TREE	3 0
ROSES AND DAISIES. Illustrated	3 0	MAGGIE'S SECRET. Sung by Mdme. SAINTON-DOLBY	4 0
THE LOVE TEST	4 0	MILLY'S FAITH	3 0
MAGGIE'S WELCOME. (Answer to "Maggie's Secret")	3 0	MY BRILLIANT AND I	3 0
WE'D BETTER BIDE A WEE. Sung by Mdlle. LIEBHART	4 0	NORAH'S TREASURE. Sung by Madame SAINTON-DOLBY	4 0
WEEP NO MORE, DARLING	3 0	MARION'S SONG	3 0
KATHLEEN'S ANSWER. Reply to "Come back to Erin"	3 0	THE LIFEBOAT. Words by Lord STRATFORD DE REDCLIFFE	4 0
STRANGERS YET. Sung by Madame SAINTON-DOLBY	4 0	TAKE BACK THE HEART	4 0
ALL ALONG THE VALLEY. Poetry by TENNYSON	3 0	THE BELLS' WHISPER	3 0
WALTER'S WOOING. Composed for Mdme. SAINTON-DOLBY	4 0	PRIEZ POUR ELLE	3 0
ONLY A LOCK OF HAIR	3 0	SUSAN'S STORY	3 0
SECRETS. Sung by Mdme. SHERRINGTON	4 0	THE BLUE RIBBON. Illustrated	3 0
SILVER CHIMES. Sung by Madame SAINTON-DOLBY	4 0	THE BROKEN SIXPENCE. Illustrated	3 0
COME BACK TO ERIN. Sung by Mad. LEMMENS-SHERRINGTON	4 0	THE TWO NESTS. Illustrated	3 0
I CANNOT SING THE OLD SONGS	4 0	THE OLD PINK THORN. Illustrated	3 0
DO YOU REMEMBER?	3 0	WONT YOU TELL ME WHY, ROBIN?	4 0
GOLDEN DAYS	3 0	"YOU AND I." Sung by SIMS REEVES	4 0
BLIND ALICE	3 0	MOUNTAIN MABEL	3 0

SONGS BY VIRGINIA GABRIEL.

	s. d.		s. d.
THE PRISONER AND THE LINNET	4 0	THE LADY OF KIENAST TOWER	4 0
THE SURPRISE. Sung by Mdlle. LIEBHART	4 0	NIGHTFALL AT SEA. Reverie	3 0
SOMEBODY'S DARLING	4 0	DREAM, BABY, DREAM. Sung by Miss BANKS	3 0
ONLY AT HOME. Composed for Madame SAINTON-DOLBY	4 0	THE SKIPPER AND HIS BOY	4 0
BYE-AND-BYE. Sung by Madame SAINTON-DOLBY	4 0	THE LIGHT IN THE WINDOW	4 0
WHEN THE PALE, PALE MOON	4 0	I WILL NOT ASK TO PRESS THAT CHEEK	3 0

SONGS BY ELIZABETH PHILP.

	s. d.		s. d.
WHEN ALL THE WORLD IS YOUNG	3 0	SLEEP, BABY, SLEEP. Sung by Madame RUDERSDORFF	3 0
BREAK, HEART, THY LOVE CAN NE'ER RETURN	3 0	'TIS ALL THAT I CAN SAY. Poetry by THOMAS HOOD	3 0
WHAT IS LOVE?	3 0	THE RIVER RAN BETWEEN THEM	3 0
THE GOLDEN PAST. Sung by Mr. W. H. CUMMINGS	3 0	GATHERED TREASURES. Poetry by TOM HOOD	3 0

SONGS BY ARTHUR S. SULLIVAN.

	s. d.		s. d.
[O SWEET] AND FAIR!	4 0	WILL HE COME? Sung by Madame SAINTON-DOLBY	4 0
[BAC]K TO ROCK. Words by F. C. BURNAND	3 0	GIVE. Sung by Miss EDITH WYNNE	3 0
[I]F WIND SIGHS ALONE. "	3 0	SHE IS NOT FAIR TO OUTWARD VIEW	3 0
[GE]NTLE MAIDEN. "	3 0	THOU ART LOST TO ME	2 6
. WE'LL MEET AGAIN. ("He will return") "	3 0		

SONGS BY "DOLORES."

	s. d.		s. d.
SLEEP	3 0	THE FAIRIES	4 0
O, MY LOST LOVE	3 0	UNCHANGED	3 2
"CUSHA"	3 0	CLEAR AND COOL	3 0
GOLDILOCKS	4 0	SONG OF A NEST	4 0
THE FOOLISH SHEPHERD	3 0		

NEW VOCAL DUETS.

		s. d.			s. d.
DAY DREAMS	CLARIBEL	3 0	THE ANGELS' HOME	SAINTON-DOLBY	4 0
THE CHIMES OF ST. MARY'S	CLARIBEL	3 0	OH! MAYST THOU DREAM O: ME	GABRIEL	2 6
	MY ROSES BLOSSOM THE WHOLE YEAR ROUND. GABRIEL. 3s.				

BOOSEY AND CO., HOLLES STREET, LONDON, W.

A list of Boosey's 'Popular Songs' from the late 1860s.

followed. Three years later, as a well-known name, she had to pay to have her cantata *Dreamland* printed privately. Cantatas and oratorios, the major musical forms of British concert life, and the forms which gave composers real stature, were a male preserve. Publishers were falling over each other, however, in competing for the rights to print Gabriel's ballads. A well-defined area in the ballad market had opened up to women composers in the 1860s. At the close of that decade, Boosey & Co. were making a specific point of advertising songs either sung or composed by women in their lists of 'popular songs'.

Gabriel was driven to writing ballads in order to achieve any reputation as a composer. In her early career she was fond of composing in the Italian style (probably under Mercadante's influence), as in her canzonetta 'Se mi perdi', published by C. Londsdale of London in 1854. But when she wrote 'The Skipper and His Boy' for the celebrated ballad singer Charlotte Sainton-Dolby in about 1860, she was given clear proof of the acclaim which she might receive by concentrating on this genre. It was her first big success: Brinley Richards made a piano transcription in 1861, and the song itself was in its third edition in 1865. Composing ballads did not mean 'selling out' by tailoring her music to a perceived market: in 1865 she merely adapted to words by Arthur Matthison an 'Ave Maria' she had composed in 1857 and produced the successful ballad 'Nightfall at Sea'. Gabriel's compositional training constantly shows in her ballads. Sometimes it is evident in the form: 'When Sparrows Build' (published by Metzler & Co., *c.* 1870) is a modified sonata-form such as was often found in the slow movements of contemporary symphonies. Sometimes it is evident in the harmony: 'Alone' (published by Boosey & Co., undated) shows her harmonic skill and adroit use of minor inflexions to create a sensitive response to the words.

Sometimes it is evident in the rhythm: 'Only' (published by Duff & Stewart, 1871) has uncommon rhythmic verve for a drawing-room ballad.

It is not just a matter of vigorous accompaniment; the rhythmic exhilaration pervades the melody too: note the singer's tiny but effective break before 'nothing more'. The extrovert style is undoubtedly related to its having been written for a male singer (something unusual for women composers to do at this time). The song shows her continuing interest in the *bel canto* style. The words (unattributed) have been carefully written to allow 'weak' phrase endings, a feature of Italian song deriving from the natural stresses of the Italian language. The melody concludes with a strikingly Verdian cadence.

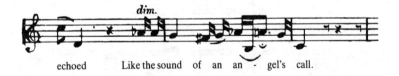

Gabriel's influence was widespread in the 1860s, and some of her procedures later became better known in association with the names of Sullivan and Cowen; for instance, the device of changing key from minor to tonic major coupled simultaneously to a direction to deliver the music with heightened expression.

The example on page 73 is from 'Ruby' (published by Metzler & Co., *c.* 1865). Gabriel, herself, may have derived the idea from Schubert or Italian opera, though examples which closely resemble the given extract from 'Ruby' are rare ('yearning' sections in Italian arias tend to be in the relative, rather than tonic, major).

The opening up of the ballad market to women composers in the 1860s probably owed most to the exceptional commercial success of Claribel's ballads. Charlotte Alington Barnard, née Pye (1830–69) may have taken the pseudonym Claribel from a poem of that name by a fellow native of Lincolnshire, Tennyson.

Unlike other women composers who seem to have thrived in the absence of male partners (and in this respect it is noteworthy that Virginia Gabriel was already well established before marrying George March in 1874), Claribel apparently only began to write songs after her marriage to the Rev. Charles Barnard. Her marriage does not appear to have been a close one, however, and her true feelings may have always been attached to the barrister to whom she was engaged for a year before giving in to her father's demands to call it off. It is surely not entirely coincidental that Claribel had some of her greatest successes with jilt songs, like 'Oh, Mother! Take the Wheel Away' and 'Won't You Tell Me Why, Robin?'

Claribel was enabled to turn to composition by her removal, after her marriage, from Louth to London. There she received a little instruction from the piano virtuoso W. H. Holmes and took singing lessons from some of the finest women singers of the day. The most influential of these must have been Charlotte Sainton-Dolby (1821–85), not only because of her skill as a contralto, but also because she was interested in composition herself. She had enjoyed a modest success with her ballad 'Lady, I Think of Thee' which was published by Leader & Cock in 1856, the year before Claribel arrived in London. Sainton-Dolby had the advantage of being able to promote her own songs at concerts and soirées, and she extended this facility to Claribel.

Claribel nearly always provided her own words to her ballads; in this she no doubt benefited from the advice and encouragement of her close friend and cousin, Jean Ingelow (1820–97). Ingelow, who had also moved to London from Lincolnshire, was one of several women poets building reputations in the 1860s; others included Elizabeth Barrett Browning and Christina Rossetti. Adelaide Procter (1825–64), whose poem 'A Lost Chord' was later to become one of the most famous of all drawing-room ballads in the hands of Sullivan, was already a well-known figure in the London Portfolio Society. Claribel occasionally set Ingelow's verse, and Ingelow's poetry soon became a storehouse for ballad composers; sometimes, as in the case of 'O Fair Dove! O Fond Dove!' and 'When Sparrows Build', spawning several versions.

Claribel's songwriting career was eventually halted by a combination of ill health and the disaster of her sudden loss of respectability. Her father, Henry Pye, absconded as a bankrupt in 1868, having made fraudulent use of public funds (he was, amongst other things, County Treasurer of Lincoln). Her own financial loss as a result of this was £30,000; but worse, she was 'no longer the popular song-writer Claribel, at whose house the leading poets of the day gathered to drink tea, and talk. She was the daughter of Henry Pye, swindler'.[15] She left for the continent, the usual step in such circumstances, but died in January 1869 shortly after returning.

Claribel's first success was with 'Janet's Choice', written for Sainton-Dolby in 1859. It is a typical ballad of its time, consisting of a sixteen-bar verse and an eight-bar refrain. The tune is attractively memorable throughout: there is never a feeling that Claribel saves her best melodic ideas for the refrains of her songs. In this respect, nothing has changed since Bishop's 'Home, Sweet Home!', and so the situation continued until the heyday of the Boosey Ballad Concerts, when the refrain develops from a standard eight bars (commonly derived from previous material) to the largest and most musically important section. In Claribel's day verse and refrain form was by no means the norm; in fact, Claribel did much to make it the norm, since she used it more than other composers at this time.

'Five o'Clock in the Morning'

Writing her own words, she had the option of using this form whenever she desired. Strophic settings were still the favourite: a frequent procedure was to extend the basic sixteen-bar tune to twenty bars by repeating the last line (both words and music). Claribel adopts this method in 'Five o' Clock in the Morning' (1862), subtly deflecting the tune from an anticipated close in bar 16. See the musical example on page 74.

Claribel's sustained commercial success is indicated by her being one of the first ballad composers to make a royalty arrangement with her publisher, rather than selling her copyrights for a fixed sum. Her importance to Boosey's song catalogue is evident both from the space she occupies and Boosey's care to try to accommodate a song with a wide range, like 'Maggie's Secret' (1863), to the amateur voice by offering it in three different keys instead of the customary two.

Claribel's natural melodic flair had as one of its chief attractions the mixture of the predictable and the unpredictable. 'Mountain Mabel' (1864), for example, is a strophic song in the familiar twenty-bar span, but although the harmonic movement of the closing bars comes just as expected, the shape of the melody avoids the obvious.

'Mountain Mabel' shows Claribel widening her harmonic vocabulary and developing confidence in handling dissonance; yet, formally, as remarked above, it follows a conventional pattern. 'Come Back to Erin' (1866), written after she had taken some more lessons in composition, has greater breadth and subtlety in its design. The structure is ternary: the middle section consists of a minor variation of the melody used in the outer sections. Thus the song has a unity lacking in her previous attempt at a broad ternary structure, her waltz song of 1864, 'Take Back the Heart' (composed to words by the Hon. Mrs G. R. Gifford).

Claribel's reputation spread to North America, where her songs, if anything, exceeded the popularity accorded them in Britain. Both the last-mentioned songs were particular favourites. On her death the New York publisher B. W. Hitchcock introduced several of her songs into his 'half dime series of music for the million', thereby making them even more widely known. Even in 1883, fourteen years after her death, she is still one of the best represented composers in Thomas Hunter's *Song Folio*, an American collection of vocal music by 'favourite composers'.

Claribel's elegantly crafted melody and melancholy charm is typified by her song 'Oh, Mother! Take the Wheel Away'.[16]

> Oh, mother, take the wheel away, and put it out of sight,
> For I am heavy hearted, and I cannot spin tonight:
> Come nearer, nearer yet I have a story for your ear,
> So come and sit beside me, come and listen, mother dear;
> You heard the village bells, tonight, his wedding bells they were;
> And Mabel is his happy wife, and I am lonely here;
> A year ago tonight, I mind, he sought me for his bride,
> And who so glad at heart as I, that happy Easter tide?
>
> But Mabel came among us, and her face was fair to see,
> What wonder was it, mother, that he thought no more of me?
> When first he said fair words to her, I know she did not hear,
> But in the end she listen'd, could she help it, mother dear?
> And afterwards we met, and we were friendly all the same:
> For ne'er a word I said to them of anger, or of blame,
> Till both believed I did not care, and maybe they were right,
> But mother, take the wheel away, I cannot spin tonight.

Of thirty-two bars of melody, half that number begin with what is technically known as an *appoggiatura*, a note dissonant with the harmony which is made concordant by falling on to the harmony note one step below in pitch. The effect of this constant contrast of tension and falling release is to create a kind of musical sighing, which is here suggestive of the jilted woman's disappointment. At 'I am lonely here' (and the equivalent place in the next stanza), the melodic phrase ends on a discord, a procedure of some novelty at this time and furthering the yearning mood by its prolongation of musical tension. If each line of the song is given a letter name to indicate melodic repetition, then the unusual pattern AABBCDEA results (though the climax is reached at a conventional point). The evenly measured rhythmic movement is less likely to be a sign of banality than a simple convenience of notation which offers the possibility of interpretive flexibility on the singer's part. The accompaniment can only be described as basic, but enough variety is present to maintain interest. Claribel's songs stand or fall by the strength of their tunes: one of the keys to her popularity must have been the ease with which it was possible to transmit her tunes orally; songs like 'Come Back to Erin' were not long confined to the drawing rooms of the musically literate.

The text of 'Oh, Mother! Take the Wheel Away' is both a simple narrative and a lesson in correct behaviour to the young middle-class woman. In a time of emotional turmoil she should confide in her mother. Hysterics are out of the question; she must exercise disciplined restraint, although she may be forgiven for not being able to concentrate on other things the day her former sweetheart marries. Jealousy is irrational: if Mabel is prettier, then it is only natural for the man to prefer her. Malicious feelings about the rival should be quashed; how could Mabel help listening to the 'fair words' being spoken to her? Finally the young woman should react to being jilted by keeping up appearances and assuming the quiet dignity that Millais portrays in *The Wedding Card* (1854). The song presents an ideal of middle-class social mores, though the scene is rural and the girl may be spinning to earn money. Claribel is fond of rural life in her songs, and equally fond of using it to articulate bourgeois values. As mentioned in Chapter 1, the idyllic rustic cottage was already a myth when it was eulogized in 'Home, Sweet Home!'

Images of women in drawing-room ballads

The type of woman who appears in Claribel's ballads, and indeed in all drawing-room ballads, tends to be a representative of bourgeois values in the form of 'perfect lady' or honest country maiden, simply because this kind of woman can be portrayed with less hypocrisy than the working-class woman, whose life points to the contradictions in those values. On the rare occasions when the plight of poor working-class men and women finds its way into these songs, then it comes in a package heavy with sentiment. Women are generally depicted as romantic objects, or placed in the context of the family. A woman is associated with the role of home-maker. Nothing in the words of 'Home, Sweet Home!' necessarily implies that the gender of the singer should be female, but it is the combination of female voice with its homesick melancholy which gives it potency:

> The mem'ries of that night of bliss,
> Will never from me part,
> She sang a song of 'Home sweet home',
> The song that reach'd my heart.
> (from *The Song That Reached My Heart*, words and music by J. Jordan)

Women appear in many songs as mother: for example, 'The Emigrant Mother', 'A Mother's Song' and 'The Mother's Dream' (dates, writers and composers may be found in the Song Index). An important aspect of the maternal role is the opportunity it gives to minister to loved ones, one of the highest duties of a woman. Some songs are concerned with the sorrow felt by men when death has robbed them of a mother's loving care for their moral and physical well-being: for example, 'The Old Arm Chair' and 'I'm Lonely Since My Mother Died'. Grandmother occasionally appears, as in 'Grannie's Story' and 'Grandmother's Chair'; so too does the maiden aunt, who invariably possesses a crotchety character arising from her disappointment at having been deprived of the blessings of marriage and motherhood. F. E. Weatherly offers rare sympathy when in 'Auntie' (music by A. H. Behrend) he includes the lines,

> Old maids have hearts, my darling,
> Whatever the world may say.

Songs about boys far outnumber those about girls, and the latter are portrayed as extremely vulnerable when outside the setting of a 'normal' home: for example, the lonely girl in 'Ora Pro Nobis' and 'The Children's Home'. If girls are working, they are usually doing something associated with female domesticity, as in, for example, 'Knitting'. Boys can demonstrate spirited independence, as do 'The Little Hero' and 'Little Drummer'. In general, songs about the deaths of children concern boys: for example, 'Close the Shutters, Willie's Dead' and 'Put My Little Shoes Away'. A dead baby may be of unspecified sex, as in 'The Empty Cradle'.

Women as romantic objects are often pictured in Victorian literature and the visual arts as angelic characters or as temptresses; very few sirens, however, find their way into drawing-room ballads. Songs suitable for the parlour or drawing room were wholesome entertainment for family and friends: music-making here was a celebration of home and family life. Suggestive songs were the province of music-hall (for example, 'Saucy Betsy Gay', or 'It's Naughty But It's Nice'); in the drawing room only the barest hint of disruptive female sexuality was tolerated, in songs such as 'Florence Vane' and 'The Picture with Its Face Turned to the Wall'. Young women are either serenaded, as in 'Come into the Garden, Maud' and 'The Bloom Is on the Rye', or they are the subject of tearful partings, as in 'Goodbye!' Older women either appear as wives, as in 'Darby and Joan', or widows, as in 'She Wore a Wreath of Roses', or mothers (already referred to above). If a young wife appears in a ballad, she is almost certain to be married to a sailor, as is 'Nancy Lee'. A woman who is the subject of a passionate love song is often dead, as in 'Alice, Where Art Thou?', 'Looking Back', and 'The Fisher'. Because the woman is dead, ruling sex out of the question, a more uninhibited quality is permissible than in the case of songs about living women: there, tasteful restraint is necessary, unless the lovers are parting for ever. There are few examples of songs concerning a woman losing a husband or sweetheart, as occurs in 'She Wandered Down the Mountainside', but there are plenty of songs about mothers losing sons. When Felix McGlennon attempts to describe the nature of true love, in his song 'That Is Love', his first example is of mother and son:

> See a mother gazing on her baby boy,
> With ecstatic eyes and heart that fills with joy,
> He to her is purest gold without alloy,
> For him how she prays to Heav'n above.

How she guides his footsteps through this vale of strife,
Watches o'er his bedside when infection's rife,
Risking for her baby boy her health, her life,
That is love, that is love!

It was sentiments like these that enabled McGlennon to invade the middle-class parlour, in spite of his being a music-hall performer. Not only could songs of love pierce class barriers, but they acknowledged within themselves the possibility of love's breaking down class distinctions. It ought to be noted, however, that it is invariably the woman who belongs to the subordinate class in this type of song, as in 'The Beggar Maid'. The poor artless maid who wins the heart of a nobleman is really used as a critique of urban sophistication rather than an advertisement for marriage between the classes.

It should be borne in mind, while considering the limited roles allotted to women in drawing-room ballads, that women as pianists in the home also learned pieces which endorsed these roles: for example, 'The Maiden's Prayer' by Thekla Badarzewska; 'The Fairy Wedding Waltz' by J. W. Turner; and 'The Bridal Polka' by Charles D'Albert. Just as Badarzewska, a young woman composer, acquiesced in the stereotype of the praying maiden when she gave a title to her theme and variations for piano, women ballad composers and authors also portrayed the same stereotypes as are found in ballads by men. Furthermore, these stereotypes remain constant irrespective of which side of the Atlantic the ballad originates; indeed, some of the examples given above are of American ballads.

The favourite subjects chosen by women composers fall into four main categories: religious songs, jilt songs, genteel love songs, and songs about children. Religious songs were accorded such respect that a woman composer had no qualms about using her married name on the sheet music, rather than using her maiden name or adopting a pseudonym. Maria Lindsay proudly announces herself to be Mrs J. Worthington Bliss on ballads like 'Absalom'. A certain delicacy arises with genteel love songs, since, no matter how polite their style, the possibility of arousing the erotic interest of men in their female creators always remains. Jilt songs are safer terrain, although, when Lord Arthur Hill heard 'In the Gloaming', he boasted he would marry its female composer; and so he did. More often than in men's songs about children, in women's songs the singer is cast in the role of mother, as in 'Destiny' or 'Alone'. Women composers in the 1860s and 70s see themselves, in the main, as providing songs for women; this is an attitude which begins to change only with the arrival of the 'new woman' of the 1880s. There is a dearth of music by women, for instance, written for the low male voice; Sheard's largely retrospective *Baritone's Song Folio* of 1903 contains not a single song by a woman composer. In the 1860s women composers were something of a novelty with which to stimulate the market and appeal to its many female consumers; in the middle of the next decade there seems to have been a slackening of interest, and songs by women were given no special promotion. Nevertheless, in the late Victorian and Edwardian period women again come to the fore, with such names as Hope Temple, Guy D'Hartelot, Maude Valerie White, Liza

Lehmann, Teresa Del Riego, and Amy Woodforde-Finden. There are few alterations to female stereotyping in Edwardian ballads, however: for example, 'The English Rose' contains references to 'the perfect English rose' which recall the early Victorian ideal of the 'perfect lady'. Even in the year the Edwardian period closes, Liza Lehman's ballad 'Daddy's Sweetheart' carries a familiar warning to women of independent disposition:

> Mary Jane told me this morning
> Something which made me afraid;
> She said I'd have to marry a man
> Or be a cross old maid.

4   *Cultural Assimilation*

Throughout the nineteenth century musical features from a variety of ethnic cultures were introduced from time to time as exotic decoration to drawing-room ballads. Afro-Americans and Celts, however, were subject to cultural assimilation on a broader scale: no one could mistake a drawing-room 'Hindostanee' ballad for the real thing, but many blackface minstrel songs and pseudo-Celtic songs came to be accepted as the authentic cultural expression of black Americans and of Irish and British Celts. As a consequence of cultural assimilation, the true voice of these peoples was almost silenced. That it survived is a tribute to the fierce independence of those who fought to preserve it, and to whom it held meanings closely allied to a sense of community and racial identity. The present chapter, though, is only incidentally concerned with trying to define authentic culture; the subject under consideration is the process of part appropriation and part invention which went into the creation of fake ethnic songs.

Afro-Americans

In the eighteenth century curiosity was occasionally shown in the culture of African slaves working on colonial plantations. Dibdin developed a black character in his act named Mungo; he first appeared in Dibdin and Bickerstaffe's opera *The Padlock* (1768). Mungo was used to preach contentment with one's lot: for example, in 'Kickaraboo' (from *Christmas Gambols*, 1795) he sings,

> One massa, one slave, high and low, all degrees,
> Can be happy, dance, sing, make all pleasure him please . . .

and the song 'Negro Philosophy' (from *The General Election*, 1796) contains the lines:

> Then let um wait till that world come,
> Where overseers no jerk ye.

Mungo is a mixture of clown and 'noble savage'; he is not used, as are the blackface-minstrel corner men, to deflate high culture. That is the province of the comic Irishman: Dibdin's 'Irish Italian Song', for example, is intended to poke fun at Italian opera. This song is in Dibdin's Table Entertainment *The Wags*

(1790), which also includes 'The Negro and His Banjer', a song demonstrating an early appreciation of the importance of the banjo to black culture. Thomas Jefferson was one of the first to describe the instrument, calling it a 'banjor', in his *Notes on the State of Virginia* (1784).

Before the minstrel show, a blackface performer would normally be found in a circus; additionally, in Britain, there were blackface 'folk' customs. Until the end of the War of 1812 in America, the dominant attitude to the black slave was similar to that of Dibdin's. When the war with Britain ended in 1815, a demand grew for a specifically American form of culture. Contained within that demand was the need for a better understanding of the cultural significance of the Afro-American. The Yankee, however, beat the Afro-American as the first stereotype to tread the stage, a figure courageous and simple, patriotic and strong in moral fibre. The key moment for blackface performance came when Thomas D. Rice took a song and dance, 'Jim Crow', from a black street performer in 1828, and acquired overnight fame. The details concerning his discovery of the song and his first performance of it have passed into legend and are surrounded by conflicting evidence and competing claims.[1] Rice was not the first to appropriate black culture (the first definite example was the Englishman Charles Matthews's use of 'Possum up a Gum Tree' in his entertainment *A Trip to America*, 1823), but his unique success came from his developing an entire entertainment based on close imitation of an actual black performer. He thus set a precedent for the mediation of black culture by white entertainers which has continued to the present (blues, jazz, reggae, hip-hop, etc.).

Credit for turning blackface performance from a solo entertainment into a minstrel show is generally given to the Virginia Minstrels. They were formed by Daniel Emmett in New York in 1843 and began as a quartet (violin, banjo, tambourine, and bones). The market swiftly opened up for minstrelsy: black-face performance may have started in the South and Mid-West, but blackface minstrelsy was concentrated in the industrial North-East (New York, Philadelphia, and Boston). The class orientation of the early minstrel show is difficult to assess: Toll sees it as 'unabashedly popular in appeal',[2] yet notes that it was performed by 'middling' Americans. It is not a simple question of judging which theatres minstrels performed in, because each American theatre was divided up internally on clear class lines – boxes for the élite, the pit for the 'middling' class, the gallery for the lower orders. The images of plantation slaves, moreover, were not shaped by class consciousness and black realities, but by racial consciousness and white prejudices. The minstrel show enabled the already racially mixed white Americans to develop a sense of national identity, and to perceive the place of black Americans within that identity. While guarding against the pitfall of presentism by being wary of applying today's attitudes on race to the nineteenth century, it is none the less evident that minstrel shows were racist in suggesting the superiority of one race to another.

At the same time, minstrel racism was full of contradictions: patronizing mockery, for instance, became ambiguous when black culture proved to be thrilling (as was the concluding minstrel hoe-down, based on the black ring-shout). Minstrels were picking up ideas for dances from black slaves in the South throughout the 1850s; the texts of songs, too, often demonstrate an African interest in animal fables and fantasy. There was a shifting level of identification with the blackface performer which related to the meaning of his mask. The mask is a traditional means of obliterating the individual personality; it requires that the character be seen as symbolic of something that extends beyond the purely personal. It does not need to be an actual mask: Buster Keaton's blank expression was a mask, and so is the blacked-up face in minstrelsy. The blackface minstrel denoted a particular kind of theatricality. The adoption of the blackface mask allowed the loss of inhibition without the loss of dignity: once the burnt cork was applied, a transformation of character could take place. This helps to explain why minstrelsy was as popular in Britain as in America. In an age of inhibitions and social restraint, it was desirable to have a valve for letting off steam. For the bourgeoisie this must have been a major factor in minstrelsy's appeal; certainly there were great numbers of middle-class minstrels who lacked all but the slightest acquaintance with the behaviour of black Americans.

It is unlikely that the minstrel projection of the African as a person in need of paternalistic care from a civilized slave owner would work on the same level of recognition in Britain as in America. Wilberforce, after all, had fought for years against just that sort of image (and the contrast, made with hypocritical concern, between poor white workers and happy black slaves) before his bill for the Abolition of the Slave Trade was passed in 1807. For the British working class, the minstrel show must have been attractive, not so much in its caricatures of a little-known Afro-American population, but in its inversion of much of the dominant ideology of the day, an inversion which inevitably posed challenges to the values by which they were asked to live (for example, the Protestant work ethic). There is no doubting that the minstrel show had the broadest cross-class appeal of any Victorian entertainment. Yet there is surely no one who doubts, either, that blackface minstrelsy did help to promote ruling-class interests by contributing to the growing racism of nineteenth-century Britain. Notwithstanding the general rejection of paternalistic arguments for slavery, many came to accept the idea of a paternalistic *Pax Britannica*, notions of 'responsible governments' abroad, and then the need for imperialist expansion and the scramble for Africa. In America it is noteworthy that before the Civil War Indians were represented in minstrel shows as 'noble savages', but during the big push west in the 1870s, when Indians blocked white expansion, they became 'scalping savages'. The racist side to minstrelsy, therefore, should not be wholly dismissed in the face of the accusation 'presentism'.

Blackface minstrelsy developed chronologically in the same manner in Britain as in America: 1836–50 saw the progression from solo performer to minstrel troupe; 1850–70 was its hey-day; 1870–1900 was the period of growing lavishness and gimmickry, the buying up of troupes and the formation of bigger and fewer companies. Minstrelsy, therefore, followed the ordinary course of evolution of capitalist consumer industries. Minstrelsy, in a form mixing blackface men and whiteface women, has not entirely disappeared in Britain: a 'Black and White Minstrel Show' was presented at the New Theatre, Hull, in 1986. Rice was as big a sensation when he performed in Britain in 1836 as he had been in America.

Coincidentally, he appeared in London the same year as Henry Russell made his début in New York. Russell was the first Englishman to build a repertoire of 'Negro melodies', although he did not perform in blackface. An open champion of the abolition of slavery, Russell points to further contradictions in the ideological significance of this sort of material. Most of the early minstrels were pro-slavery, yet they often sang the same songs as Russell. In Russell's repertoire was 'Dandy Jim of Caroline', which, along with 'Zip Coon', established the stereotype of the black dandy, holding up to ridicule his strutting around in patent boots, pantaloons, and long-tailed blue coat. Dandy Jim's girlfriend has the obligatory enormous feet – 'eighteen inches from de heel to de toe' – and his male potency is beyond dispute (he intends to have twenty-four children). Yet, while on the one hand the song can be seen as satirizing an Afro-American trying to rise above his station, on the other hand it can be interpreted as a universal indictment of vanity, begging the question why anyone at all should dress in such a manner.

The melody of 'Dandy Jim' is typical of early minstrelsy in owing much, if not everything, to Afro-American music-making. Unlike the thematic style of Western European song, the fondness for broad archlike shapes, and the careful positioning of climax, 'Dandy Jim' is constructed in short melodic and rhythmic cells and generates excitement through repetition. The two motives, or cells, are marked (a) and (b) in the complete tune given below.

Cell structure, which may be presumed to be of African origin, characterizes many of Russell's 'Negro melodies' as well as many of the songs sung by early troupes like the Virginia Minstrels, the Ethiopian Serenaders, and the Christy Minstrels. Other features which suggest appropriation of black culture are syncopation ('Buffalo Gals', 'Old Dan Tucker') and an absence of modulation. Often the leading-note is absent too (though strict pentatonicism is rare), or the leading-note is flattened, 'blue note' fashion. The distinctive effect of the latter, plus one or two other resemblances, helps identify a kinship between Russell's 'De Merry Shoe-Black' and the Ethiopian Serenaders' 'My Old Aunt Sally'. Compare the following extracts (Russell's tune has been transposed up one semitone to facilitate the comparison):

'De Merry Shoe-Black'

'My Old Aunt Sally'

Comparing the two songs reveals some of the changes, especially those resulting from adding new texts, which might be wrought upon the same ethnic material; but which song is closer to that material in its original appropriated form is impossible to say (though a guess would naturally favour the Ethiopian Serenaders' version for its avoidance of the leading-note amongst other things).

The 'call and response', common in the black religious rituals of the South, also finds its way into minstrel song. Stephen Foster (1826–64) uses cell structure and 'call and response' in his famous song of the late 1840s, 'Gwine To Run All Night' (or 'De Camptown Races'). He carefully marks the verse to be sung as solo, alternating with chorus every two bars. Foster became familiar with black culture as a boy, when his father regularly allowed him to visit 'a church of shouting colored people'.[3] The other features 'Gwine To Run All Night' shares with typical minstrel songs of the 1840s are a near pentatonic tune and simple duple metre. Absence of modulation and 2/4 time are ideally suited to the banjo: the former because of the banjo's drone string (it is not certain whether this was added by Joel Sweeney of Virginia in 1831, or whether he added the lowest string[4]), and the latter because it is the rhythm of the basic banjo strum. That this strum, inherited by today's clawhammer banjoists, was the same as that used in the first minstrel shows, is confirmed by Foster's song 'Way Down in Ca-i-ro' (1850) which imitates a banjo in its piano accompaniment.

Foster's involvement with minstrel songs demonstrates how quickly they were accepted into bourgeois culture, for he writes to E. P. Christy in 1852, saying:

> I had the intention of omitting my name on my Ethiopian songs, owing to the prejudice against them by some, which might injure my reputation as a writer of another style of music, but I find that by my efforts I have done a great deal to build up a taste for the Ethiopian songs among refined people.[5]

Two-thirds of Foster's output is unconnected with minstrelsy: 'Jeanie with the Light Brown Hair' (1854) typifies his drawing-room manner – wider range, modulation, gentle pace, flowing phrases, pervasive melancholy – but in the 1850s these two styles began to intermingle. His letter to Christy in 1852 was written to ask if he could be given credit for having written 'Old Folks at Home', which had appeared, by agreement, under Christy's own name in the previous year. It must have been obvious to Foster that there was no great divide between a song like this and a genteel ballad like Bayly's 'Long, Long Ago!' Indeed, the use of repetition in the latter even suggests 'call and response' form (compare it, for example, with the spiritual 'Zion's Children'). Bayly's song, incidentally, was converted into a popular song entitled 'Don't Sit Under the Apple Tree', in 1942. In 1850 Foster must have already had his sights on the domestic market when he arranged the chorus of 'Nelly Bly' for two harmonizing sopranos for the sheet music published by Firth, Pond & Co., New York. The song had been written for the Christy Minstrels who, like all the troupes at that time, were entirely composed of men. Foster became uncertain about the use of dialect: in 1853 he wrote 'My Old Kentucky Home' first in dialect and then without. He began to avoid dialect in other songs, for example, 'Old Black Joe' (1860), and finally abandoned it altogether after 'Don't Bet Your Money on de Shanghai' (1861).

There was in America, besides the minstrel show, a tradition of respectable entertainments given by travelling families, who offered simple, catchy songs as well as melodramatic pieces. The teetotal Hutchinson Family, for example, sang short, lively tunes like 'Cape Ann' as well as long, dramatic ballads of the *gran scena* type like 'The Vulture of the Alps' (a harrowing tale of a father who finds his child has been eaten by a vulture – the bird has considerately left the boy's cap on his skull to aid identification). The humour and rhythmic drive of 'Cape Ann' are not far removed from contemporary minstrel songs and, just as the sentimental minstrel song was a blend of parlour and plantation, the exuberant minstrel song must have combined black culture with the more vigorous elements of the white tradition represented by the Hutchinsons. Furthermore, the text of 'Cape Ann' is full of the nonsense humour and exclamations of early minstrelsy (though obviously related to English 'folksongs' like 'The Three Huntsmen'):

One said it was a frog,
But the other said nay;
He said it was a canary bird,
With its feathers washed away.
Look ye there!

The Hutchinsons were accompanied by an ensemble with the European tone colour of violins, cello, and guitar; the minstrel ensemble was dominated by the African sound of the banjo and percussion.

The minstrel show won respectability in Britain as quickly as in America: the Ethiopian Serenaders performed at the White House in 1844, and on their British tour in 1846 they performed before Queen Victoria at Arundel Castle. Barlow's *Nigger Melodist* was published in 1846, claiming to provide a 'choice collection of all the original songs' including those of the Ethiopian Serenaders and celebrated (unnamed) banjo players. In the early 1850s Davidson was marketing his *Cheap Edition of the Songs of the Ethiopian Serenaders* alongside his 'cheap editions' of Russell's songs, Dibdin's songs, and Jenny Lind's 'Swedish Melodies'. Although the Ethiopian Serenaders prided themselves in being the most refined of the troupes, the Virginia Minstrels were also at pains to avoid anything which might be considered vulgar, and the Christy Minstrels spoke of their 'unique and chaste performances' which had been 'patronized by élite and fashion'.[6] It was the last-mentioned troupe whose name became almost synonymous with minstrelsy in Britain, the name 'Christy' being used like 'Ethiopian' merely as a convenient label for blackface minstrels.

The rapid acceptance of the minstrel show as respectable entertainment contrasts with the bourgeois reception of music-hall. In spite of its broad cross-class appeal, however, it was 'just as much about English social relations as it was about a scantily known Afro-American population'.[7] The black struggle in America may have held very different meanings to the different classes in Britain, as does, say, the struggle for free trade unionism in Poland today. Minstrelsy's links with bourgeois humanitarians like Russell gave it a more elevated status than music-hall, but it would be wrong to identify the blackface minstrel too closely with the Afro-American plantation slave. Again, it must be stressed that the blackface mask denoted a certain kind of theatricality, and when genuine black performers confirmed the minstrel stereotypes, it was because they needed to adopt the conventions of blackface entertainment to enjoy success.[8] The black stereotypes projected by the minstrel show had their repercussions in other musical genres: no longer was it possible in 1870, as it had been in 1770, for a black actress to take the part of Polly in *The Beggar's Opera*.

The two biggest British troupes, both based in London, were the Moore and Burgess Minstrels and the Mohawk Minstrels. The former were formed in 1857, the year that E. P. Christy's Minstrels visited London, and they also named themselves 'Christy Minstrels'. The Mohawk Minstrels were formed in 1867.

The British minstrel show came to maturity during and after the American Civil War, and its heavy content of sentimentality derives as much from the changes wrought upon minstrelsy by that conflict as from a deliberate appeal to the bourgeois drawing-room market. In the 1850s minstrels were continuing to paint a picture of contented black slaves, perhaps playing the occasional prank on an overseer (something they did not do in the 1840s), but happy with their families, and needing to be supervised by whites for their own good. When George Aiken's stage version of Harriet Beecher Stowe's *Uncle Tom's Cabin* was greeted with enthusiasm in New York in 1853, minstrel shows began to include parodies of it (Barnum also staged a pro-Southern version at his American Museum). *Uncle Tom's Cabin* was a more uniform success in Britain, Henry Russell and Eliza Cook responding to it with particular warmth. All the same, the majority of minstrel troupes found themselves out of favour in the South immediately before the Civil War despite their pro-plantation ideology; the reason was simply that they came from the North. Towards the middle of the Civil War, minstrel shows were dominated by patriotic Unionism: gaiety passed into martial vigour, and the sentimental songs now reached out to the audience's concern for friends and relatives in the war. Foster remarks in 'That's What's The Matter' in 1862 (a song for Bryant's Minstrels):

We live in hard and stirring times,
Too sad for mirth, too rough for rhymes.

An irony of the conflict, which emerges unspoken from such songs as 'Dear Mother, I've Come Home to Die' (words by E. Bowers, music by H. Tucker), is that brother fought brother while both sides believed in family values. It was only in 1863 that the emancipation of slaves became an issue, partly because Lincoln needed to recruit blacks into the Union army. Till then the cause had been simply the restoration of the Union, a thing minstrels had always supported. Reluctantly minstrels began to accept the need for emancipation when it became impossible to overlook the part played by black soldiers in fighting for the Union. A key moment arrived when minstrels felt able to sing songs by the fervent abolitionist Henry Clay Work (such as 'Kingdom Coming') whose family home in Illinois had been a station on the underground railroad for runaway slaves. Sentimental songs, however, never concerned dying black soldiers, and they never consisted of a blanket condemnation of war (which would have been unpatriotic). It was the Hutchinson Family who sang Walter Kittredge's anti-war song 'Tenting on the Old Camp Ground', a song which was revived by Pete Seeger in the 1960s as part of the protest movement against the Vietnam War. The American Civil War drew out further contradictions in minstrelsy when the South adopted as a favourite patriotic song 'Dixie's Land', written and composed as a minstrel walk-around by the patriotic Northerner Daniel Emmett in 1860. In Britain Foster's minstrel songs were thought to be Confederate ballads, but some of his other songs, such as 'We Are Coming Father Abraam, 300,000 More' (1862) and 'Nothing but a Plain Old Soldier' (1863), prove he was a committed Unionist. The Christy Minstrels made their allegiance public by singing 'John Brown's Body'. To British publishers all this was irrelevant: Hopwood & Crew published the latter – advertised as 'Federal Hymn' – as well as *Celebrated Songs of the Confederate States of America.*

The minstrel show and the Civil War gave the two biggest boosts to American music publishing in the nineteenth century. Federal ballads outnumber Confederate ballads like Harry Macarthy's 'The Bonnie Blue Flag' (1861) for the reason that all the major publishing firms were in the North. After the War there was a slump, and minstrels faced competition from new variety shows offering wholesome family entertainment. Minstrel shows were therefore under pressure either to compete in terms of respectability, or to take an opposite direction. An example of the second option was the female minstrel show, which would nowadays merit the description 'soft porn'. Perhaps in reaction, the respectable minstrel show remained exclusively male, although the female impersonator (for example, Francis Leon) became an important character in the show. The lachrymose minstrels of this period, obsessed with morbidity and 'Old Black Joe' nostalgia, were eventually reinvigorated by more black culture which filtered through to them via the black-minstrel shows.

Black-minstrel troupes had emerged in 1855 but did not establish themselves until after the Civil War. Unfortunately, the necessity of making money drove them to confirm the minstrel stereotype at first. Again, it must be emphasized that this was because people expected a particular kind of entertainment when they went to a minstrel show; in different circumstances, the African Theatre in New York had flourished (it was here Charles Matthews heard 'Possum up a Gum Tree' in 1822) and was, in fact, forced to close by whites envious of its success. Black troupes got into the business of minstrelsy by capitalizing on the authenticity of their material, and by stressing slave connections. Whites started to take over ownership of black troupes in the 1870s. Sam Hague organized a ten-man 'Slave Troupe' for a British tour in 1866. J. H. Haverly's Colored Minstrels came to Britain in 1881 and received acclaim; they were presented as spontaneous and natural, as opposed to his artistically refined blackfaced Mastodon Minstrels.

James Bland (1854–1911) of Callender's Georgia Minstrels, the finest minstrel composer of the 1870s and 80s, was black. The texts of his songs (he wrote both words and music), however, express the dominant culture and endorse black stereotypes in just the same way as the songs by women, discussed in the previous chapter, confirmed female stereotypes. 'Carry Me Back to Old Virginny' (1878), the official state song of Virginia, has been attacked in recent years as racist. Bland's 'Oh, Dem Golden Slippers!' (1879) shows the effect of the conventions of blackface minstrelsy on a black minstrel: it adheres to the limits of what was felt to be comfortable when the subject of religion entered the songs of blackface minstrels. It seemed incongruous for certain subjects to be sung about in blackface; on these grounds Pickering feels that minstrel comic love songs subvert the parlour ballad.[9] However, love songs of the serenading type were not so common in the home as those love songs concerning separation and death, and here minstrels acquiesced in the same kind of sentimentality from the days of 'Lucy Neal' onwards. Indeed, one of the most famous parting songs was 'Darling Nelly Gray' (1856) by the abolitionist Benjamin Handby. Its serious intent is evident from its avoidance of dialect, and the directness of its third verse:

> One night I went to see her but 'she's gone!' the neighbours say,
> The white man bound her with his chain,
> They have taken her to Georgia for to wear her life away,
> As she toils in the cotton and the cane.

There was undoubtedly a widespread feeling of incongruity at blackface minstrels singing religious songs, and a reluctance on the part of publishers to categorize a minstrel song as sacred: for example, 'Still Watch o'er Me Little Star' (which is certainly religious in its content) was listed in London publishers Howard & Co.'s 'Musical Library' under the category 'song' rather than 'sacred song'. Here is further evidence that the blackface mask did not operate on a realist level, for whereas blackface minstrels rarely sang religious songs, one of the most successful groups of black musicians in the nineteenth century was the Jubilee Singers, who sang almost nothing but religious songs (see the following chapter).

The musical style of minstrelsy during its British heyday in the 1860s and early 70s points to the diverse class character of its audience. The songs of Harry Hunter, a celebrated 'interlocutor' (a minstrel master of ceremony) of the period, illustrate the *rapprochement* with music-hall: 'The Doctor Says I'm Not To Be Worried' is musically indistinguishable from a music-hall song. It has the music hall's 6/8 jollity (inherited from the comic 'Irish song') rather than the 2/4 vivacity of early minstrelsy, and it follows a typical music-hall form of eight-bar introduction, sixteen-bar verse, and eight-bar refrain; considered harmonically, too, it employs the passing modulations characteristic of music-hall song. There is nothing in the music which sets the song apart from, say, George Leybourne's 'That's Where You Make The Mistake'. The crucial difference with Hunter's songs was that they could be assumed to be, in the language of the day, entirely devoid of all vulgarity in their texts. An advertisement for his song 'Little Joe' declared with wry humour: 'the song suits both dark and fair singers, as it may be appropriately sung either in evening dress or nigger costume.'[10]

Hunter also sang parody songs: for example, 'I Dreamt That I Dwelt on the Top of St Pauls', a parody of Balfe's 'I Dreamt That I Dwelt in Marble Halls'; and 'Just Behind the Battle, Mother', a parody of George Root's American Civil War ballad 'Just Before the Battle, Mother'. The last-mentioned parody is a good example of minstrel inversion, and the challenge it could pose to dominant ideology; consider verse 3 and chorus:

> Gently falls the night, dear mother,
> Gently slopes the battle plain,
> While I glide from sight, dear mother,
> Gently *sloping* home again.
> I care not for wars and quarrels,
> Or for laurels on my brow,
> I'd prefer to see the laurels,
> In your kitchen garden now.

(CHORUS)   Dearest mother, here the hissing
           Of the bullets is too plain,
           So I'll be numbered with the missing,
           But oh! never with the slain.

Compare this with the message of the original song, which is summed up in the first four lines of verse two:

        Oh, I long to see you, Mother;
        And the loving ones at home;
        But, I'll never leave our banner,
        Till in honor I can come.

Minstrel parodies had a double-edged appeal, which again relates to the cross-class nature of their audience: to some they would appear to deflate, to others they would seem to flatter (the parodies tended to be affectionate). Whichever was the response, the songs Hunter parodied must have been well known to his audience for the humour to work. Minstrel parody songs are a key to discovering to what extent familiarity with the drawing-room genre was spread among the working class. Moreover, they lend further emphasis to the speed with which minstrel shows associated themselves with bourgeois song, since even in the early 1850s there were parodies of Tom Moore ('The Young May Moon' became 'De Big White Moon') and Henry Russell ('A Life on the Ocean Wave' became 'A Life by de Galley Fire'). In their turn, minstrel songs might be parodied in the music-hall: for example, at the Oxford, W. Randal sang of a seaside holiday in Margate in 'On the Sands', a parody by J. Caulfield of 'Dixie's Land'. When minstrels were not actually performing there, minstrel songs also found their way into the music-hall in medley songs, such as Harry Clifton's 'Robinson Crusoe'.

While some minstrel songs parodied drawing-room ballads, with much of the humour resulting from the contrast of the polite musical style with the new text, other minstrel songs embraced the genteel idiom and squeezed the utmost sentiment out of it. Horace Norman, the lyric tenor of the Moore and Burgess Christy Minstrels, sang ballads like 'I'm Lonely Since My Mother Died' which made Cook and Russell's 'Old Arm Chair' seem positively restrained. The English Buckleys, who emigrated to America and formed one of the first minstrel troupes, also specialized in the polite style and returned to make a triumphant British tour. Apart from songs like J. R. Thomas's 'The Cottage by the Sea', which is a ballad of the Claribel type, they included burlesque opera in their programmes. Their wholesomeness is epitomized by the song which gave them their 'greatest hit', 'I'd Choose To Be a Daisy'. The Musical Bouquet, which concentrated on publications aimed at the drawing-room market, published all the Buckley Serenaders' songs. Hopwood & Crew, who had an extensive music-hall catalogue and therefore lacked the genteel status of the Musical Bouquet, were keen to point out that the Moore and Burgess Christy Minstrels' songs, too, were 'ever welcomed and highly appreciated in the drawing room'.[11]

One effect of the acceptability of minstrel songs in the drawing room was that it became fashionable to play the banjo. The Prince of Wales took banjo lessons from James Bohee (of the genuinely black Bohee Brothers), and middle-class males throughout the land were eagerly taking up the instrument. Walter Howard's *Banjo Tutor and Banjo Songs* catered for the demand for tuition; it was advertised without undue modesty as 'the best instruction book in the world, combined with an unequalled budget of popular songs & ballads'.[12] Walter Howard was a member of the Mohawk Minstrels, and his tutor was published by Francis Bros. & Day, London, who also published the *Mohawk Minstrels' Magazine* and *Mohawks' Annual*. Harry Hunter's Balfe parody, 'I Dreamt That I Dwelt on the Top of St Pauls', was sung by Walter Howard, and the sheet music was available in a version for voice and banjo (also published by Francis Bros. & Day). Another effect of the respectability of minstrelsy, and tied to the fashion for the banjo, was the emergence of 'plantation songs' targeted straight at the drawing room rather than being directed there via a minstrel show. Alfred Scott Gatty's *Plantation Songs*, which consist mainly of his own verse and music, show that the assimilation of Afro-American culture into English bourgeois culture has reached its final stage. He had four volumes published in the 1880s, the first three giving an option of piano or banjo accompaniment. The first song of volume 1, 'Click! Clack!', reasserts, in spite of recent history, the preferred view of the plantation as a lost Eden of uninhibited joy.

> De oberseer he turn him back,
> Click! clack! clatter go de clogs!
> De banjo out in half a crack,
> Click! clack! clatter go de clogs!
> Den Joe, he lead out lubly Nell
> Tho Jim swear Dinah am de belle,
> And off to de dance dey run pell mell,
> Click! clack! clatter go de clogs!

Celts

Before discussing the way in which Celts were subject to cultural assimilation, it must be pointed out that there was some fusion of Afro-American and Celtic culture in the nineteenth century, probably originally as a result of cultural interaction between black and white on the American Southern Frontier. The black dancer William Henry Lane, for example, combined African dance with the Irish jig to produce his acclaimed stage jig as 'Master Juba'. Since the minstrel show developed during the years when large numbers of Irish immigrants were arriving in America, Irish songs were found to be a popular part of the show, particularly new songs calling for the liberation of Ireland. The Irish side to minstrelsy was adopted by the British troupes, but with an emphasis on 'traditional' song: no. 14, vol. 5, of the *Mohawk Minstrels' Magazine* is actually labelled 'Special Irish Number', and includes seven Tom Moore ballads. Thus the ground was already laid for some of the remarkable Afro-American/Celtic fusions of the present century, such as the bluegrass style of Bill Monroe.

Celtic culture is not, of course, solely Irish but includes Scottish, Welsh, Manx,

Cornish, Breton, and Galician cultures. In this chapter, however, for reasons of space, the main concern is Scotland and, to a lesser extent, Ireland. Scotland is important because it occupied a special place in the fascination of the Victorian bourgeoisie with the Celt's culture and environment. The debt owed to Scotland by the Romantic movement has long been acknowledged: a frequently quoted musical example of this debt is Mendelssohn's overture *The Hebrides* (1830). Queen Victoria's first visit to Scotland was in 1842, and then, with the development of rail travel, so popular did it become among the middle class that, in 1866 alone, Thomas Cook catered for 40,000 tourists. It became an escapist world of romance to the industrial bourgeois; even if not all of them went as far as the mill-owning Bullough family from Lancashire, who bought the Isle of Rhum in 1888, built a castle there (paying the workmen an extra shilling a week to wear kilts!), and paid £2000 for an organ to be installed in it. Meanwhile, Highlanders were emigrating, some as a result of the blight which destroyed the potato crop in Sutherland in the 1840s (those who stayed were set to work building 'destitution roads'), and others driven out because they could not afford to remain once the leases on their tenancies expired and Lowland farmers competed for the land in order to place profitable Cheviot sheep there. The Highlands were in the hands of a few vast landowners, and what was not leased out to farmers was treated as a huge recreation park. Deer stalking was perhaps the favourite pastime among wealthy Highland landlords and their business friends, many of whom would have made their fortunes selling the new whisky, blended from Lowland grain (mostly unmalted) and Highland malt. This state of affairs did not continue for the whole century: the Highland Land League was formed in 1882, and by 1886 crofters had won security of tenure. However, even at the outbreak of World War I the land question and the problems of Highlanders had still not been resolved. Such, then, is the background against which the Victorian image of the romantic tartan-clad Highlander must be viewed; that image owed much to Scott's Waverley Novels and little to contemporary realities.

Either writing verse to Scottish airs contemporaneously with Burns, or following in his immediate footsteps, like Nairne, Hogg, and Scott, were dozens of others. Among the most prominent were Mrs Grant of Corran (1745–1814), Hector MacNeill (1746–1818), Susanna Blamire (1747–94), Mrs Grant of Laggan (1755–1838), Joanna Baillie (1764–1851), William Smyth (1766–1849), and Sir Alexander Boswell (1775–1822). Some, like the last three, were prepared to set verse to a variety of Celtic airs, Irish and Welsh as well as Scottish, while the market for them thrived. Furthermore, Joanna Baillie, although born in Scotland, spent most of her life in Hampstead (she did not even visit Scotland once in the last thirty years of her life), and William Smyth was a Liverpudlian who, from 1807 till his death, occupied the chair as Professor of Modern History at the University of Cambridge.

'Scotch songs' were great favourites in the early Victorian drawing room and were still very much 'the rage' in the 1850s, when singers like Mr Wilson and Mme Sainton-Dolby introduced them into their concerts. Just what made them so much admired may be gleaned from an article printed in *Eliza Cook's Journal* in 1852, which picks out characteristic features for approval: they are 'morally healthy' in advocating contentment with one's lot; they abound in pictures of domestic peace and comfort; and they show joy in the beauties of nature. Scottish songs are felt to be non-élitist:

> The writers of the words for the songs – the Scottish poets – have written them for the people – for the nation – for the many – not for the few.[13]

The music is thought to demonstrate honest heart-felt expression, but it has to be considered lacking in refinement:

> Scotch songs are not 'pretty'. Though they have been the rage in drawing-rooms, they are yet born of the people. They were not meant to be merely ornamental; they were the growth of simple taste, of true feeling, often of intense passion.[14]

The suggestion is that the Scottish people are a homogeneous mass, that their songs spring from the people and are for the people, hence they have a universal appeal. Indeed, the writer goes on to advise Tennyson to be less classical and strive for universality. The organic Scottish society was, of course, a myth, and Scottish song which was not actually bourgeois in origin still only reached the drawing room after bourgeois mediation. By 1852, not only were most of the texts of Scottish songs the product of the Lowland middle class, or members of the old Scottish aristocracy with a sentimental attachment to Jacobitism, but many tunes had been freshly composed or modernized. The extent of this rewriting may not have been obvious to the writer quoted above, because in the first half of the nineteenth century any song text which was written by a woman would be published without attribution. Therefore, anyone keen to be reassured of the naturalness of bourgeois values might be ready to believe that these anonymous songs had sprung from untutored Scottish peasants. There was a ladies' musical society in Edinburgh which encouraged anonymous songwriting (Lady Nairne was a leading member).

It was mentioned in the previous chapter that Felicia Hemans played a key role in the emergence of women songwriters into the drawing-room ballad market; two features of her work should be stressed, since they mark her out from the Edinburgh ladies: she did not write in dialect and she did not publish anonymously. Anonymity was respectable (because modest) but worked against the economic interest of women. Lady John Scott, née Alicia Spottiswoode (1810–1900) was composer and author of several successful ballads, but because she remained anonymous until the mid-1850s her influence on other women was slight compared with that of Caroline Norton and Maria Lindsay. Also it meant that, because she had no personal reputation, anything she did outside the realm of 'Scotch song' was liable to be overlooked. One of her most well-known songs today, 'Think on Me', a straightforward Bayly-style drawing-room ballad, was first published ten years after her death.

Before turning to Alicia Scott's output, there is an intermediate stage in the assimilation of Scottish song into English bourgeois culture which needs to be considered. Stage one was the writing of new or improved verses to old airs; but many were of the opinion that these airs were not 'pretty' long before the writer in *Eliza Cook's Journal* and regarded this as a fault. Major keys were the norm for genteel music, yet Scottish tunes might be modal (Skirven's 'Johnnie Cope' and Burns' 'Highland Mary'), or have a pentatonic shape which shifted ambiguously between major and relative minor (Blamire's 'What Ails This Heart o' Mine' and MacNeill's 'Come Under My Plaidie'), or the melody might pivot more strongly around the dominant than the tonic (Nairne's 'The Land o' the Leal' and Glen's 'Wae's Me for Prince Charlie'). It is, of course, unhistorical to talk of keys when discussing the older Scottish tunes; nevertheless, in the drawing room those tunes would have been perceived against a background of music with which the Victorian middle class was familiar. Hence, rather than accept them on their own terms, there was a tendency to see the tunes as crudely groping after the refinement of the classical key system. The first thing that could be done to 'improve' matters would be to provide classical harmonies and decorate the melody with classical ornamentation. Here is a mid-century version of the opening of a pentatonic Gaelic air, 'Crodh Chailein' it is from Mrs Grant of Laggan's song 'Flora to Colin', a translation of the Gaelic original (Burns reused this tune for 'My Heart's in the Highlands').

It will be seen that the melodic decoration (∗) is designed around the concept of underlying harmonies, except for the trill in the penultimate bar, and that calls for classical vocal technique. Compare this version of the tune with the way it might be tackled by someone playing an instrument with a drone accompaniment. Here are the first four bars with some typical Highland bagpipe ornaments.

Now, in complete contrast, it would be difficult to find harmonies to suit the grace notes.

Sometimes the whole tune was modernized, as was 'The Flowers of the Forest' by Mrs Cockburn (see Chapter 1). Very soon there was an urge to compose fresh tunes to those songs which presently consisted of old tune and fresh words. An early example of this is the Rev. William Leeves' setting of 'Auld Robin Gray', published in 1812. The words were by Lady Anne Barnard, née Lindsay

(1750–1825), the eldest daughter of the fifth Earl of Balcarras. Living in Fifeshire, but spending winters in town, as was customary among the aristocracy, she was probably encouraged to try her hand at a 'Scotch song' as a result of mingling in Edinburgh society. However, like all lady songwriters, she kept her authorship a secret. She finally confessed to writing it in a letter sent to Walter Scott two years before her death. A Captain Hall relates that Scott told guests at his home in 1825 that, when Anne Lindsay first heard the tune, it was accompanied by 'words of no great delicacy, whatever their antiquity might be'.[15] Her letter to Scott, dated 8 July 1823, declares that she longed to sing the tune to different words, 'and give its plaintive tones some little history of virtuous distress in humble life, such as might suit it'.[16] Written in 1771, 'Auld Robin Gray' became such a favourite that in 1780 it formed the basis of an entire ballad opera, *William and Lucy*, complete with new happy ending. However suited Anne Lindsay's words were meant to be to the 'plaintive tones' of the tune, the old modal melody was immediately banished from the drawing room when Leeves' version became available. Today, the song invariably begins at the second stanza ('Young Jamie lo'ed me weel'), since Leeves began his setting with a recitative. He relies on classical procedures for expressive effect, such as the contrast of major and minor key, and the use of chromaticism; his Scottish flavouring is limited to one or two snap rhythms. Mrs Gibson of Edinburgh (1786–1838) must have experienced similar feelings to Leeves when she contemplated the gloomy minor melody which accompanied Byron's poem 'Lochnagar' (from *Hours of Idleness*, 1807).[17] Her bright and mellifluous alternative soon became a favourite tenor song. Although a dubious tribute to 'dark Lochnagar', it creates a Scottish atmosphere by plentiful use of pentatonic shapes.

Thus, the foundation was laid for Alicia Scott to both write and compose original Scottish songs. Her best-known song is 'Annie Laurie', which consists of two stanzas rewritten from an earlier song and a third stanza of her own, all set to her own music. She found the words in *Songs of Scotland* (1825), edited by Allan Cunningham, but felt they were in need of 'improvement'. A comparison of the original second stanza with her version gives an insight into drawing-room propriety.[18]

She's backit like a peacock,	Her brow is like the snaw-drift,
She's breastit like a swan,	Her throat is like the swan,
She's jimp about the middle	Her face it is the fairest
Her waist ye well may span;	That e'er the sun shone on;
Her waist ye well may span,	That e'er the sun shone on,
And she has a rolling eye,	And dark blue is her e'e;
And for bonnie Annie Laurie	And for bonnie Annie Laurie
I'd lay down my head and die.	I'd lay me doune and dee.

It is noteworthy that Lady Scott's version sounds a great deal more Scottish than the original; but her attachment to the Lallans dialect derives from her sentimental Jacobitism rather than an interest in ordinary Scottish people, so expressions which seem to her vulgar, like 'backit', 'breastit', and 'jimp about the middle' are dropped. For the latter she substitutes 'Her face it is the fairest', but in the 1854 version she forgoes her alliteration in order to translate the English 'fairest' as the Scottish 'bonniest'. It is a telling change; indeed, throughout the Scottish songs for which she provided texts, Lallans is treated merely as a vocabulary of romantic words, rather than a dialect with its own syntax. Musically 'Annie Laurie' is typical of her style: it is a simple strophic song which sets the words syllabically to a sixteen-bar diatonic melody decorated with an occasional 'Scotch snap'. The word 'pretty' would not be inappropriate as a description of its elegantly crafted tune. Its tonality is unambiguously major, and its musical tensions rely on changes of harmony: for example, the tension on the word 'bonnie' in the first line, 'Maxwelton braes are bonnie'. Lady Scott used to sing her songs to a harp accompaniment, though she seldom wrote down anything but the melody.

Her songs were published anonymously in arrangements by others: 'Annie Laurie' first appeared with an accompaniment by Finlay Dun in *The Vocal Melodies of Scotland*, volume 3, 1838, published by Paterson and Roy, Edinburgh. It has been noted that it was customary for women songwriters to remain anonymous at this time, whether they had written words, music, or both. As the ballad market began to open up for women in the mid-century (see Chapter 3), attribution was no longer thought immodest. When Lady Nairne died in 1845, and her authorship of songs was acknowledged, the situation must have eased a little. Lady Scott was first given credit as a songwriter when she published six songs in 1854 for the benefit of the wives and families of soldiers who had been sent to Crimea (the songs included 'Annie Laurie' and 'Katherine Logie'). A song often attributed to her is 'Loch Lomond'; however, its earliest known appearance is in W. Christie's *Traditional Ballad Airs*, volume 1, 1876. Its largely pentatonic character seems stylistically unlike Scott, and lends credibility to the argument that it is a modern version of 'Robin Cushie', first printed in McGibbon's *Scots Tunes Book* of 1742. The words are another possibility, since they are very much in her English-with-a-Scottish-accent style. This might also serve as an appropriate description of her music. She embraces the major key world of the drawing room, avoiding 'antiquated' modality (the musically unpalatable equivalent of words like 'breastit'?), and applying dabs of regional colour with the odd pentatonic turn of phrase and snap rhythm.

It may have been noticed that, with the exception of 'Crodh Chailein' ('Colin's Cattle'), all the Scottish songs discussed so far have been Lowland songs. Some Gaelic songs were published in the early nineteenth century: 'Crodh Chailein' appeared in Fraser's *Airs Peculiar to the Scottish Highlands* (1816), and another all-Gaelic collection was Alex Campbell's *Albyn's Anthology*, which came out in two volumes (1816–18). Gaelic songwriters, a large proportion of whom, incidentally, were women, continued to produce new songs throughout the century. Some even wrote new words to old tunes, as had happened with Lowland songs; 'An-t-Eilean Muileach' ('The Isle of Mull'), penned by a homesick Dugald MacPhail in Newcastle, is an example. Gaelic music divides not into 'serious' and 'popular' but into big (*ceol mor*) and small (*ceol beag*). The absence of 'high' and 'low' categories reflects the socio-economic basis of Gaelic society, which was comprised of clan communities led by chiefs, and kept in existence by subsistence agriculture (based on cattle) and, in the case of some clans, fishing. There were inequalities of wealth and status within the clan, but it saw itself as a cohesive whole. Little Gaelic song entered the drawing room because in a capitalist society art is part of leisure, but to the Highlanders art was a part of work as well, and their types of song reflect this – waulking songs (three speeds, depending on the weight of the cloth), nurses' songs, milking songs, rowing songs, etc. Even where a Gaelic song might be thought to have a universal appeal – laments for lost loved ones, such as Christina Fergusson's lament for William Chisholm, or songs of emigration, such as 'Gur Moch Rinn Mi Dusgadh' ('Early Did I Awaken') – the authentic voice of the Gael was rejected in favour of an invented voice (for example, C. Mackay's 'The Highland Emigrant' of 1861). Eventually Gaelic song was to find a form suitable for drawing-room consumption this century, mainly owing to the mediations of Marjorie Kennedy-Fraser and the interest among the English middle class in 'Celtic Twilight' romanticism.

The general opinion in the mid-nineteenth century was that Gaelic culture was crude and unimportant: 'The Highlanders, who inhabit the mountainous and picturesque part of Scotland, have added very little to its stores of national music, except a few wild pibrochs, befitting the uncouth instrument on which they are usually played – the Highland bagpipe.[19] An invented culture filled the gap created by ignorance of the Highlander's culture. Highland dress, for instance, was no longer regarded as subversive; but, in order that it might fit in with the construction of a romantic Highland mythology, dozens of colourful fraud tartans were produced. Queen Victoria's desire for a personal piper owed more to Highland romance than to an interest in *piobaireachd*. The changes in pipe music illustrate how Gaelic culture was part marginalized and part assimilated in the nineteenth century. Angus Mackay, Queen Victoria's first piper, was an authority on the great music (*ceol mor*) of the Highland bagpipe, but by the 1880s the craze for the 'competition march' had marginalized this music. The official recognition given to pipers by the War Office in 1854 acted as a stimulus to the formation of pipe bands, and they, in turn, developed a repertoire distinct from that of the solo Highland piper (who originally played only *piobaireachd* or jigs).

Only when the socio-economic foundation of Gaelic communities was being almost everywhere undermined (even Lewis found itself host to British Aluminium in 1896) was there a rush to document and preserve their disappearing culture. According to John Blackie, who initiated the Gaelic *mod*, there is evidence in 1885 of 'enlarged public sympathy' in welcoming Gaelic song, although a 'great army of tourists and travellers' still comes to Scotland and thinks no more of inquiring into the social conditions of Highlanders 'than they would into the economy of a few sparrows on the roadside'.[20] Part of the interest in Gaelic culture was motivated by an interest inherited from German theorists of *Volkslied*; this is shown by the use of terms like 'folk's song' and 'popular song' (the later term 'folk-song' is not identical to *Volkslied*, since the latter did not necessarily imply anonymity).[21]

While Gaelic culture in the Highlands and Islands of Scotland managed to survive the nineteenth century in an attenuated form, the Gaelic culture of Ireland was all but wiped out. This was a result of the changes in social relations which followed on the heels of the political defeats of the late eighteenth century.

Bunting had collected the music of an almost defunct bardic tradition, which he published in three collections in 1796, 1809, and 1840. The other major nineteenth-century collection was that published by Petrie in 1855, initiated at the request of the Society for the Preservation of Irish Music. While collecting, Petrie discovered that the art of harp playing had died out: 'The Irish harp cannot be brought back to life; it is dead forever.'[22] In Ireland the harpist was the musician who held the highest social rank. Pipers were of much lower status, but their instrument, too, was found to be 'rapidly disappearing in favour of the flute and violin'[23] in 1890. The method of tuning the Irish harp favoured the pentatonic scale, while allowing the possible use of other notes. This state of affairs finds an echo in the scale of the Highland bagpipe (a scale ideally suited to three varieties of pentatonic tune) and thus may account for some of the similarities between Irish and Scottish music.

The Irish music which found its way into the drawing room followed, more or less, the same stages as Scottish music. There were one or two differences: for example, in the second half of the eighteenth century the Irish comic song had become established. As usual, Dibdin was to the fore, with songs like 'Paddy O'Blarney'; indeed, it is unlikely that most Irish comic songs were anything but English in origin, but the nineteenth century inherited the tradition. Another difference was that Moore showed greater concern for the suitability of his songs to the drawing room than did his Scottish counterpart, Burns. An example which demonstrates his sure understanding of that taste is his song 'The Meeting of the Waters', which uses the tune 'The Old Head of Denis' but converted from the old Aeolian mode into a modern major key.

Moore had disciples waiting to assume his mantle in the same way as Burns had his followers. Moore's most important successor was Samuel Lover (1797–1868), the son of a Dublin stockbroker. Lover at first took up his father's profession, but finding it was not congenial decided to become a portrait painter. In addition to painting, he proved to be a man of many skills: for example, he turned his successful ballad 'Rory O'More' (1826) into an equally successful novel (1836) and then into a play (1837). His reputation for miniature portraits encouraged him to move to London in 1835, where *Songs and Ballads* was published in 1839. Then, in 1844, his eyesight failing and threatening his income as a painter, he devised a one-man show called *Irish Evenings*, consisting of his own poems, songs, and stories. After returning from a lengthy tour of Canada and America, 1846 – 8, he gave a new entertainment entitled *Paddy's Portfolio*. Lover's songs reveal a similar stage of fusion between drawing-room idiom and Celtic music as that attained by the songs of Alicia Scott. In 'Rory O'More',[24] for example, he writes a jig incorporating the typical repeated tonics which originally served the function of emphasizing the pitch of the drone; at the same time, his melody shows little pentatonic influence or any disposition to avoid or flatten the seventh. Another song of his, 'Molly Bawn', from his burlesque operetta *Il Paddy Whack in Italia* (1841), mixes pentatonic writing with occasional chromaticism and passing modulation. As far as subject matter is concerned, Lover shows an interest in romance, character, and a desire to perpetuate the myth of the comic Irishman.

An 'Irish song' from the late 1830s, 'Kathleen Mavourneen', was an enormous success: D'Almaine & Co. issued the twentieth edition in 1850, and the song remained a favourite in the drawing room for the entire century. The words are commonly attributed to Mrs Crawford, although not without some misgiving,[25] and the music was composed by Frederick Crouch (1808–96). Its contrast of major and minor tonality is very much in the European classical mould, and its suggestion of an Irish quality is only evident from two or three pentatonic turns of phrase, an occasional drone bass, and the typically Irish use of triple time for a love song (the most famous example being 'Eileen Aroon', attributed to the sixteenth-century bard Gerald O'Daly). Apart from this, the modulations, chromaticism, and sobbing dissonances (implying the need for classical harmony) mark it down as a sentimental ballad for the middle-class home. Ironically, as a song of leave-taking, it adumbrates the mass exodus from Ireland a few years after it was written.

Ireland did not figure so prominently in the Romantic movement as Scotland, though the novels of Maria Edgeworth (1767–1849) may be seen as in some ways an Irish equivalent to Walter Scott's Waverley Novels. Moore's *Irish Melodies* were perhaps the most influential contemporary literature to come out of Ireland: Berlioz composed nine fresh settings of Moore's verse in 1830, and Mendelssohn based his *Phantasie über ein Irländisches Lied* of the next year on 'The Last Rose of Summer'. However, the extent of poverty in Ireland, the constant agitation for land reform and for repeal of the Union did not encourage tourism. Finally, the Great Starvation 1845–51 made it impossible to see the beauties of the country without witnessing the barbarous treatment of its people by those who owned the land. During these years a million died and a million emigrated (followed by another million in the 1850s). The famine was partly the result of a potato blight, but more importantly the result of having to sell off other crops to pay rent to landlords. Songs of farewell were numerous, not written by starving Irish emigrants, but by bourgeois songwriters and, in the case of Lady Dufferin, the Anglo-Irish aristocracy.

Lady Dufferin, née Helen Sheridan (1807–67) was the elder sister of Caroline Norton and moved to Ireland when her husband succeeded his father as Baron Dufferin in 1839. Her song 'The Irish Emigrant' views the desperate situation in Ireland from the perspective of the Anglo-Irish peerage.[26] The sufferings of the poor are only hinted at ('I'm very lonely now Mary, for the poor make no new friends') and so too is the lack of food and employment (in the land the emigrant is going to 'They say there's bread and work for all'). The impression given by the song is that the man is leaving Ireland not for his own survival, but to make a fresh start after the death of his wife: he goes because 'There's nothing left to care for now.' There is no suggestion, either, that his wife has died as a result of the famine. Yet Lady Dufferin was not ignorant of, nor unsympathetic to, the problems facing her Irish tenants; the land question long occupied her husband, and in the year of her death he published a book entitled *Irish Emigration and the Tenure of Land in Ireland*. George Barker, who provided the music to 'The Irish Emigrant', had acquired celebrity as a drawing-room composer with 'The White Squall' (*c.* 1835), and, as may be guessed, the song is not remotely Irish in character. The musical setting merely serves to emphasize that this is a ballad for the English middle class; it was, in fact, published in London by Chappell in 1846 and made available with either piano or guitar accompaniment to suit home music-making. In 'Terence's Farewell to Kathleen' (1848), Lady Dufferin chooses to fit her words to a traditional air, and also attempts an Irish dialect; the result is a cross between a serious farewell (the girl is leaving to find work in England) and a comic song like 'Katey's Letter' which she also wrote in dialect. The emphasis falls not on the departure but on the attention Terence's sweetheart will have from 'iligant boys' in England, and how she will come back 'spakin' sich beautiful English'. Lady Dufferin decided, like her Scottish female counterparts and not like her sister, that she would publish anonymously, although her identity as a songwriter began to be known in the 1850s and attributions given to her.

It was during the process of cultural assimilation described in the previous pages that Celtic song evolved into just one more species of the genus of the drawing-room ballad. The English composer and publisher Sydney Nelson (1800–62) may be used to illustrate the point: he had only four lasting ballad successes, two Scottish ('Mary of Argyle' and 'The Rose of Allandale'), one Irish ('Oh! Steer My Bark to Erin's Isle'), and one English ('The Pilot'). It was not just that Celtic features were incorporated into imitation 'Scotch' and Irish songs for the drawing room, sometimes a supposedly Celtic musical feature could be invented in the same way as a new tartan: for example, the change from major key to relative minor for a middle section, as in 'Rory O'More', 'Kathleen Mavourneen', 'The Irish Emigrant', 'The Rose of Tralee' (words by E. Mordaunt Spencer, music by Charles Glover), and 'Come Back to Erin'. Here the drawing-room Irish ballad has established its own tradition.

While enthusiasm for Scottish song began to wane in the 1860s, interest in Irish song was sustained by the popularity of the minstrel shows and a craze for Irish melodrama. Balfe's 'Killarney' comes from *Peep o' Day* (1861), one of Edmund Falconer's several Irish melodramas. Falconer had acquired an appetite for this theatrical genre after acting in Boucicault's *The Colleen Bawn*. The latter was set in Killarney, and the most famous music it inspired was Benedict's opera *The Lily of Killarney* (1862).

As mentioned earlier, there is no room to deal with other Celtic cultures in any detail in this chapter, but a few words may be said here. Some well-known Welsh airs, like 'Ar Hyd y Nos' ('All Through the Night') and 'Gorhoffedd Gwyr Harlech' ('March of the Men of Harlech'), were first published in Edward Jones's *Relicks* in the late eighteenth century. 'The March of the Men of Harlech', incidentally, was a favourite harp or piano piece which only had words put to it in the 1860s.[27] Dibdin, predictably, seems to have been the first Englishman to write 'Welsh' songs, for example, 'Taffy and the Birds'. Many other familiar names also appear in connection with Welsh songs (Joanna Baillie, Felicia Hemans, William Smyth, Mrs Grant), some of them involved in 'improving' enterprises such as the Beethoven *26 Welsh Songs*. Welsh music remained popular in the drawing room as long as the harp was in favour. John Parry of Denbigh (1776–1851) was a highly regarded figure; he published a collection of Welsh melodies entitled *The Welsh Harper* (volume 1, 1839; volume 2, 1848) and also adapted Welsh airs to English words.

Manx music was virtually ignored until the 1890s,[28] although a collection of inaccurately notated Manx tunes, *Mona Melodies*, had been published in London in 1820. The research into Manx music, Gaelic music, and even Indian music, which began in the 1890s, was a response to the growing interest in the field-collecting of 'folk-song'.[29] From now on there was a change of direction in cultural appropriation: less and less were people to see their musical culture absorbed into the bourgeois form of the drawing-room ballad; instead, their music would be variously selected and mediated according to bourgeois values, then accepted in the drawing room as 'folk-song'.

5   *Sacred Songs*

A branch of the drawing-room repertoire which grew in importance throughout the nineteenth century was the sacred song. The term 'sacred song' could be used to denote anything from a simple hymn to a complex ballad of the Russell *gran scena* variety based on a religious theme. In the last quarter of the century, some ballads cannot be readily separated into straightforward sacred or secular categories: it is debatable, for instance, which of these labels would best describe 'The Lost Chord', 'The Better Land', or 'The Holy City' (three ballads discussed in detail in Chapter 7). Part of the problem is that the entertainment of the drawing room came to uphold 'the ideal of the week of seven Sabbaths'.[1]

At first, sacred songs were thought of as part of Sunday evening's entertainment in the home. An early publication aimed at this market is James Hook's *Sunday Evening's Recreation* (1806), a collection of hymns, solos, and duets with piano arrangements; it sold well enough to be reissued two years later. More activity is discernable in the 1830s, with music being produced for Sunday Schools, and further voice and piano arrangements of hymns being provided for home use (for example, *Family Hymns*, published by Chappell in 1837). The market for hymns at this time was located among the Dissenting middle class; in the Anglican church, music had become a wayward affair, and in some parishes non-existent. Greater interest in Anglican church music was shown in the 1840s, when societies were formed to promote church music, recruit choirs, and throw out the village band (or at least insist that they play only sacred music).[2] Much of the impetus came from Tractarians, who emerged as a potent force in what was called the Oxford Movement (since it was in Oxford that Keble delivered his influential sermon on 'The National Apostasy' in 1833). A debate over the nature of religious authority split the Anglican church between Evangelicals and Tractarians, the latter moving ever closer to Rome (and, in the case of Newman, all the way). The 'high church' Tractarians stressed the importance of Communion as the Christ-given service of the church and placed great weight upon the choir and music during services. The 'low church' Evangelicals, whose leading spokesman was Charles Simeon, had been concerned to contain religious fervour within the Anglican church rather than move to Dissent. The original spur to the Evangelical movement had perhaps been the perceived threat of French Republican atheism and Jacobinism; this certainly accounted for the involvement of influential laymen like Wilberforce. The feudal character of the

Established Church, seen in the yawning gap between wealthy bishops and poor curates, was in urgent need of reform.

The majority of the middle class, for historical reasons, were nonconformists. The unwillingness of early Dissenters, such as Quakers, to take loyalty oaths had restricted the career opportunities available to them. Quakers Lloyd, then Barclay, took banking to the provinces; other Dissenters formed companies to pay 'navigators' (gangs of workers who, in the 1830s, came to be known as 'navvies') to build canals and, later, railways. Industry was a career for which pupils at Dissenting schools were well fitted: these schools had the advantage of up-to-date equipment. Dissenters held most of the mining concessions in the country, something which proved immensely valuable with the development of coke-fired furnaces. The religious character of industrial capitalism was, therefore, Dissenting; furthermore, 'Nonconformist strength went on increasing, as the middle and working classes of the new industrial order continued to grow in numbers, wealth, political power and social esteem.'[3] In industrial districts there were often either Dissenting churches or none at all. The relationship of the class division between aristocracy and bourgeoisie to the religious division between church and chapel was made transparently clear when the bishops tried to stop the Reform Bill in 1831. Once that Bill was passed, the Dissenters, in their turn, fully expected the disestablishment of the Anglican church to follow; instead, various Parliamentary reforms took place.

Hymns and sacred solos

Nonconformist hymns were a transforming influence on church congregational music: the hymns of Isaac Watts (1674–1748) and Charles Wesley (1707–88) challenged, then superseded the metrical psalms previously sung in church. Watts worked in the Calvinist tradition of close adherence to the Biblical text but differed in allowing personal reflection, as in 'When I Survey the Wondrous Cross'. Watts was an Independent, and his hymns became popular with Baptists and Presbyterians. Charles Wesley, the brother of John Wesley, was actually the one who founded the 'Holy' Club, the original Methodists. Strong emphasis on the personal was a constant feature of his hymns, and it accorded well with a burgeoning middle-class individualist ideology. The idea of God's caring love for the individual was also a comfort to the poor. 'Jesu, Lover of My Soul' was a favourite; this hymn also shows that Wesley's novelty lay not only in his content, but also in his experiments in metre and verse structure. The unusual trochaic metre for 'Jesu, Lover of My Soul' set a precedent for Toplady's equally personal 'Rock of Ages'. Melodically he made a conscious gesture in the direction of the middle class by employing tunes which resembled the musical style of contemporary theatre, in particular that of oratorio (the tunes to Methodist hymns became broader in popular appeal as time went on). The English oratorio, as established by Handel, was written in a style associated with secular musical practice and performed in the theatre, a fact which had brought Handel into early confrontation with the Bishop of London.[4] Recognition of the crucial importance of Handel to the development of English sacred music is given in a large Edwardian song collection:

> Since the time of *The Messiah* [*sic*], sacred music in England has been utterly unlike what it was before. We had nothing remotely comparable, in melodic character, to such airs as, 'He shall feed His Flock', 'I know that my Redeemer liveth', and other airs which have long been installed as first favourites of English speaking nations throughout the world.[5]

Handel made much use of the Italian operatic style in his oratorios, but the influence of Purcell is not negligible. Charles Wesley also shows his familiarity with Purcell by parodying the air 'Fairest Isle' (words by Dryden, from the 'semi-opera' *King Arthur*) in his hymn 'Love Divine All Loves Excelling'. Compare the first stanzas of each:

> Fairest Isle, all isles excelling,
> Seat of pleasures and of loves;
> Venus here will choose her dwelling,
> And forsake her Cyprian groves.

> Love Divine, all loves excelling,
> Joy of heaven, to earth come down,
> Fix in us thy humble dwelling,
> All thy faithful mercies crown.

Wesley thus sets a precedent for 'divine parodies' of music from the stage, a practice usually associated with the Salvation Army.

In the 1840s the hymns sung by families on Sunday evenings began to be supplemented by more and more of the solo songs coming on to the market. At mid-century, these newcomers fell into three recognizable types: the short strophic song resembling the hymn, the song modelled on the solo found in oratorio, and the genteel style of ballad already familiar in the drawing room. Caroline Norton's 'No More Sea' (1853), No. 2 of her *Sabbath Lays*, shows where the hymn stops and the drawing-room ballad begins. Structurally, it is not unlike a hymn, being a sixteen-bar melody in regular phrases. However, it differs in a crucial respect: it is composed for a solo voice. The hymn's function as a vehicle for collective expression holds consequences for its musical form:

> The hymn tune is even more shackled in regard to verbal expression than its secular counterpart, the ballad. A ballad singer can vary the length of notes from verse to verse, so as to improve the elocutional force of the words. Metrical irregularities can be accommodated. But in the case of the hymn tune this is not possible. The hymn tune is for the congregation, a vast unyielding mass . . .[6]

The tune of 'No More Sea' does, indeed, contain adjustments to suit the slight differences between various stanzas, either in numbers of syllables or change of accent. The words themselves reflect upon a Biblical text (Revelation 21: 1 and 4) in a manner common to hymns. The melody is described as an 'Arab air', introducing an exotic element which would have held connotations both sacred and secular. On the one hand there would have been a suggestion of Palestine and things holy, and on the other an association with exotic theatre sets (Weber, for example, had included an 'Arab melody' in the Finale of Act I of *Oberon*). Norton's tune turns out to be a precursor of that familiar today as the 'Hootchy Kootchy Dance', supposedly composed by New York Congressman Sol Bloom for an Egyptian dance at the Chicago World's Columbian Exposition in 1893.

Like the wild   cease-less   mo-tion, Of the   deep   heav-ing   waves,   Is   the heart's   rest-less

beat-ing From our birth,   to   our   graves,   Toss'd by strong   stor - my   pas - sion,   In   the (*etc.*)

Although this tune can be found circulating in the 1890s in profane form, as a *danse du ventre* (belly dance), the reverse also happened, and sacred versions supplanted secular ones, as when Mendelssohn's 'Gutenberg der Grosse Mann' became 'Hark! The Herald Angels Sing'. In the nineteenth century it was generally acknowledged that music 'in itself is neither secular nor sacred, and each piece must be judged upon its merits';[7] but dispute about those merits might focus on the extent to which a tune's secular associations create distractions to worship. The piano accompaniment was very much an integral part of Norton's *Sabbath Lays*, highlighting their character as Sunday drawing-room ballads. Their appeal to the home-music market was further enhanced by their being published by Chappell separately with colour lithographs on their front covers.

A colourful and richly decorative cover also adorns Maria Lindsay's 'Resignation', published by Robert Cocks & Co. in 1856. Cocks divided up his publication list of Lindsay's songs into sacred and secular categories and gave many of the former 'elegantly illuminated titles', which lent a gothic splendour to her work. Musically, 'Resignation' is indebted to the English oratorio as established by Handel and given fresh impetus in the 1840s by Mendelssohn. The latter's *Elijah* had been received with enormous acclaim at the Birmingham Triennial Festival in 1846. One air from the work, 'O Rest in the Lord', became a particular favourite in the drawing room; its narrow compass and uncomplicated technical demands were admirably suited to the amateur performer. A combination of simplicity and musical subtlety was what was so highly esteemed in Handel; a critic notes with regard to 'He Shall Feed His Flock' (from *Messiah*): 'A boy of ten may sing this air with effectiveness, while the greatest artist may find in it scope for the highest intelligence of expression.[8] Its ease of execution for the performer is not a universal feature of Handel's music, but where it existed it found a ready market: for example, between 1815 and 1905 a new edition of the air 'Angels Ever Bright and Fair' (from Theodora) was issued, on average, every five years. Lindsay's 'Resignation' has exactly the same compass (ten notes) as 'Angels Ever Bright and Fair' but does not possess the fluidity of musical phrasing found in this and other music by Handel. Some flexibility is, however, necessary to meet the demands of Biblical prose, which does not offer the regular patterns of metrical verse. Lindsay employs repetition of words as well as the declamatory device of recitative, a traditional means of accommodating the difficulty presented by a prose text; yet the end result of these compositional techniques is often nothing more than a constant succession of two-bar phrases.

him ____   I __ shall go __ to him   to   him   but

con espress.

he __ shall not re __ turn   to   me   I   shall go   to

The text is taken from II Samuel 12: 22–23 and concerns the need for resignation following the death of a beloved child. Sacred songs for the home dealing with the deaths of children are not uncommon; their quantity is probably related to the high infant and child mortality rate (from which the middle class were not immune)[9] and the family's need to come to terms with their bereavement, or that of their close relatives. There would have been few without the experience of attending a burial service for a young child. A favourite text, suggesting, perhaps, an added importance attached to the male child, was David's lament for Absalom; a setting made by Lindsay of these words in 1868 (again, in oratorio manner) was particularly highly regarded. It is difficult, now, to perceive the 'originality, sweetness, and extreme pathos'[10] which her sacred songs were thought to possess, since her melodic lines seem so plain and predictable. Yet perhaps her achievement in adapting the refined and professional medium of the oratorio to the capabilities of the home circle was felt to offer new dignity to Sunday-evening music-making.

The third variety of sacred song at mid-century has its roots in the 'improving' ballad of the Henry Russell type. There is no difference in style between Joseph Knight's genteel settings of Bayly's verse and his setting of Emma Willard's 'Rocked in the Cradle of the Deep', published in London in 1846.[11] The same slow rate of change of harmonies, sentimental chromatic inflexions to the melody, and gentle pace are present. If there was some doubt as to whether or not 'Rocked in the Cradle of the Deep' was a sacred song, since it resembled neither a hymn nor an air from an oratorio, it is strange that no such doubts applied to Stephen Glover's duet 'What Are the Wild Waves Saying?', published by R. Cocks & Co. in 1849.[12] It may be that Glover's success with his *Songs from the Holy Scriptures* of the preceding year inclined people to think automatically in terms of the sacred category, even though there is no more of Holy Writ in this duet than in 'Rocked in the Cradle of the Deep'; it is, in fact, based on a scene from Charles Dickens's

Dombey and Son. A sick Paul Dombey demands of his sister Florence, 'I want to know what it says – the sea – what is it that it keeps on saying?' Dickens fails to give a precise enough answer in his novel, but this defect is remedied by J. E. Carpenter who wrote the words to the duet. He has Paul and Florence proclaiming together ecstatically,

> The voice of the great Creator
> Dwells in that mighty tone!

Again, a slow harmonic rhythm (generally one or two chords per bar), a sentimental sprinkling of chromatic notes in the tune, and a modest tempo reveal its ancestry in the polite style of the drawing room. A kinship with Russell's ballad style is especially noticeable in the accompaniment, which is in places identical to the pattern used in 'Woodman, Spare That Tree!'

In the 1860s hymns began to be marketed in a more decisive manner: some publications targeted the church or Sunday School, and others the home. In 1861 Novello published *Hymns Ancient and Modern*, a collection inspired by the Tractarians, but in the variety of its contents displaying a desire to attract the custom of churches generally. It was so successful in this aim that by 1895 around 75 per cent of English churches had adopted it, and a remarkable 60 million copies had been sold by 1912.[13] In contrast, Chappell clearly intended their *100 Sacred Songs* of 1861 to find a market in the home, since they were available in arrangements for clarinet, cornet, concertina, flute, sax-horn, or violin. New hymns for the church which proved popular were packaged for the home in small collections, or even as single sheet-music items. The setting of F. Lyte's 'Abide with Me' by William Monk (editor of *Hymns Ancient and Modern*) circulated in an arrangement by A. F. Mullen in *A Collection of Popular Sacred Melodies* in 1863; four years later it was issued as a separate sacred song (also arranged by Mullen) and as a duet. The Victorian hymn had a broad appeal which set it apart from earlier church music; the difference can be readily perceived by trying to imagine a Sternhold and Hopkins metrical psalm being sung at a Wembley Cup Final as an alternative to 'Abide with Me'. Another difference can be found by comparing 'Eternal Father, Strong to Save' with 'The Old Hundredth' ('All People That on Earth Do Dwell'); the former achieves its emotional impact through a modern use of expressive chromaticism (for example, at the words 'O hear us when we cry to Thee'), while the latter's austere majesty comes from its strong, plain harmonic progressions.

Although interest in German sacred song had grown in the 1850s (benefiting, in addition to Mendelssohn, the lesser-known Franz Abt), the most successful solo sacred ballad of the 1860s was French in origin. Charles Gounod's *chant évangélique* 'Jésus de Nazareth' (words by A. Porte) had appeared in Paris in 1856 but was first published in London by Schott & Co. in 1862. It was printed with English words only (by H. F. Chorley), was entitled, more guardedly, 'Nazareth', and was available with an *ad libitum* harmonium part. Its popularity is indicated by the quantity of different arrangements which became available – piano transcriptions, a violin and piano duet, a version for piano and harmonium, and many others. 'Nazareth' contains features which differ from what was the norm in vocal music for the British drawing room and which indicate the song's foreign origin: it is written for bass voice and, because the accompaniment is designed to make the most of this, it is unsuitable for any other voice; moreover, the compass of the song and the technical difficulties for singer and accompanist make it awkward for amateurs. This is not to say that display pieces for a particular voice never found a footing in the drawing room (Shield's 'The Wolf' is an early example of a bass song which was well established there), but publishers favoured songs which could be sold to both male and female singers and, as a further boost to sales, be offered in at least two keys to cater for low and high voices. Schott & Co., of course, were not to be deterred by arguments on purely aesthetic grounds from offering 'Nazareth' for other voices; once they realized they had a runaway success, they offered it in five different keys. This was clearly an attempt to reap profit from the home market; the only orchestral concert versions available were both for low male voice. In retrospect, the success of 'Nazareth' can be attributed to its standing at the head of a line of 'big' sacred songs, which culminate in the ballads of Adams and Cowen and extend well into the Edwardian period. In some respects, 'Nazareth' is like a sacred counterpart to the famous tenor display piece 'Come into the Garden, Maud': they are both in rondo form, and both save their passionate climaxes till the end.

Virginia Gabriel's setting of Adelaide Procter's 'Cleansing Fires', published in London by Cramer & Co. around 1869, is a more typical sacred song of its time. Its musical style shows a homogeneity which cannot easily be broken down into any of the previously discussed categories which were prevalent at mid-century. Gabriel extracts the maximum drama from a strophic setting by giving a strongly contrasted musical treatment to the first and second half of each of Procter's stanzas. The first half of each stanza is set to an austere, mainly unison, minor melody; the second half moves to a bright tonic major with the melody soaring ever higher to emphasize Procter's optimism concerning the moral benefits which accrue from suffering. The stark unison treatment suggests an association with oratorio, for example, 'The People That Walked in Darkness', from *Messiah*; the throbbing triplets of the second half, on the other hand, are a familiar feature of drawing-room music. Because each stanza falls into two sections, the effect is of verse and refrain, but it is not without ambiguity. A glance at Procter's verse would suggest a refrain for the last two lines of each stanza where she repeats her rhymes and image of gold being tried by fire. Gabriel, however, moves to her major section two lines earlier, when the mood of each stanza turns to one of optimism; moreover, a refrain would normally begin with tonic harmony, but here she dovetails the first and second halves by prolonging an inconclusive dominant harmony from the former into the latter.

The sentiments of *Cleansing Fires* accord with a common Victorian preoccupation with trial and the winning of moral strength from having been tried. There is, in fact, nothing strongly religious about the song, which compares the casting of gold in a furnace with a heart's emerging cleansed from 'the furnace of living pain'. A middle-class audience for Procter's text is plainly assumed in verse 3, which begins:

> I shall know by the gleam and glitter
> Of the golden chain you wear,
> By your heart's calm strength in loving,
> Of the fire they have had to bear.

'Cleansing Fires' has drawn together various threads of sacred music-making in the home, but, importantly, the result is a song that need not be confined to Sunday evening.

Boosey & Co. woke up to the realization, in the 1870s, that this kind of sacred song could be marketed in the same fashion as the rest of their drawing-room ballads. In the previous decade they were unsure of the relationship of the sacred song to the other ballads they published. This may be gleaned from the fact that, although Claribel was their best-selling songwriter, her *Sacred Songs and Hymns* were published posthumously in about 1870. In 1875 Boosey's *Sacred Musical Cabinet* was begun (running to twenty-eight parts before its termination in 1885), and in the later 1870s they published *Sacred Songs, Ancient and Modern* (edited by J. Hiles). Other ballad publishers were also taking a keen interest in this field: Metzler published *Forty Sacred Songs* as the second of their *Popular Musical Library* (1873); Charles Sheard, who had taken over the *Musical Bouquet*, published *Sacred Songs* with accompaniments for piano or harmonium in 1874; and A. Hammond & Co., who had succeeded to Jullien's firm, published, as part of their 'Musical Presentation and Circulating Library', *Sabbath Strains* (a collection of solos and duets) and *Sunday at Home* (piano pieces).

Gospel song

The 1870s also saw an attempt to broaden the popular appeal of sacred song for ideological reasons; this tendency had its origins in the Sunday School movement and the spread of American religious revivalism, particularly the second wave of fundamentalism which came after the Civil War. Before the Civil War, American sacred songs divided into those sung at the 'fire and brimstone' camp meetings of the earlier fundamentalist revival, and those with 'chaste and popular tunes' for 'family and social worship', as the contents of Thomas Hastings' edition of *Sacred Songs* published by the American Tract Society in 1842 are described. There were, in addition, collections of songs being published for Sunday School use from the 1830s onward which proved influential. The need for simplicity and directness in these songs for children was an important ingredient of the gospel-hymn style. It was even possible for a child's hymn to end up as a full-blown drawing-room ballad, as happened in Britain with Gounod's setting of Mrs C. F. Alexander's hymn for 'little children' 'There Is a Green Hill Far Away' in 1871. Itinerant preacher Dwight L. Moody (1837–99) led the post-Civil War revivalist movement. It was pervaded by a new mood, which to some extent echoed the new mood of blackface minstrelsy: no more was the atmosphere one of hellfire and hysteria; instead, a mixture of heavy sentiment and stirring songs of hope prevailed. The new style can be seen emerging in hybrid hymns such as 'Oh, You Must Be a Lover of the Lord', a song popular in revival meetings in the American South and Mid-West. It links an Isaac Watts hymn, 'Am I a Soldier of the Cross?', to a rousing camp-style chorus, the whole set to the same music, with no regard for the crude contrast in diction:

> Am I a soldier of the cross?
> A follower of the Lamb?
> And shall I fear to own His cause,
> Or blush to speak His name?
>
> Oh, you must be a lover of the Lord,
> Oh, you must be a lover of the Lord,
> Oh, you must be a lover of the Lord,
> Or you can't go to heaven when you die.

The published music of 1866 is credited to J.N.S., who almost certainly was an arranger; it was common practice for publishers to employ house musicians to arrange gospel hymns as separate songs with piano accompaniment. No one knows who the arranger was of the most famous hybrid hymn, 'Battle Hymn of the Republic'. When the sheet music was first published, by Oliver Ditson & Co. of Boston in 1862, it carried the information that Julia Ward Howe's verses had been 'adapted to the favourite melody of "Glory, Hallelujah".' In similar fashion to 'Oh, You Must Be a Lover of the Lord', the poetry is crammed into an unsuitable tune and punctuated at each stanza's end with a trite, repetitive refrain. The tune originally accompanied G. S. Scofield's Methodist hymn 'Say, Brothers, Will You Meet Us?' (1858), but became widely known as 'John Brown's Body' in 1861. Songs moved back and forth between sacred and secular versions during this period; another famous song of the Civil War, 'Tramp! Tramp!. Tramp!' by G. F. Root, gave its melody to the Sunday School hymn 'Jesus Loves the Little Children'.

American ballad composers like G. F. Root and J. P. Webster were now taking an interest in gospel hymns; the latter's 'Sweet By and By' (words by S. F. Bennet) almost equalled his wartime 'Lorena' in popularity. It was originally published in *The Signet Ring* (1868), a collection of hymns, but was soon made available in a separate sheet-music version. The first large collection of gospel hymns was compiled by Ira D. Sankey (1840–1908), who joined Moody in Chicago in 1870. *Sacred Songs and Solos* was published by Morgan & Scott in London in 1873, the year Moody and Sankey made their triumphant tour of Britain. In America, Sankey collaborated with another evangelical singer, Philip Paul Bliss (1838–76), to produce *Gospel Hymns and Sacred Songs*, published in New York in 1875. The compositions of Bliss typify the new sentimental style of gospel song. One of his first songs (for which, as so often, he wrote both words and music) was 'If Papa Were Only Ready!', a short solo which he sang to the accompaniment of an American reed organ. The song concerns the hopes and fears of little Willie. At this time, the name 'Willie' usually proved fatal for any character in a song, and here is no exception; the song begins, 'I should like to die,' said Willie, 'if my papa could die too.' As well as solos, Bliss wrote fully harmonized hymns, but the songs which are richest in the characteristics of the new gospel style are those which follow the pattern common in minstrel shows of solo verse and harmonized refrain. For example, 'What Shall the Harvest Be?' (words by E. A. Oakley) has many typical features: a melody coloured by sentimental chromaticism and expressive dissonance; a dancelike rhythm; and harmony which embraces the 'modern' vocabulary of the drawing room (passing diminished sevenths, dominant extensions, and pedals). Here is the opening of the verse:

A favourite device used in the choral refrains of gospel songs is that of 'echo voices', usually male voices echoing a phrase sung by female voices. In the present song, the soprano moves through the text at a slower speed than the other voice parts, which might more accurately be called 'anticipating voices'.

Another characteristic of gospel style, seen to some extent in this song, is the tendency to favour parallel movement for the top three voices of a four-part harmonization. The form of 'What Shall the Harvest Be?' is more expansive than the norm; it has a twelve-bar verse and sixteen-bar chorus, rather than eight bars

for each. Besides the evangelical enthusiasm of their texts, it is just this compact-
ness of musical form which separates many gospel songs from songs of the
minstrel stage, not the use of anything strikingly different in their melodic,
harmonic, or rhythmic departments; a comparison of Foster's 'De Camptown
Races' and Bliss's 'Look and Live'[14] shows how close together on occasion they
could come. While being infused with the sentimentality of post-Civil War song,
some of the vigour of pre-Civil War minstrelsy also seems to have passed into
gospel music. This vigour is apparent in the fondness for questions and exclamations as titles.

The texts relate to the Bible in three main ways: they may illustrate and
confirm, as happens in 'What Shall the Harvest Be?', which takes as its departure
point 'Whatsoever a man soweth, that shall he also reap' (Galatians 6:7); they
may use a Biblical quotation as a basis for personal confession, as occurs in 'The
Wandering Sheep', which quotes at its head, 'All we like sheep have gone astray'
(Isaiah 53:6), and begins, 'I was a wandering sheep, I did not love the fold'; or
they may offer individual witness to the truth of a Biblical statement, as does 'The
Sands of Time', verse 3 of which testifies to the truth of the assertion 'Thine eyes
shall behold the land that is very far off' (Isaiah 33:17):

> Amid the shades of ev'ning,
> While sinks life's ling'ring sand,
> I hail the glory dawning
> From Immanuel's land.

It was Bliss and Sankey's desire that their music, and gospel music in general,
should reach into every corner of society. As mentioned before, this was born of
ideological rather than commercial reasons; they refused, in fact, to take any
personal profit out of their editing or songwriting. Revivalism was nothing new to
Britain. The Primitive Methodist church had its origins in the first English camp
meeting held at Mow Cop on the Staffordshire–Cheshire border by 'Crazy
Alonzo' Dow in 1807.[15] William Booth began holding services in the open air and
in tents from 1864 onwards, although he did not create the Whitechapel Church
Mission, and with it the Salvation Army, until 1878. However, Moody and
Sankey arrived in Britain in 1873, a year of industrial crisis. The middle class no
doubt welcomed the distraction offered to an increasingly discontent working
class who now had the electoral franchise and had forced the Liberal government
to give full legal recognition to trade unions just a few years after an attempt to
re-enact the Combination Laws. But even in the most respectable middle-class
quarters a fervent religious strain was already to be found. In 1860 Miss Lindsay
had a notable success with her setting of Tennyson's 'Too Late!', which in parts
reads like a revivalist hymn:

> Late, late, so late! and dark the night and chill!
> Late, late, so late! But we can enter still!
> Too late! too late, ye cannot enter now,
> Too late! too late, ye cannot enter now.

The songs of P. P. Bliss certainly found their way into middle-class homes in
Britain; some of them were published separately in the *Musical Bouquet*, in

arrangements by T. Westrop. In this connection, also, it is worth noting that No. 111 of Sankey's *Sacred Songs and Solos*, 'Farewell Hymn', is a divine parody of 'Home, Sweet Home!'

The Negro spiritual

The combination of enthusiasm for sacred song and for blackface minstrel song prepared the ground for the visit to Britain of the Jubilee Singers, also in 1873. Although the early camp meetings showed the influence of black religious practice, an interest in publishing and disseminating the religious music of Southern slaves only awakened with their emancipation, the first collection being *Slave Songs of the United States* (1867). The Jubilee Singers were students of Fisk University, Nashville, an institution founded in the late 1860s with funds mainly from the American Missionary Association. The idea behind its inception was that emancipated slaves should be given access to a Christian education, 'or the nation must suffer far more in the future than in the past from the curse of slavery'.[16] George White, who was indeed white, organized the Jubilee Singers, who were all black, to raise funds for the University in 1871. Lord Shaftesbury, in his capacity as President of the Freedmen's Mission Aid Society (the English sister organization of the American Missionary Association) arranged their first concert in Britain, in London, in 1873. The following day they were invited to perform in the drawing room of the London home of the Duke and Duchess of Argyll. There they received a visit from Queen Victoria, to whom they sang the nowadays well-known spirituals 'Steal Away' and 'Go Down, Moses'. They went on to perform in other drawing rooms, including that of the Prime Minister, Gladstone. Yet, like Moody and Sankey, they saw their audience as encompassing the whole of society. Hence they not only performed in the drawing rooms of the rich and in chapels but also had the idea while in Hull on their tour north of giving concerts in the open air. Rather than charge for their concerts, they took collections; all money raised was to help pay for the completion of Jubilee Hall at Fisk University. In Newcastle upon Tyne they encountered Moody and Sankey and immediately joined their efforts to the 'great work'. Whether in England or Scotland, the Jubilee Singers were warmly welcomed wherever they toured, and it is noteworthy that they met with very little racial prejudice:

> In no way were they ever offensively reminded, through look or word – unless by some rude American who was lugging his caste conceit through a European tour, or by a vagrant Englishman who had lived long enough in America to 'catch' its color prejudices – that they were black.[17]

On their second visit to Britain, ten strong, in May 1875, they again gave some joint performances with Moody and Sankey in various halls, or in tabernacles erected specially for Moody's meetings. Sunday School parties would be taken to these meetings; in Liverpool, 12,000 children from ninety different schools turned up.[18] After the Jubilee Singers returned from a European tour in 1878, Fisk University disbanded them, and the following year they set themselves up as a joint stock company. In 1882 they reorganized and embarked upon a six-year world tour, this time under a black musical director, Frederick J. Loudin.

The songs they sang, which came to be known as 'Negro Spirituals', make much of the contrast between unison and harmony, usually in order to underline a 'call and response'. Like the Moody and Sankey repertoire, a favourite structure is eight-bar verse and eight-bar refrain, except that the song commonly begins with the refrain rather than the verse. They are also distinguished melodically in their use of pentatonicism, syncopation, and cell structure. Nevertheless, there are some songs with solo verse and choral refrain which show a close relationship to the Sankey gospel style, for example, 'The Gospel Train' and 'In the River of Jordan'. Some are harmonized throughout, and others, for example, 'I've Been Redeemed' and 'He Rose from the Dead', have the typical gospel feature of 'echo voices'. The Jubilee Singers sometimes supplemented their Afro-American repertoire with blackface minstrelsy ('Old Folks at Home'), patriotic Unionism ('John Brown's Body'), and white gospel (Bliss's 'Grace Before Meat'). Even in their own songs, the influence of nonconformist preaching is obvious and is pointed to directly in verse 24 of 'Go Down, Moses':

> I'll tell you what I likes de best,
> Let my people go;
> It is the shouting Methodist,
> Let my people go.
>
> Go down, Moses, etc.

Only a few of the Jubilee Singers' songs were published in separate sheet-music versions with piano accompaniment. Like a lot of Afro-American music, it was difficult to capture on paper what was so thrilling in performance. Even though they were self-consciously refined, and sometimes used a piano themselves, the harmonies they used would have looked very plain in a drawing room of the 1870s. With the development of impressionistic and 'jazzy' harmonies, the Negro Spiritual gained access to the twentieth-century drawing room.[19] Those chosen last century for publication by John Church & Co. of Cincinnati either resemble an early minstrel song (though dialect is little used), as does 'Reign, Master Jesus', or resemble a gospel hymn, as does 'I'm Going To Sing All the Way'.

Without an understanding of the importance of religion, and particularly nonconformist religion, in the middle-class home, a full appreciation of the meaning of drawing-room ballads of the second half of the nineteenth century is often impossible. Take Michael Watson's ballad 'Anchored' (words by S. K. Cowan), for example; it can easily be read as a conventional tale of a shipwreck, with a clever twist at the end when the father's home the sailor thought he was heading for turns out to be the Heavenly Father's home. However, the very title of the ballad would have called to mind the promise of salvation, 'Which hope we have as an anchor of the soul, sure and steadfast' (Hebrews 6:19), or perhaps the gospel hymn 'The Anchored Soul' (words by W. O. Cushing, music by R. Lowry). The carved anchor and the quotation from Hebrews was often placed on the tombstone of a wealthy seaman in a church graveyard or private cemetery. One of Bliss's best-known sacred songs, 'The Life Boat', makes metaphorical use of the sailor's life: here a shipwrecked sailor jumps into a life-boat, determined to 'pull for the shore'. Bliss has no need to explain the metaphor which extends throughout his song, that the wrecked ship is the body, that the life-boat is Christ, and that the shore is heaven. The Rev. E. S. Ufford's 'Throw Out the Life-Line!' plays upon the same theme. Given the close relationship between gospel hymns and sailors, it was perhaps fitting that the band of the *Titanic* should have chosen to play a Moody and Sankey favourite, 'Nearer, My God, to Thee', as she went down.

Roman Catholicism

So far, Roman Catholicism has not been mentioned except as a passing reference in connection with the Oxford Movement. Before mid-century no publisher saw much potential for sales of songs espousing Roman Catholic sentiment, however attractive the music, and despite the Catholic Emancipation Act of 1829. Of course, the tradition of comic monks and friars continued to resonate in nineteenth-century song: for example, 'The Syren and the Friar' (1842), 'The Monks Were Jolly Boys' (1862), Friar Cupid (1884); and for the whole century a perennial favourite was 'The Friar of Orders Grey', from O'Keefe and Reeve's opera 'Merry Sherwood' (1796). Sometimes a means could be found to draw attention away from Roman Catholic sentiment by emphasizing that the text came from a Romantic literary source. Schubert's 'Ave Maria' was published by Wessel & Co. of London in the early 1840s as 'Ellen's Hymn! Ave Maria!' from Sir Walter Scott's *Lady of the Lake*. Today, ironically, the fact that Schubert set a German translation of Ellen's 'Hymn to the Virgin' from Canto III of that work is almost unknown.[20] Another way Roman Catholicism might find favour in the drawing rooms of the 1840s was if it arrived in the form of a prayer or aria from a Romantic opera; hence, 'Holy Mother, Guide His Footsteps', from Wallace's *Maritana* (1845), was accepted as a delightful and inoffensive duet. In the 1850s, with the drift towards Catholicism of many Tractarians, the climate was sufficiently changed for settings of the actual *Ave Maria* prayer rather than the outpourings of a fictional character to prove capable of attracting large sales. Such a one was Virginia Gabriel's 'Ave Maria' of 1857, though Boosey sought to boost sales figures by issuing it as 'Nightfall at Sea' with secular words by A. Matthison in the mid-1860s. The famous 'Ave Maria' melody by Gounod, composed to the accompaniment of a Bach prelude, also belongs to the 1850s; it was published in London in 1859. However, even when the sacred song was a well-established species of drawing-room ballad in the 1870s, the content was still strongly Protestant. James Molloy, one of the best-selling ballad composers of this period, and a Roman Catholic, very obviously steers clear of religious subject matter in his output.

In the 1880s the ballad of Roman Catholic character gains an unshakable footing in the drawing room, thanks to the efforts of Theodore Auguste Marie Joseph Piccolomini (1835–1902). Piccolomini, who, incidentally, was born in Dublin, had his first real success in 1884 with a song of broad religious sentiment, 'Saved by a Child' (words by 'Nemo').[21] In 1889 he made his religious convictions plain in what became his most celebrated song, 'Ora Pro Nobis' (words by A. Horspool). In a previous ballad, 'The Toilers' (1888), for which he had provided his own words, he had had the idea of making the refrain a prayer. There he quoted part of the Lord's Prayer; but in 'Ora Pro Nobis', the words of the title, which form the refrain, are part of a uniquely Catholic prayer, the *Ave Maria*. The combination of dramatic *gran scena* treatment and lyrical effusiveness had also featured in some of his earlier ballads, but the touching tale of an orphan girl who dies at her mother's graveside contrived to make this one irresistible. There is a difference, although it may be only of degree, between ballads of this nature, designed largely for the sentimental self-indulgence of a drawing-room audience, and ballads such as John Blockley's setting of Longfellow's 'The Reaper and the Flowers' (1855) where the intention seems to be to provide comfort for those who have lost children of their own. The character of the angel is worth noting in this respect, too. In both Britain and America, where urbanization took a similar toll of young lives, there developed an image of the angel as a quite specific kind of being. Many sheet-music covers of songs about dying show a pretty, white-robed girl with large feathery wings, who may be playing a harp, or carrying a child to heaven. That these comforting creatures were invariably feminine in the nineteenth century, thereby reflecting gender roles in the earthly home, was as true of nonconformist angels as of Roman Catholic angels ('Queen of Angels' is the title of a 'Vesper Song' composed by Piccolomini to words by 'Nemo' in 1897).

Christmas

Finally, some words need to be added concerning the special religious festival of Christmas. The Victorian period certainly saw the construction of a new meaning and ritual around Christmas, and many of the changes in celebrating Christmas may be related to the need to organize and control the leisure activity of a large urban population. The slow build-up to the festival, however, and the vast display of conspicuous consumption are of more recent date. New publications of old carols began to appear in the 1840s and were soon being aimed at the family; the ideology of the family was reinforced at Christmas by the example of the Holy Family. *Songs of Christmas for Family Choirs*, selected and adapted by 'a Clergyman of the Church of England' was published in London in 1847. Henry John Gauntlett then published some new carols, in *Christmas Carols, Old and New* (1850); his most well-known carol is 'Once in Royal David's City', a setting of verse by Mrs C. F. Alexander. In the same way that one of the early varieties of sacred song for the drawing room developed from the hymn a related kind developed from the carol. One of the first to win widespread favour was Brinley Richards' 'Christmas Chimes' (words by R.B.), published by A. Hammond & Co. in 1854, and reaching its twelfth edition before being reissued by Chappell in the late 1860s. In the last quarter of the nineteenth century, the Christmas theme, like any other sacred theme, was just one more option open to songwriters, as the diverse musical strands of the drawing-room ballad moved towards a uniformity of idiom under the influence of Boosey's Ballad Concerts (see Chapter 7). One of the most celebrated of the ballads from this period to deal with Christmas time was 'The Star of Bethlehem' (1887), words by Frederic Weatherly, music by Stephen Adams.[22]

6   *Promoters, Publishers, and Professional Performers*

The amount of concert promotional activity taking place in Britain multiplied rapidly in the second half of the nineteenth century. It was symptomatic of the increasing commercialization of music during this period. Ballad concerts may have begun in London but were soon found spreading to all major cities, and also to holiday resorts, where the spa orchestras 'were in part heirs of the ballad concerts, the "Grand Morning Concert" or "Soirée Musicale" which for long delighted middle-class Londoners'.[1] 'Morning' performances, incidentally, were conventionally given in the afternoon, a practice which continued when the word 'matinée' was substituted for 'morning' in the 1880s. A seaside resort within easy travelling distance from London by rail, like Brighton, found it a simple matter to attract money into the town during the lean winter months by presenting a concert season. This was good news, too, for the railway company who could advertise a range of special offers for the Brighton Season and fill up their Pullman Drawing Room Cars which would otherwise have lain empty in February.

Many commercial and industrial centres started up festivals – often, as in the case of Leeds (1858), Bradford (1853), and Huddersfield (1881), to promote their new town halls. Birmingham boasted a festival which could be traced back to 1768, but most of the festivals which dated from before the nineteenth century were cathedral festivals, such as the Three Choirs Festival and the Norwich Festival. In the industrial North the sponsors of festivals would generally be a combination of business magnates, local traders, and the local authority. Sometimes the landed gentry might offer support to a rural festival: the Worsley family, for instance, sponsored a festival in the small Yorkshire village of Hovingham (1887–1906). Sometimes a festival was begun by moral crusaders; the Harlech Festival was organized by a group of temperance choirs in 1867. New festivals usually trumpeted the fact that, like the cathedral festivals, they were taking place for a charitable rather than a business purpose: the Glasgow Festival of 1873, for example, raised £1000 for the Infirmary, and the Birmingham Triennial Festival traditionally handed over its profits to the General Hospital.

Festivals were just one part of the rapid spread of concert activity, however, and the lack of a festival did not necessarily mean a city lacked music; Liverpool, for example, never managed to get a regular festival off the ground, but that may have been because there was already so much happening there, including a thriving Philharmonic Society. In Hull, a city which never had a festival, regular concerts were promoted by local traders and others. The music shop Gough and Davy brought up Edward Lloyd in February 1893 to sing his latest ballad-concert success, 'The Holy City', accompanied by its composer at the piano. Although many concert promoters were keen to offer cheap rates (the standard cheap rate being 1s.) in order to increase the size of the audience – and this was a concession normal at promenade concerts which had developed from pleasure-garden music-making – there remained a few élitist bodies who were concerned to keep out even the lower middle class, let alone the working class. The Philharmonic Society in London, which long enjoyed a monopoly in orchestral performances, refrained from offering cheap rates during the entire time they played at the aristocratic Hanover Square Rooms; they did, however, change their policy when they transferred to St James's Hall in 1869. In Manchester entrance to the 'Gentlemen's Concerts' was by old-fashioned subscription only, and patrons were required to wear full evening dress. Ironically, the organizers of the massive triennial Handel Festivals held at the Crystal Palace, occasions which seemed designed as an illustration of the classless universality of Handel's genius, never made seats available at a cheap rate: in 1857 admission was 10s. 6d. and reserved seats cost 1 guinea. Jullien mounted a rival cheap festival that year in the Surrey Gardens Hall.

The majority of promotional bodies were on a constant look-out for new ways to entice more people into concerts. Promoters in the London suburbs had to put on programmes of great diversity to fill halls. The Beaumont Institution in the East End endured much ridicule in 1860 for a programme mixing items from opera and oratorio with drawing-room ballads, organ music, and other musical fare. The directorate responded to criticism by saying, 'the hall was packed, the audience encored half the pieces, and – we paid our expenses'.[2] Smoking concerts were started in London in the 1880s; those who wished to luxuriate in tobacco smoke while listening to 'good' music now had only to look for an advertisement such as 'Grand Cigarette Concert'.[3] Founded in the same decade was the Coffee Music Halls Company, Limited; the first venue they acquired for a coffee music hall was the then run-down theatre known as the 'Old Vic'.

There were also new developments in theatrical performance. A large portion of the bourgeoisie had always eyed the theatre with suspicion as a place of dubious propriety (see Chapter 1); it was to overcome just this fear of offended respectability that Thomas and Priscilla German Reed opened their 'Gallery of Illustration' in Regent Street in 1856. They aimed to provide impeccably wholesome entertainment and pointedly refrained from calling their premises a theatre, although it was, in fact, licensed as such by the Lord Chamberlain.[4] Advertisements announced their dramatic performances as 'Mr and Mrs German Reed's Entertainment', a phrase suggestive of 'at home' functions among polite society. In the early days the entertainment simply consisted of the husband-and-wife team singing and acting, Thomas adding musical accompaniment when needed on piano or harmonium. After 1868 the company increased and included, among others, their son Alfred and the barrister turned musical mimic, Corney Grain. They were now able to mount a variety of small-scale burlesques and operettas. Both Gilbert and Sullivan had independently supplied material for the Gallery of Illustration before their first formal introduction to each other there in 1871.[5] The German Reeds' provision of wholesome comedy for the middle class proved to be a great influence on the later development of the Gilbert and Sullivan partnership and, indeed, on the acceptance of comic song in the drawing room, till then almost solely represented by 'Simon the Cellarer'. In the last decade of the century another new form of salubrious entertainment, the pierrot show, was developed at seaside resorts to serve the leisure-time interests of the lower middle class who were by then confirmed in the custom of taking an annual seaside family holiday. Dressed as clowns the actors may have been, but tearful ballads were sung in plenty.

Prominent among concert promoters were the music publishers themselves. Tom Chappell of Chappell & Co. financed the building of St James's Hall in 1858 and the presentation of the Monday and Saturday 'Pops'; he may have found inspiration for these 'popular concerts' in the well-attended Wednesday Concerts at the Exeter Hall (started in 1848). Naturally the opportunity was not missed to display the firm's instruments and sheet music at St James's Hall. Speculation also played a part in Chappell & Co.'s success; Tom Chappell bought the publishing rights of Balfe's *The Bohemian Girl* and Gounod's *Faust* before either of them had been staged in London (though *Faust* had actually been given a concert performance at the Canterbury music-hall). The risks involved in this sort of speculation could be high: Tom Chappell had paid around £100 for *Faust* which was expected to fail, but John Boosey paid £1000 for Gounod's next opera, *Mireille*, which was expected to be a triumph, yet turned out to be a flop.[6] Publishers looked upon operas as storehouses of profitable individual sheet-music items. In a notorious case a publisher forced Jullien to take off an acclaimed production of Donizetti's *Lucia di Lammermoor* at Drury Lane in December 1847 and replace it with Balfe's new opera, *The Maid of Honour*. Jullien had signed a contract committing him to a penalty of £200 if he failed to put on Balfe's work as soon as it was ready, and the publisher was keen to bring out the 'favourite airs' in time for Christmas. Chappell & Co.'s sphere of influence extended beyond their own publications and promotions: Tom Chappell was one of the original directors of the Royal College of Music and one of the original governors of the Royal Albert Hall. Chappell & Co. also helped to finance the first D'Oyly Carte Company, though they soon acquired a deeper vested interest in its success by publishing almost all the Gilbert and Sullivan operettas.

The new series of Saturday afternoon 'Pops' begun by Chappell in 1865 may have influenced John Boosey's decision to establish the London Ballad Concerts at St James's Hall in 1867. The market for the 'popular concert' could be seen to be growing, and the profitable ballad catalogue Boosey had built up no doubt suggested an area for further expansion. The main factors in Boosey's success seem to have been the mixture of well-known songs among the new, the engagement of celebrated singers, and the lack of 'heavy' items in his programmes. A reviewer in 1871 picks up on these points:

> Mr Boosey has been giving on successive Wednesdays a new series of these highly popular entertainments, and by a judicious admixture in the programmes of things

new and old, as well as by securing the services of many of our principal public performers, has made them thoroughly attractive. There are thousands who would never go to St James's Hall to hear a quartett [*sic*] or a sonata, that can thoroughly appreciate a 'good old song'; and for this numerous class the Ballad Concerts supply exactly what they like.[7]

In their turn, the Boosey Ballad Concerts were later emulated by Chappell; in fact, William Boosey, the adopted son of John Boosey and well-versed in ballad affairs, was engaged to run their first series in 1894. William Boosey, who went on to join Chappell & Co., almost single-handedly built up their ballad catalogue. The suggestion that he do so came from himself:

> Mr Chappell's first idea was to engage me to run a series of ballad concerts. I explained to him, however, that he was securing the least valuable half of the loaf, and that the concerts would be of no use to him unless he could count on me to provide him at the same time with a new ballad catalogue.[8]

Besides Chappell and Boosey, the other member of the big three British music publishers of the nineteenth century, Novello, also promoted concerts. Having an enormous choral catalogue, it is no surprise to discover that they were especially keen to promote oratorio concerts. That Bach's *St Matthew Passion* was being so widely taken up in the 1870s demonstrably owed more to Novello's new cheap octavo edition, coupled to their promotional efforts, than to the earlier and more musicologically celebrated Mendelssohn revival of the work. Novello also showed business acumen in taking over the firm of Ewer & Co. who possessed the publishing rights to Mendelssohn's *Elijah*, a work which held second place only to Handel's *Messiah* in relation to its frequency of performance.

Before the opening up of the country by rail, the market for sheet music was fraught with transport difficulties. These problems account for music publishing outside London having reached its peak in the early industrial period of 1790–1830. Even then, the publisher outside London was often a branch of the publisher in London: William Power of Dublin, for example, who published Moore's *Irish Melodies*, was related to James Power of London. George Thomson of Edinburgh (mentioned in Chapter 1 in connection with Beethoven's arrangements of Scottish airs) was independent, but his business ended in bankruptcy. Bremmer and Cori in Edinburgh were branches of their respective London firms. After 1830 Edinburgh and Dublin were the only serious rivals to London as places for music publishing. It should be pointed out, however, that a fair amount of publishing activity did take place in Bath, Cambridge, Leeds, Liverpool, Manchester, Oxford, York, and Aberdeen. Many music publishers relied on sales of instruments as well as sheet music; salient names here are Chappell, Metzler, D'Almaine, and Boosey (the latter began manufacturing wind instruments in the 1850s and moved into brass also when they bought up the business of Henry Distin and Co. in 1868). Those companies concentrating on sheet music sales alone had to pin-point their market with care. In the publication of drawing-room ballads, George Davidson (who set up business around 1833 and became 'The Music Publishing Co.' in 1860) targeted the cheap end of the market, cutting costs by using musical type; by 1870 he was able to offer songs in his *Musical Treasury* at a fraction of the price of his rivals (though, naturally, both print and paper were of poor quality): 'Popular Songs, in threepenny sheets, many with elegant illustrations and portraits in colours . . . The original and only genuine music for the million.'[9] In the middle of the market was the Musical Bouquet which flourished under the proprietorship of Charles Sheard who took it over in 1855. At the top of the market was Robert Cocks who had the prestige of royal patronage and of owning the lease of the Hanover Square Rooms. The carving up of the market in various layers of price relates to the increasing commercialization of music and the interaction of supply and demand. Back in 1811, for example, Chappell had begged leave 'to aquaint the nobility and gentry'[10] that he had set up in business, a statement indicative of the restricted market at that time. By 1870 no publisher catered exclusively for the aristocracy and wealthy bourgeoisie, and all the larger publishers were selling internationally. For international sales a publisher had no need of a branch in every country: in the colonies, for instance, companies could be found specializing in importing music, like Harold & Co. Ltd, the 'Musical Depot' of Calcutta. Boosey & Co. did open a New York branch in the 1890s, but Chappell waited until 1906 before following suit.

Perhaps because of growing demand (the entertainment industry was booming in a time of recession, as it has done since), perhaps because of increasing standardization of publishing format (particularly applicable to music-hall songs), or perhaps because of innovative technology (the rotary press was but one method of faster production), the price of sheet music was being pushed down in the later nineteenth century. Nor must one ignore the general economic background of continually falling prices from 1873 to 1896, and factors such as the money supply (gold reserves) which also may have had a bearing on commodity prices, such as paper.[11] Drawing-room ballads were falling in price from an average 4s. in the 1860s to 3s. in the 1870s and to 2s. in the 1880s, and this was only the marked price; most publishers had an arrangement to sell at half the nominal price. There were cheap postal arrangements, too, some sheet music stockists even offering to supply music post free. In the 1880s Moutrie and Son of Baker Street were charging a maximum of 1s. 6d. per item, post free, and a further reduction was made for soiled copies.[12] Not to be overlooked amongst all the bargains were the albums of 'standard works' and the 'cheap editions' that were being produced in great quantity.

In respect of the biggest ballad successes the market for transcriptions and arrangements was vast: in the case of 'The Holy City' (1892), for example, Boosey published a whole range of spin-offs from the original, including a German translation, 'Die Heilige Stadt' (1896), a version with chorus parts (1894), a military-band arrangement (1892), and an organ transcription (1894). Note that the military-band version appeared in the same year as the ballad's first publication; Boosey's connection with wind instruments made them eager to publish 26-part band versions of their ballad triumphs (the vocal melody often being carried by a solo cornet or euphonium). Having been the first to see the potential of the drawing-room-ballad market, Boosey & Co. were also in a position to avail themselves of their extensive back catalogue and reissue former favourites for a new generation of consumers. 'Come Back to Erin', reissued in

1893, proved more profitable over the next two decades than it had been in the late 1860s and 70s.

The curse of the publisher was the pirated edition. An area particularly vulnerable to piracy was blackface minstrel song. Where the composer was assumed to be an anonymous black American, any number of authorized editions might appear, but even as eminent a composer as Henry Clay Work was not safe from such treatment. In the 1870s the reputable publishers H. D'Alcorn & Co. produced a 'Grandfather's Clock' which purported to be the 'authorized version' of 'The Great Song, sung with unbounded applause in Uncle Tom's Cabin.' Only the work of an arranger, J. E. Mallandaine, was credited. Hopwood & Crew advertised an 'authorized edition' of Christy's Minstrels songs and ballads, but it did not prevent the more up-market Musical Bouquet from publishing many of the same songs in versions by their own house arrangers. Publishers were treading on each other's toes because the market for minstrel songs was so extensive, reaching into drawing room, music-hall, and even the classroom. H. D'Alcorn included minstrel songs in their albums of *Easy Piano Music for Children* (while they felt unable to include items from their huge music-hall catalogue), and Hopwood & Crew pointed out that their minstrel songs were 'ever welcomed and highly appreciated in the drawing room, and the greatest favourites with teachers in Class Instruction'.[13]

Copyright was often either not strictly enforced or offenders were treated leniently in the nineteenth century. Moreover, there was a degree of confusion about some of the terms of the Copyright Act of 1842. Under that Act copies had to be registered at Stationers' Hall to protect copyright; it would then last for a period of forty-two years or the author's lifetime plus seven years, whichever was longer. A question arose, however, concerning the copyright of titles. The last page of 'It's Just As Well To Take Things in a Quiet Sort of Way' bears a warning from the publisher H. D'Alcorn against any attempt to pirate 'the Words or Title of this Song'. Yet one judge expressed grave doubt 'as to whether copyright could be claimed at all to a mere title'.[14] Another problem was in deciding how much imitation could be allowed before a composer was liable to the charge of plagiarism – Sullivan's 'When a Merry Maiden Marries', for instance, begins in almost identical manner to the refrain of Molloy's 'Love's Old Sweet Song' ('Just a song at twilight'). A further problem arose concerning the distinction between copyright and performing right (known then as 'acting right'). Note the following caution which appeared on Hopwood & Crew's publication of Harry Clifton's 'Pretty Polly Perkins of Paddington Green': 'This song is legally protected, and cannot be sung in Public without the written permission of the Author.' In this case, presumably, Clifton had sold only the copyright to the publisher and not the performing right. Many singers assumed that they purchased their songs from publishers who owned both copyright and performing right; it was certainly in the publisher's interest to own both, since a song that could not be performed in public without special permission would not sell as well as one which could. Under the strict terms of the Act, however, the performing right needed to be entered separately at Stationers' Hall. There was a notorious Mr Wall who managed to purchase performing rights from impecunious composers or their descendants, register them, and then have singers and bands prosecuted for performing them. The following throws light on his method:

> There is a certain old song, for instance, 'She wore a wreath of roses', which had been sung for a great number of years publicly in all kinds of concert-rooms, and no one ever dreamt of stopping the singing of it; it was sung by Phillips, Rudersdorff, and many singers of the time gone by, and then all of a sudden, not the publisher, but Mr Wall, secures the reversion of the words, I suppose, and registers that reversion, and immediately comes down on singers singing his song who have been singing it all their lifetime, and compels them to pay forty shillings.[15]

The activities of Wall led to publishers like Boosey attaching the comment 'May be sung in public without fee or license [*sic*]' to their ballads (although Boosey was adamant in prohibiting parodies). Today, it is necessary to apply for permission to perform copyrighted songs in public to the Performing Right Society Ltd, the independent body now serving the interests of composers and their descendants. Ironically it means that some Boosey ballads, previously published with a disclaimer, cannot now be performed in public without a fee, since under the terms of the 1911 Copyright Act copyright protection was extended to the author's lifetime plus fifty years.

Until the reforms of 1902, 1906, and 1911, copyright legislation was largely ineffective in the face of the massive piracy of the late nineteenth century. In consequence, it was not only publishers who suffered; composers paid on the royalty system were inevitably deprived of part of their rightful income. John Boosey had been the first to allow composers a royalty on all copies of their music sold.[16] The very first composer to benefit from the royalty system is said to be their number one ballad composer of the late 1860s, Claribel.[17] Before the existence of the royalty system, copyrights were sold outright, and sometimes brought little to the composer, as Henry Russell explains:

> I have composed and published in my life over eight hundred songs, but it was by singing these songs and not by the sale of the copyrights that I made money. There was no such thing as a royalty in those days, and when a song was sold it was sold outright. My songs brought me an average price of ten shillings each, that is to say, my eight hundred songs have represented about four hundred pounds to me, though they have made the fortune of several publishers.[18]

Russell's celebrated precursor, Charles Dibdin, did somewhat better for himself when he sold his entire stock of 360 songs to Bland & Weller of Oxford Street for £1800 with £100 per annum for three years after, for such composition as he might produce during that period.[19] In the 1860s the outright fee for a song could vary from £1 to £10. When royalty payments gained ground – most publishers being forced to follow Boosey's example in order to compete for the best-selling composers – there was also a variety of payments negotiated. The norm was around 10 per cent, but some terms could be very generous: a contract from Hopwood & Crew, who were moving up-market in the 1870s with their take-over of the firm of Charles Coote, offered John Hatton a royalty of 7*d.* on each copy sold of his ballad 'Faithful Ever' (1875), the value of one copy of which was registered at 1*s.* 0*d.*[20] Royalties were also negotiated for arrangements: a letter from Sullivan to Arthur Boosey, dated 21 April 1877, expresses the former's willingness to accept 3*d*. a copy for the piano arrangement of 'The Lost Chord'.[21] The same letter brings up a problem related to the aggressive ballad marketing of the 1870s and beyond; Sullivan discovered that old songs of his were being dished up with new words by his previous publisher, Metzler, and then advertised as new songs in order to cash in on his Boosey ballad-concert successes.

Professional singers were crucial to sales promotion in two ways: first, they were necessary in making the ballad known, and second, their association with the ballad could be used as a recommendation. Thus, it was important for publishers to include in advertisements of their ballad successes details of who they were sung by. Each ballad would normally have a back page devoted to the publisher's catalogue, with singers' names listed against each item. On the front the singer(s) associated with the ballad in question would be identified after some such phrase as 'Sung with Brilliant Success by', or, if the publisher favoured a softer sell (like Boosey), a modest 'Sung by'. A sales promotion technique well underway in the 1860s, and probably in existence before, was the payment to singers of a fixed royalty for a term of years on each copy of a ballad sold, on condition that they plugged it at all their concert engagements. Publishers had, of course, interested themselves in the repertoire of singers well before the rise of the 'royalty ballad' – it was John Boosey who had sent Tennyson's 'Come into the Garden, Maud' to Balfe, asking him to set it for Sims Reeves[22] – but the crude inducement of hard cash raised fiercely debated matters of taste. The acceptance of a royalty threw doubts on the artistic integrity of the singer:

> whether honest art is not more important than the twopence or threepence a copy is a serious question . . . I strongly urge that musicians should elevate the taste of the public, and should guide it. They can do it, and they have a moral duty to do so, especially those who are not obliged to work for the penny that brings the bread, and who can afford to refuse the bait.[23]

Some singers hit back with their own moral arguments, portraying themselves as public servants and placing the onus for questions of taste on the audience: 'the public which remunerates the singer . . . has a right to demand whatever will amuse it . . . I cannot enter into the question of public taste here; being public property I have no right'.[24] The attitude above, however, can easily slide into contempt, best exemplified by the notorious, though probably apocryphal, advice Nellie Melba is supposed to have given Clara Butt on the eve of the latter's Australian tour: 'Sing 'em muck; it's all they can understand.'[25] The castigation of singers who accepted payment for promoting songs has persisted in modern surveys of the period (though under different guises, like accreditation with part of the composition, the practice has continued to embrace singers as different as Al Jolson and Elvis Presley): 'It was not to the credit of celebrity singers of the time that they rushed on to the band wagon, sponsoring drivel because the chore was well-paid, bribed to insert new drawing-room ballads in their programmes.'[26]

The question arises, however, as to whether or not singers saw themselves as 'sponsoring drivel'. The tenor Edward Lloyd expressed surprise that he should not sing 'popular songs', provided one or two conditions were satisfactorily met:

'Why not popular songs? The people like them, and if the words have a good tone and the music is pleasing to the audience, why should I not sing them?'[27] In her later life, Clara Butt, the last celebrity singer engaged to promote 'royalty ballads', found it impossible to recollect any drivel she had sponsored: 'I have sung many hundreds of songs during my career, and I do not think I have sung any bad ones.'[28]

The 'royalty ballad' system did not always operate as smoothly as publishers wished, either. At first they assumed that only the leading singers needed to be paid royalties, and that lesser-known singers would automatically take up the same songs. Nevertheless, it was not long before a small publisher, Hutchinson, started paying those lesser singers to promote his own firm's songs, a move which forced the big publishers into this area as well. Another problem was created by the very public whose taste so many were avowedly eager to please. When William Boosey started the Chappell Ballad Concerts, his business instinct told him to engage the well-known names from the Boosey Ballad Concerts, yet it is apparent, reading between the lines of the following comment, that problems ensued regarding the introduction of sufficient new material: 'I used to find ballad concerts handicapped by it being necessary so very frequently to repeat the same songs and solos over and over again.'[29] The audience were naturally insistent that these singers perform their 'greatest hits', most of which were in the Boosey and not the Chappell catalogue. Furthermore, singers tended to have only a handful of encore pieces, often dating back to the days when they first built their reputation, which served them for an entire career: for example, the tenor Sims Reeves sang 'The Death of Nelson', 'The Pilgrim of Love', 'The Bloom Is on the Rye', and 'The Bay of Biscay' as his standard encores for thirty years; none of these were 'royalty ballads'.

Sims Reeves (1818–1900) has been disdainfully marked down as 'an all-round singer who went wherever the pickings were greatest';[30] but is this fair? Unlike the famous visiting Italian tenors, Reeves could not make his money on a few months of opera in London and spend the rest of his time performing at aristocratic functions. He did show great enthusiasm and skill as an opera singer, but no English tenor could compete with the status accorded to Italian tenors, like Mario, and he was seldom given opportunity to display his talents in that field. Where Reeves sang, then, cannot be exclusively attributed to personal greed; moreover, at times he took a principled stand which cost him dearly. A controversy raged in the late 1860s and throughout the 1870s concerning the height of English as opposed to Continental pitch. In 1868 Reeves made a resolution not to sing except at Continental pitch. It was a decision which caused consternation: 'Those who regarded musical art as a matter of pounds, shillings, and pence could not understand how a singer could forgo such a comfortable source of income.'[31] All the same, he stuck by his refusal for over three years, fruitlessly as it turned out, since orchestras were not willing to spend money on the purchase of lower-pitched Continental wind instruments. Another point of honour for Reeves was his determination never to sing if he felt unable to do justice to his art; since he was plagued with a delicate throat, this meant the surrender of fees which 'amounted during his career to no less than £90,000'.[32]

Sims Reeves

In the late 1870s Reeves shared with the young American contralto Antoinette Sterling (1850–1904) 'the chief place amongst our ballad singers'.[33] Sterling, far from jumping at the chance to promote new 'royalty ballads', was renowned for the careful perusal she gave, particularly to texts, before agreeing to perform them. Even the penetrating critic Shaw was drawn to the artistic honesty of her singing:

> Ballad singing is usually accompanied by coquettish smirks, a smile at the end of each stave, and an absurd prolongation of the pathetic phrases . . . These petty practices Madame Sterling has never condescended to employ . . . but relies simply on the rapid sympathy inspired by her voice's strange tone quality.[34]

Sterling's technique was not without its faults, however; Shaw criticizes her for occasional incorrect phrasing and a lack of fluent execution. Her early vocal studies had been in New York, and the further tuition she received on the continent was unusual in not including study in Italy. When she settled in England in her mid-twenties, she developed an individual and virtually self-taught style. Here she was breaking new ground and forming a closer relationship

Antoinette Sterling

to the drawing-room amateur than to the sophisticated concert artist. Study in Italian vocal techniques was an almost mandatory requirement for concert singers. Her most prestigious contralto predecessor in ballad singing, Charlotte Sainton-Dolby (1821–85), who had retired from professional performance in 1870, had been coached by Crivelli at the Royal Academy of Music. Reeves himself had studied in Milan, and his great predecessor, Braham, had studied with Rauzzini in Bath. An Italianate technique was expected and continued to carry the highest status, even when many ballads were moving, under the influence of Molloy and Adams (not to mention blackface minstrelsy), away from an Italian style. The status of things Italian had its origin in aristocratic taste (see Chapter 1), and it is to be noted that Queen Victoria was taking lessons in singing from Tosti in the 1880s. Some singers were still adopting Italian names at this time: for example, the bass Signor Foli (Allen Foley, 1835–99).

In the early century the pre-eminent voice range was that of the soprano. Even in mid-century, at the Norwich Festival, Reeves was unable to negotiate a higher fee than 100 guineas, while the committee were willing to pay 300 guineas for soprano soloists. The rise of the tenor soloist was related to middle-class distaste for the castrato voice, which was suggestive of the aristocratic effeminacy they so despised (it was not a quality which could be squared with bourgeois ideology). Braham did more than most at the beginning of the century to create the image of the tenor 'superstar'. He was almost certainly the only tenor at that time to command fees like the 2000 guineas Dublin Royal Theatre were prepared to pay for a fifteen-night engagement in 1809.[35] In *The Enterprising Impresario* (1867), Walter Maynard (Thomas Beale) recommends organizers of touring concert parties to calculate on the following basis:

	£
Soprano	200
Contralto	25
Tenor	200
Bass	15
Pianist	50
Violinist	30
Conductor	25
	£545
Hotel, travelling and servants, say . . .	£150[36]

By the mid-1860s sopranos and tenors were deemed to carry equal status as major attractions; the alto and bass merely make up the full quota of voice ranges normal in a concert party so as to cater for four-part harmony. In later years, though sopranos and tenors continued to command high fees, especially if celebrity had been achieved – Adelina Patti's standard fee was £1000 – altos and basses began to better their status as some of their number won fame in ballad concerts. Perhaps they found ready employment in these concerts because they had more time available for such work, or because they were at first cheaper to engage on the 'royalty ballad' system. Whatever the reason, in the 1880s Antoinette Sterling and the baritone Charles Santley (1834–1922) were as acclaimed as any soprano or tenor ballad singer. In a concert given in Hull's Public Rooms on Monday 19 October 1885 it was Sterling and the baritone Michael Maybrick who constituted the main draw, not the soprano or tenor. Another explanation for the enthusiasm for altos and basses may be that the lower voice range is more easily emulated by amateurs; a failed attempt at a low note usually results in a hoarse growl, a far less embarrassing sound than the agonized yelp that attends a cracked high note. One fact is indisputable: the best-known songs of the first half of the century were almost always originally written for soprano or tenor, whereas after 1870 the best-known ballads were almost always for alto or baritone.

Maynard's book had been written before any concert agencies existed in Britain. This state of affairs, however, lasted for barely a year after its publication. Rudall & Co. claimed they were founded in 1868, with the intention of bringing continental fashion to Britain:

> Although nearly all Engagements in Italy, France, Germany and Spain, have long been arranged by Agencies, any extensive development of the 'Agency' system as applied to first-class musical performances, was unknown in England till introduced by Messrs. Rudall & Co.[37]

Concert agencies proliferated in the 1870s and formed a bridge between concert promoters and performers, taking up the negotiation of fees and organizing the details of tours.

Agencies thrived by easing some of the problems created by the complex and rapid commercialization of music in the 1870s. As concert affairs grew ever more intricate, specialists moved into more and more areas. This often meant new ways of making money: for example, programme notes (a rarity before this decade) were soon a regular feature and, although trivial in content, they were expensive in terms of cost, 6*d.* – 1*s.* being the norm. The commercialization of music was conspicuously evident in the spread of the musical press, which had expanded enormously from the 1840s. Periodical issues of music were the forerunners of the musical periodical, the magazine or journal consisting of articles, criticism, and musical news. Periodical issues of music had begun to make room available for theoretical articles and reviews; an early example of this was *The Harmonicon* (1823–33). The first periodical, in the sense of a musical journal, was *The Musical World* (1836–91). In the 1840s periodicals were springing up around the sight-singing movement; Novello, however, made a particularly influential move by taking over Mainzer's periodical and turning it into *The Musical Times* in 1844. The age of the music publisher's periodical was now under way. It was, of course, useful to have a magazine which could promote the firm's products, but it was not necessary to turn it over entirely to this end; the status of issuing a well-read and respected periodical was itself a form of self-promotion. Robert Cocks started a *Musical Almanack* in 1849, Boosey took over *The Musical World* in 1854 and started a *Musical and Dramatic Review* in 1864, and Augener started *The Monthly Musical Record* in 1871. Periodicals were important both in terms of their influence and in the stimulus they gave to the supply-and-demand nexus of consumer capitalism. Wherever there was a sufficient expression of minority interest to intimate the possibility of profitable publication, a new specialist periodical was born. From the late 1870s onwards there were even periodicals aimed at those engaged in the music trades themselves. Between 1870 and 1900, all told, over a hundred different musical periodicals were started up at one time or another.

All this, furthermore, occurred simultaneously with the production of new publications performing the traditional service of a periodical issue of music, like Chappell's *Musical Magazine* and Boosey's *Musical Cabinet* (both started in 1861), and (also in the 1860s but more down-market) Hopwood & Crew's *Bond Street*, a monthly magazine of 'popular songs' and dance music. Not to be neglected in this connection was the use made by publishers of the attraction of a musical series to boost sales; there was an obvious appeal to the collector, for example, in Boosey's *Royal Edition* of operas. Finally, mention must be made of the nineteenth-century equivalent of the compilation album, the speciality now of record companies like K-tel; an example was *The Musical Circle*, begun by H. Vickers of London in 1881 as a 'fortnightly journal of copyright and standard music, both vocal and instrumental'.

Other branches of the music trades, such as instrumental manufacture and printing technology, have been dealt with in Chapter 2; but the present chapter cannot close without a few words on the subject of industries clinging to the periphery of musical commerce. The tobacco industry, for instance, was keen to push the idea that cigarette smoking was good for the voice and throat. Some celebrity singers did smoke – the tenor Edward Lloyd was one[38] – but truth was not to stand in the way of good advertising, and even the non-smoker Clara Butt was enlisted to endorse their products. The glamour of singers could be guaranteed to boost sales of appropriate products: Adelina Patti was expounding the virtues of Pears' soap in the 1880s.[39]

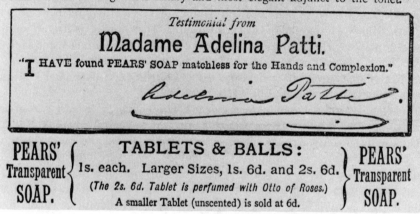

Fry's employed musical metaphors in advertisements for their cocoa ('Strikes the keynote of health' and 'Keeps you up to pitch'). Perhaps cigarette manufacturers did not actually think of themselves as providing medicine – though Wilcox and Co. sold their cigarettes, for the relief of bronchitis, in chemists – but 'musical medicine' was another area for imaginative marketing. Endless products were claimed to improve vocal production and to be conducive to the well-being of the singer. Voice lozenges were being pushed continually in the 1880s; manufacturers quoted eloquent testimonials from singers and reported the award of gold medals for their wondrous lozenges. Despite the sales drive, however, none of them caught on. Most bizarre of all was the attempt to market Italian air. A certain Dr Moffat had voiced the opinion in 1884 that 'the presence of peroxide of hydrogen in the air and dew of Italy had some connection with the beauty of Italian vocal tone'.[40] Marchesi, in *Singer's Pilgrimage* (1923), describes 'amoniaphone' (allegedly compressed Italian air) which was sold in 5s. tubes. One is reminded of Frank Owen's remark in *The Ragged Trousered Philanthropists* that capitalists would bottle the very air and sell it if it were possible to do so.

7   A Best-selling Formula?

Until the 1870s there were a number of different musical forms which could be found in songs labelled as 'popular' or 'drawing-room ballads': Shield's 'The Wolf' is a through-composed aria; Moore's 'The Last Rose of Summer' is a strophic air; Bishop's 'Home, Sweet Home!' has verse and refrain; Horn's 'Cherry Ripe' is a roundelay (rondo); Russell's 'The Maniac' is like an entire operatic mad scene. Minstrel forms have been dealt with in Chapter 4, and sacred styles in Chapter 5. 'Respectable' music-hall ballads are considered in Chapter 9, and Tin Pan Alley (which develops its own distinctive style later) awaits discussion in Chapter 10.

Together with the variety of forms went a variety of subject matter. A great many songs concern themselves with character, predominantly that of the adult male. In the category of songs about working men are found musical portraits of blacksmiths, bell-ringers, watchmen, and bandits, but never factory workers. No bourgeois wished to be reminded of factory hands during a musical evening. Usually a character study formed the basis of an 'improving' ballad, a song which contained a moral lesson. Genteel love songs might be romantic serenades like Bishop's 'The Bloom Is on the Rye', jilt songs like Claribel's 'Won't You Tell Me Why, Robin?', or songs of separation and death like Ascher's 'Alice Where Art Thou?' Songs of social concern are dealt with in Chapter 9 and patriotic songs in the one before. Disaster songs given the *gran scena* treatment remained fitfully popular into the 1890s. When the marketing emphasis began to shift, in the late 1860s, from songs which were aimed at the performing forces available for domestic music-making to songs which were promoted by professional singers at fashionable concerts, duets and songs with a harmonized chorus steadily declined. Religious ballads moved away from biblical episodes in favour of visionary experiences. They took on a marked secular quality as their musical style became indistinguishable from the other ballads with which they vied for success in the ballad boom of the 1880s.

Before discussing the songwriters who dominated the ballad boom, it would be helpful to look at three songs which show the diversity of approach in the composition of elevated 'art-ballads' during the mid-century. Each song was enormously 'popular'; yet none of the composers looked upon their formal design as a formula for success. The main reason for this lies in the composer's attitude to the text: each song is a setting of a poem conceived with no musical treatment in mind. Once the professional lyric writer emerges, then it becomes easier to duplicate procedures and engineer effects. Claribel, writing her own verse, took advantage of this fact; and her commercial success pointed the way ahead for others to adopt the strategy in a more blatant manner.

'The Wreck of the Hesperus' is a setting by John Hatton, dating from 1853, of Longfellow's poem written after hearing news of the tragedy in 1839. Hatton has abbreviated the poem by omitting six of the original twenty-two four-line stanzas. The only other change has been to substitute 'Oh!' for 'Christ' in the final stanza so as not to offend propriety. Longfellow labels his poem a ballad, and in doing so harks back to Bishop Percy: the direct influence of 'Sir Patrick Spens' is present in some stanzas. Hatton cannot hope to do justice to the dramatic narrative, however, by writing a self-consciously ancient air. In unaccompanied song a singer can provide immense variety of pace and vocal tone; but no piano accompaniment can hope to compete with the flexible nuances of the human voice in sixteen stanzas of identical melody. Hatton, therefore, opts for the *gran scena* approach, responding to the text in a dramatic manner and making use of musical motives for unity.

Example 1

The extract on the previous page shows the use of piano chords to mimic the skipper's laughter, descending arpeggios for the rain, vigorous counterpoint for the schooner's shuddering, and a sudden loud chord to indicate the shock of its leaping. Other effects follow in plenty: imitation of the fog bell, dramatic pauses, a tense operatic *tremolando*, hymn-like chords as the maiden prays, rushing downward scales as the vessel sinks, *et al.* Some examples of the way Hatton organizes motivically are given below.

'The Village Blacksmith' (1854) is a setting by the singer Willoughby Weiss of another Longfellow poem. It is an example of the improving ballad: the blacksmith's personality and way of life are held up as a model to all. Weiss decides, however, that the explicit didacticism of the final stanza is unsuitable for musical treatment.

> Thanks, thanks to thee, my worthy friend,
> For the lesson thou has taught!
> Thus at the flaming forge of life
> Our fortunes must be wrought;
> Thus on its sounding anvil shaped
> Each burning deed and thought.

This leaves him with seven stanzas of six lines each. The six-line stanza does not lend itself so readily to music as the four-line stanza: a sixteen-bar melody in four-bar phrases is one thing, but six regular phrases per musical period is another and can come to sound monotonous. Weiss does not avoid this pitfall; his entire song is in four-bar phrases. On a broader level, his setting is given shape by the use of a refrain melody for the last four lines of stanzas 2, 4, and 7; stanza 7, in fact, repeats the whole melody of stanza 2. Elsewhere melodic and rhythmic reminiscences lend a feeling of unity.

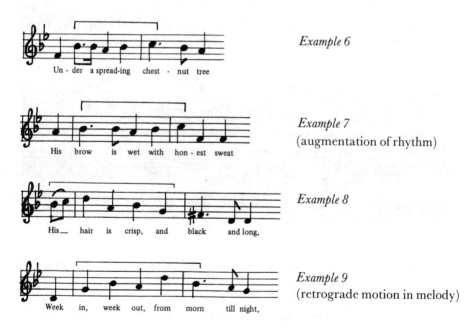

Example 6

Example 7
(augmentation of rhythm)

Example 8

Example 9
(retrograde motion in melody)

Concern for unity is not as pronounced as in Hatton's work; it is the narrative which mostly controls the musical form, prompting a variety of short-lived descriptive effects. Weiss even seeks to reinforce Longfellow's simile of the blacksmith's anvil and the sexton's bell by providing imitations of both in the accompaniment.

Example 10

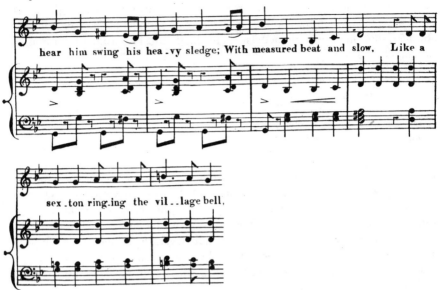

hear him swing his hea..vy sledge; With measured beat and slow,   Like a

sex..ton ring-ing the vil..lage bell,

In stanza 5, the form is dictated by the presence of the 'Old Hundredth' ('All People That on Earth Do Dwell') to accompany the scene in church.

Example 11

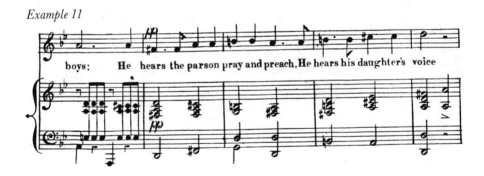

boys: He hears the parson pray and preach, He hears his daughter's voice

This drawing-room tribute to the poor but honest hard-working individual appeared in the same year that saw the defeat of the massive strike by textile workers in Preston. The song may have helped to reassert bourgeois values about the nobility and godliness of work after the recent onslaught from the forces of organized labour.

Balfe's 'Come into the Garden, Maud' (1857) is a setting of part of Tennyson's monodrama *Maud* (published in 1855). Even admirers of the poet were taken aback by his thinly veiled war-mongering in this work. Neither this aspect of *Maud*, nor any semblance of the morbid, unstable hero who delivers the verse is evident in Balfe's song. It was written for the renowned tenor Sims Reeves, who first performed it at a morning concert. Balfe's word-setting has been unjustly criticized.[1] In particular, his omission of the word 'Rose' in 'Queen Rose of the rosebud garden of girls' seems less like carelessness than a deliberate step taken to enable an abrupt modulation to achieve its maximum impact. In days when Tennyson's verse might first appear in a newspaper, Balfe's behaviour might not have seemed cavalier; in later years it seemed unforgivable. The example below shows a common Edwardian emendation: the word 'Queen' is placed on the upbeat whereas it had previously occurred simultaneously with the change of harmony at the beginning of the next bar.

Example 12

Balfe is accused of breaking the sense of two later lines.

Example 13

However, the disjointed melodic line is demanded by the singer's need to breathe. Balfe does his best to overcome the problem by breaking off on a suspension so that the dissonance propels the tune through the gap to resolve on the upbeat of the next phrase. Balfe, too, should be given credit for tackling verse which represented a continuation of the experiments in varying metrical structure which Tennyson had embarked on in *In Memoriam* (1850).

Balfe's musical structure is the old-fashioned roundelay. He was an ex-pupil of Charles Horn, and the structure of his teacher's most famous song ('Cherry Ripe') probably struck him as eminently suited to his purpose. The invitations to come into the garden are treated in the manner of a rondo theme so that the song falls into the pattern ABACA. Sections B and C are contrasted in key and melodic material. Balfe's masterstroke, the cause of his song's creating much present-day mirth, is his dramatic conclusion. The final A section is interrupted in mid-flow by a sudden diminished seventh chord and Maud's steps are heard accelerating towards the singer. Unfortunately, the contrast between the rapid 'oompahs' of the piano and the singer's reference to Maud's 'airy' tread requires earnest use of the imagination's powers of reconciliation.

Example 14

Balfe's heartbeats are more convincing; but the saving grace is the *allegro* coda which has the singer passionately holding longer notes against the 'come into the garden' theme in the piano part. It was a device not lost upon Joseph Ascher, who found an opportunity to do something similar in his setting of Wellington Guernsey's 'Alice, Where Art Thou?' in 1861.

When John Boosey took the decision to establish London Ballad Concerts at St James's Hall in 1867, the consequences for the drawing-room ballad were far reaching. The diversity of approach which has been seen in the ballads analysed above was to gradually give way to a more predictable format. Chappell's 'popular concerts' were a miscellaneous assortment of old and new music,[2] vocal and instrumental, but Boosey & Co. were determined to concentrate on the drawing-room ballad and, indeed, helped to define this genre in the shape of the songs they chose to promote in their concerts. From the 1870s onward a distinction needs to be made between the drawing-room ballad and other forms of bourgeois domestic song. The term now suggests a loftier, artier conception, as befitted its performance by internationally famous concert artists. This new meaning works to exclude songs of a more intimate manner and simpler form, the product of the blackface minstrels or the respectable music-hall entertainer. The ideology of progress in bourgeois concert music prohibited a return to the simple harmonies and textures of 'Home, Sweet Home!'

When Chappell & Co.'s fortunes began to wane, later in the century, they learnt from Boosey's success and started their own rival series of ballad concerts in 1894. But by then the most flourishing and innovative years for the drawing-room ballad were past. In the decade 1880–90 a large number of celebrated ballad singers were at the height of their powers; furthermore, these years saw the ballad apparently exhaust its formal possibilities. In the 1890s the ballad had become a standardized commodity: the industry wanted confirmation of taste, not change, and composers and lyricists tended only to look for new ways to tread familiar ground rather than to seek fresh pastures. With the arrival of the ballad concert, composers found their songs introduced in an overtly competitive manner, awaiting an instant verdict from the audience. If a song was well received, Boosey would lose no time in making this known, advertising its title on the back pages of the latest copies of sheet music. Composers were tempted to take stock of what was vigorously applauded by the middle-class audience at St James's Hall, and to try to recapture that admiration and its subsequent financial reward by writing something similar next time. The rest of this chapter will explore the output of the four enduringly popular ballad composers of the latter half of the nineteenth century, and the ways in which they attempted to reshape the elements of a successful ballad.

Sir Arthur Seymour Sullivan (1842–1900) was the son of the bandmaster at the Royal Military College, Sandhurst. As a boy he sang in the choir of the Chapel Royal; later, he studied at the Royal Academy of Music and Leipzig Conservatory. His first steady work was as a church organist in London, and he began to build a reputation in the concert hall as a composer. He supplemented his income by teaching and (later) conducting. Before Boosey & Co. began their ballad concerts, Sullivan had failed to see the potential financial returns from composing ballads: for example, he had sold his popular 'Orpheus with His Lute' to Metzler for £5 outright in 1866. On joining Boosey & Co., he arranged for publication on the basis of the royalty system. He also chose his dedicatees with care: a dedication to a famous singer, such as Mme Sainton-Dolby or Mr Sims Reeves, would enhance a song's chances considerably.

Sullivan was the most melodically imaginative and rhythmically varied of ballad composers; and he was one of the few to give a measure of independent character to his accompaniments. Yet, even in Sullivan's work, patterns of successful ballads are reused. One of his most well-known songs, 'Let Me Dream Again' (published by Boosey in 1875), follows the design of a ballad he had written five years earlier, 'Looking Back' (words by Louisa Gray). He had already tried setting a new text by Gray as a companion piece to the latter, called 'Looking Forward', in 1873. Now he chose to reuse its musical form: both songs are cast in slow triple time, verse sections are delivered in a minor key, while the refrain uses the tonic major. Use of the tonic major, rather than the conventional relative major, produces a tender and poignant effect, particularly when the tempo slows and the dynamic level falls. See examples 15 and 16.

Example 15

'Looking Back'

Example 16

'Let Me Dream Again'

After a few bars, the piano lends passionate support to the voice in octaves. The last phrase is broadened from an anticipated four bars to five and allows for flexibility on the singer's part. See examples 17 and 18.

Sullivan favours verse and refrain form in his songs of the 1870s, undoubtedly aware that the tuneful refrain of a song like 'Sweethearts' (published by Chappell in 1875) was a major factor in its success. However, when he came to compose his most famous ballad, 'The Lost Chord' (published by Boosey in 1877), he found the poem unsuitable for this treatment. Sullivan had an affinity for poetry by Adelaide Procter (1825–64); the year following her early death he composed a setting of 'Will He Come?', the last lines of which can be read as an obituary:

Example 17

'Looking Back'

Example 18

'Let Me Dream Again'

There was only a sound of weeping
From watchers around a bed,
But rest to the weary spirit,
Peace to the quiet dead!

His setting of this poem was in verse and refrain form, but it contained a harmonically adventurous and rhythmically agitated section preceding the final refrain. Sullivan may have recollected this when tackling 'The Lost Chord'. Legend has it that he was inspired to write it while watching at the bedside of his fatally ill brother.[3] By coincidence, the famous contralto Antoinette Sterling approached Sullivan with a request to set these verses. It received its first performance at a ballad concert, sung by Sterling, accompanied by Sullivan at the piano and Sydney Naylor at the organ. Its subsequent popularity was tremendous; in sheet-music sales it reached a figure of half a million before the end of the century. Yet an occasional contemporary had voiced doubts about its equalling the success of his earlier ballads; and Sullivan himself is said to have handed the manuscript to Sterling with the words 'It won't be a success, I'm afraid.'[4] Two years later, it was not only being sung all over Britain, but was also 'echoing in a thousand drawing rooms' in the United States, according to the *New York Herald*.[5]

'The Lost Chord' demands the space of a large drawing room for performance, even if the harmonium part is ignored. The widely spaced, sonorous chords at the *grandioso* climax will sound at their best on a grand piano; the harmonium player is instructed to pull out all the stops at this point, a sound which would drown out the cottage upright. Sullivan uses the harmonium to skilful dramatic effect: he blends it in with the piano in the introduction; he silences it for the first stanza, bringing it back to add colour to the words 'great Amen'; he gives it sole charge of the second stanza, playing light ethereal textures; then, after a few gentle bars of the third stanza, he silences it again ensuring maximum effect for its reappearance at the climax. The piano part shows equal imagination: the introduction and the interlude after the first stanza are written in the traditional contrapuntal texture of Anglican organ music; Sullivan thus avoids the predictability of giving dominance to the harmonium in these passages.

Example 19

(Introduction – piano part)

In the first stanza the piano gradually gathers rhythmic impetus ('my fingers wander'd idly'); sustained chords give way to a hymnlike accompaniment, the vocal melody being first reinforced in the middle of the texture and then rising to the top. In the third stanza the piano becomes increasingly agitated, tension being generated by insistently repeated notes. This whole stanza is really one long crescendo, in spite of containing the words 'trembled away into silence'. The effective use of the full sonorous range of the piano during the climax has already been noted. The crescendo may seem a cheap and obvious way of stimulating emotion, but the sustained use of the device, as seen in this ballad, was unparalleled in Sullivan's output and unknown in the ballads of his contemporaries (though not for long). The most banal effect in 'The Lost Chord' is the use of a traditional 'amen' decoration at the close of the introduction and in the song's final bars, although Frank Romer is happy to repeat this same musical cliché in his own later setting of the poem.

Striking use is made of harmony. There are some unusual pedal points set against passing chromatic chords, for example, the inner pedal at 'It quieted pain and sorrow'.

Example 20

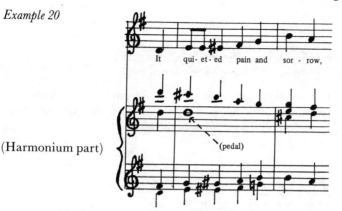

(Harmonium part)

There is a dramatic use of mixolydian modal harmony on the repeat of 'Like the sound of a great Amen'.

Example 21

There is an expressive use of the dominant minor ninth at 'I have sought but I seek it vainly.'

Example 22

The harmony contributes much of the emotional impact of the song and sometimes dictates an unusually chromatic melodic line: ten of the twelve possible notes of the chromatic scale are used at 'I know not what I was playing, Or what I was dreaming then', and they are difficult to pitch correctly without the help of the piano accompaniment.

Example 23

In the second part of the third stanza it is the voice part which dictates the chromatic harmony, the melody being designed around the idea of falling semitones. See Example 22 and its continuation below.

Example 24

Apart from the unusual degree of chromaticism which appears in the tune, its first few bars are equally unusual in being largely a monotone (again emphasizing the underlying harmony); they are suggestive of Anglican chant.

Example 25

These repeated notes find a subtle echo in the piano accompaniment at the beginning of the third stanza.

Example 26

It was probably the presence of these unconventional melodic features which made Sullivan doubtful about the ballad's success; they certainly question the idea of there being a successful formula.

The text of 'The Lost Chord' introduces a theme that lyric writers during the

Great Depression of the 1880s and early 90s were to return to frequently – the fleeting foretaste of something heavenly. In 'The Lost Chord' it is the sound of celestial harmony. In fairness, Procter only goes so far as to suggest that it *may* be a chord from heaven; later writers were prepared to assert the truthfulness of their visions more forcefully. The bourgeoisie were not interested in religious mysticism, however. The appeal of 'The Lost Chord' lies not in its depiction of a numinous experience, but in conveying a feeling of loss ('I have sought, but I seek it vainly') and an optimistic faith in death as the final comforter and the solver of all mysteries. In the later century a fondness for suggesting that problems of poverty, misery, and injustice could only be resolved in heaven took over from the earlier recommendations to trust in providence.

A sense of loss also pervades 'Sometimes', Sullivan's other ballad success of 1877. It was written for the tenor Edward Lloyd who had made 'Sweethearts' so popular. Here the elusive sound is the imagined voice of a lost loved one. Sullivan returns to verse and refrain form: the tune of the refrain, by now predictably, begins softly and gently and is then reinforced by passionate octaves on piano. He does, however, continue his harmonic adventurousness, making a distant modulation in the verse, and colourful use of chromatic harmony in the refrain. His sense of drama is still keen as he contrasts the tranquil evening with the heart leaping joyfully at the imagined sound of the 'well-known voice' in simple but evocative piano textures. Sullivan's dramatic skill was now at its peak: the following year saw the production of *HMS Pinafore*, the work which made Gilbert and Sullivan into an institution. As a result, Sullivan's ballad output dropped to less than half a dozen in the 1880s, although these included 'A Shadow' (published by Pater & Willis in 1886), a Procter setting of uncommon harmonic daring.

It is tempting to relate the taste for nostalgia in ballads of this period to the collapse of the great Victorian boom and the consequent feelings of insecurity among the bourgeoisie; but this is not the whole story, and nostalgia emerges as one of the dominant themes of the drawing-room ballad throughout the entire century. Songs about memories appeal more to the old than the young, and an explanation for their popularity may be found by examining the market. In contrast to the large teenage market targeted by the music industry of today, the nineteenth-century market was filled with older, wealthy, and status-conscious consumers (who could afford to buy sheet music). Songs sung by, for example, the young woman of a middle-class family would generally have been selected by her mother and paid for by her father; both her lack of economic independence and her parents' concern for decorum determined this state of affairs. Even songs composed by the young were likely to adopt a posture of reminiscing age: Cowen's 'It Was a Dream' sets a text referring to distant memories, yet was written at the tender age of twenty-one.

Sir Frederic Hymen Cowen (1852–1935) was born in Kingston, Jamaica, but left with his family for England at the age of four. He was a precocious child who, four years later, wrote an operetta to a libretto by his elder sister. His early career as a musician was organized by his father, private secretary to the Earl of Dudley. Cowen was involved in prestigious concerts at Dudley House as a young man.

After studying abroad, he began to make his reputation in London as a pianist and composer: he had both a symphony and a piano concerto performed when only seventeen, and his output during 1869–97 was prodigious (it included six symphonies, four operas, and four oratorios). In addition, he worked frequently as an accompanist for singers and in later years achieved celebrity as a conductor. From the foregoing, it is clear that ballad composition was not a central concern of Cowen's and, indeed, he felt embarrassed about his ballads in later life when their status as an art-form was in decline. It would be too facile to claim that this was a feeling of guilt for having wished to partake of the easy profits which flowed from successful ballads. The ballad was highly respected at the time: one of Sullivan's official appointments was as Professor of Ballad Singing at the Crystal Palace School of Art.

'It Was a Dream' (words by R. E. Francillon) was Cowen's first big seller. It was published in London in 1873 with no publisher's name given on the front page, but within two years it appeared under the imprint of Boosey & Co. Cowen went on to write most of his ballads for Boosey, so all ballads mentioned in the text below may be assumed to be published by Boosey unless specified otherwise. 'It Was a Dream' bears many Cowen fingerprints: it is in common time; the tempo is fairly slow; the refrain begins softly and ends loudly; the verse is in the minor, the refrain the tonic major; it makes use of pedal points and his favourite chromatic chords, the diminished seventh and augmented sixth; it features his favourite dominant extension, the dominant ninth; the rate of harmonic change is a basic two chords per bar; there are no 'literal' descriptive effects in the accompaniment; the latter has no real independence, being composed of chords given rhythmic impetus in a variety of simple ways such as by repeating, rocking, and spreading. Of course, many of these features are part of a common 'ballad language'; they may all, for instance, be found in Frederic Clay's 'She Wandered Down the Mountainside'. But the number of times all of these features reappear together in Cowen's ballads (and they usually include a prominent modulation to the mediant as well) does seem to indicate a feeling on his part that he needed to conform to certain procedures in order to ensure success in the rapidly expanding market.

His early ballads were performed by many of the singers associated with the name of Sullivan, and his most famous song, 'The Better Land' (words by Felicia Hemans), was composed for Antoinette Sterling some three years after she had first performed 'The Lost Chord'. The text is cast as a dialogue between mother and child and falls into three main sections. In the first two sections, the young boy demands to know the whereabouts of the radiant shore of the 'better land', a place of great beauty which he imagines to be full of such precious consumer durables as rubies, diamonds, and pearls. In the third section the mother makes it clear that the 'better land' is fairer than can be envisaged; it is a joyful, timeless world existing beyond the clouds. The song is not without drama or subtlety: in the first two sections the high-pitched accompaniment to the child's questioning is effectively contrasted with the mother's brief replies accompanied by low-pitched chords and a change of metre (see Example 27); in the third section there is an imaginative reworking of the opening of previous sections to accompany the mother's description of the 'better land' in a new metre and with low, steady harmonies (see Examples 28 and 29). The excited, questioning child and the calm, reassuring mother are therefore nicely characterized throughout.

Example 27

Example 28

Example 29

At the same time, the song is full of typical Cowen features, particularly the way the final section moves from a calm opening to a throbbing close (see Examples 29 and 30).

Example 30

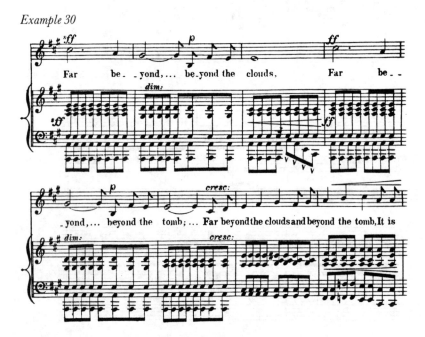

The same procedure may be seen in two of his other ballad successes of the 1880s which also fall into three sections, 'The Children's Home' (words by F. E. Weatherly, published by W. Morley & Co., London) and 'In the Chimney Corner' (words also by Weatherly). In 'The Children's Home', the addition of a harmonium increases the emotional thrill of the conclusion, playing *grand jeu* (all stops out) as in 'The Lost Chord' (see Examples 31 and 32).

Example 31 (Piano)

Example 32 (Harmonium)

In his later ballads Cowen writes mainly in verse and refrain form, placing the weight of melodic attractiveness on the refrain: he even manages to shape part of section XI of Longfellow's *The Song of Hiawatha* as verse and refrain (with some modification to the music of the second verse) in 'Onaway, Awake, Beloved' (Metzler & Co., London, 1892). Cowen remained fond of religious themes; his biggest success of the 1890s was with 'The Promise of Life' (words by Clifton Bingham). Boosey had by then expanded their business sufficiently to be able to publish it simultaneously in London and New York in 1893.

Making his reputation slightly earlier than Cowen, but exclusively in the world of ballads, was James Lynam Molloy (1837–1909). He was born at Cornalaur in Kings County, Ireland, the son of a doctor. His education took place at St Edmund's College, Ware, and at the Catholic University, Dublin. Although he graduated with an MA in 1858, degrees from the Catholic University were not legally recognized, so further study abroad was required before he was called to the English bar in 1863. He rose high in the legal profession, becoming, for a time, secretary to Sir John Holker, the attorney-general.

Molloy introduced his new songs almost exclusively at Boosey's ballad concerts where they were promoted by the same singers who performed the ballads of Sullivan and Cowen. Any publisher of a Molloy song other than Boosey will be separately attributed in the text below. After a string of ballad successes in the 1870s and 80s, he seems to have decided that to continue this activity would be inappropriate on his appointment in 1889 as private chamberlain to Pope Leo XIII.

Molloy's Irish background influenced his output both in obvious ways, such as his collection *The Songs of Ireland* (an edition mainly consisting of revamped Moore songs, published in 1873), and in the Irish character which more generally pervades his own compositions. In an early song, 'Thady O'Flinn', he set words by W. S. Gilbert in imitation of the melodic and rhythmic manner of an Irish jig.

Example 33

In the late 1860s this vigorous music, joined to humorous verse, might have been thought to herald a Samuel Lover revival. However, melancholia was restored with 'The Old Cottage Clock' (words by Charles Swain), which reflected on the transience of human affairs and adopted a high moral tone. An Irishness still filters through this piece: it is present in the pentatonic shape of the lower notes of the tune and its overall compass (reminiscent of a traditional air like 'Sly Patrick'); it also shows in the occasional use of non-functional progressions (tonic to submediant and back) and the drone effect in the bass. The rhythm may even be considered a slowed-down jig.

Example 34

A conflict is apparent in bars 7 and 11 of Example 34 between Molloy's adoption of an 'Irish' style of melody and his desire to accommodate it to classical

European harmony. The weakness of the song lies in its simple verse and refrain form which is forced to convey both a bright opening mood and a tearful conclusion. It is a defect which occurs frequently in Molloy's work. Often it is overcome by beginning the third verse in the tonic minor, as in 'Two Little Lives' of 1878 (words by F. E. Weatherly, based on Hans Anderson) and 'Mistress Prue' of 1880 (words also by Weatherly). If the song is written in the minor to begin with (fairly common with Molloy) then a Schubertian change to tonic major is called for, as in 'The Vagabond' of 1871 (words by C. L. Kenney) and 'London Bridge' of 1879 (words by Weatherly).

Molloy's Roman Catholic faith meant that religious subject matter was a delicate area; so he tended to stick to chaste love songs, improving ballads, and nostalgic memories of Irish peasants dancing in their clogs. It is small wonder Molloy should be dewy-eyed about a mythical Ireland of yore: in the 1860s the agitation of revolutionary Fenians was inspiring hate and fear in the British ruling class; and in the 1870s Ireland was in the grip of an economic crisis. Molloy's feelings of solidarity are with his bourgeois consumers who during this period were anxiously striving to forget the 'Irish question'. The only original music he had written for his collection *The Songs of Ireland* was set to Moore's words, 'Come, take thy harp, nor let us muse upon the gath'ring ills we see.' When Roman Catholicism makes a conspicuous appearance in his work, it is in a ballad which fits straight into the comic tradition of overweight monks, called 'Thursday' (words by Weatherly). Although originally published as 'Thursday' in 1884, it was retitled 'Tomorrow Will Be Friday' when its catchphrase 'Tomorrow will be Friday, but we've caught no fish today' became enormously popular.

Molloy is best known today for 'Love's Old Sweet Song', published in 1884 (words by G. C. Bingham). It is not a typical Molloy product, except in its simple verse and refrain form and the pentatonic inflexion of the melody at the beginning of the refrain. The change of metre between verse and refrain is unusual for Molloy but is suggested by the metrical structure of Bingham's poem. The words seem as if they were written in order to provide Joan with another song to sing to Darby. Not surprisingly then, Antoinette Sterling, who had introduced Molloy's 'Darby and Joan' to the audience at St James's Hall, also gave the first performance there of 'Love's Old Sweet Song'. 'Darby and Joan', written in 1878, was perhaps the most popular of the two in the nineteenth century, though the direct sentiment of Weatherly's verse did not survive long in the twentieth.

> Darby, dear, but my heart was wild
> When we buried our baby child,
> Until you whisper'd: 'Heav'n knows best!' and my heart found rest;
> Darby, dear, 'twas your loving hand,
> Show'd the way to the better land –
> Ah! lad, as you kiss'd each tear,
> Life grew better and Heav'n more near:
> (REFRAIN)   Always the same, Darby, my own,
> Always the same to your old wife, Joan,
> Always the same to your old wife, Joan.   (Verse 2)

The use of long verse followed by short refrain was also soon to sound an old-fashioned feature compared to the full-blown, semi-autonomous refrains which took over in the 1880s. 'Love's Old Sweet Song' is in the new style, with a large, melodically independent refrain which is eagerly awaited during the less tuneful verse. Another feature of Darby and Joan which was to become old-fashioned was the use of 6/8 metre; 3/4 and 4/4 became the norm in the 1890s. The 6/8 metre and regular two- or four-bar phrasing gives 'Darby and Joan' a lilting dancelike quality typical of many of Molloy's songs. His harmonies are simpler than those of Sullivan and Cowen, and so too are his modulations; he mostly favours the conventional shift to the dominant.

Example 35

Ironically, with the passage of time, this is one feature which gives his melodies a less easily dated period flavour than the frequent modulations to the mediant in Cowen. What does give Molloy's ballads their drawing-room character is the harmony, particularly his sentimental use of the subdominant minor or supertonic seventh with diminished fifth (see the chord marked * in Example 35). This character is also evident in the conflict, remarked upon earlier, between refined classical progressions and 'rustic' melodic modality (a tension which may be traced back to Haydn's and Beethoven's settings of traditional airs). Harmonically, Molloy shows no advance on Claribel, who was the composer he overtook to occupy the largest space in Boosey's lists of new songs in the 1870s. On a rare occasion a modal melodic shape inspires him to find an unexpected series of chords: Example 36 shows the aeolian close to the refrain in 'The Clang of the Wooden Shoon' (published by Metzler & Co. in 1875).

Example 36

In 'Darby and Joan' there is only the familiar pentatonic influence, heard in the last three and a half bars of the refrain.

Example 37

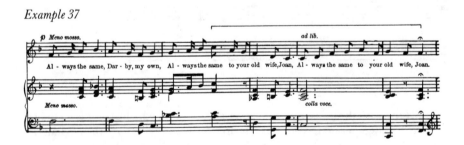

Unusually, Molloy slightly varies the accompaniment pattern in both verses 2 and 3 (the same pattern commonly suffices for the first two verses). The harmonies, however, remain exactly the same.

Like Sullivan and Cowen, Molloy was tempted to repeat a pattern which had proved successful. This can be clearly seen in 'The Kerry Dance' of 1879 which is largely a reworking of the design of 'The Clang of the Wooden Shoon'. Molloy wrote the words to these songs himself. They each consist of memories of lads and lassies dancing happily in bygone days; furthermore, they each conclude with a ghostly vision of past companions still dancing away. 'The Clang of the Wooden

Shoon' contains three stanzas sung to the same tune, the last being preceded by a short stanza sung to fresh music. The tune of the main stanzas is cast in ternary form: the outer sections are in a minor key; the middle is in the relative major (a conventional procedure for a minor key). The music which accompanies the short stanza describing the lonely present is at a slower speed and brings a change from minor to tonic major. The final stanza is introduced softly and delicately back in the minor with a new accompaniment pattern. 'The Kerry Dance' contains three stanzas sung to the same tune, the last being preceded by a short stanza sung to fresh music. The tune of the main stanzas is cast in ternary form: the outer sections are in a major key; the middle is in the dominant (a conventional procedure for a major key). The music which accompanies the short stanza describing the lonely present is at a slower speed and brings a change from major to tonic minor. The final stanza is introduced softly and delicately back in the major with a new accompaniment pattern. The resemblances do not end here: they are both in compound duple time; they both make use of fifths in the bass to suggest a piper's drone; the rhythmic setting of the words is also similar, and not just in much of the main stanzas of each song but in the short stanzas as well.

In the late 1870s, Sullivan, Molloy, and Cowen held pride of place on the back covers of Boosey's sheet music. In the 80s they found a rival in Stephen Adams (1844–1913) who, by the end of that decade, established himself as Boosey's most popular composer. One reason for this was simply that, unlike the other three, he wrote mainly for the male voice and therefore filled a gap in the market. As noted in the previous chapter, the male voice gradually rose in status during the nineteenth century, and by the 1880s there was an abundance of concert tenors and baritones ready to promote ballads. Like Molloy, Adams' reputation rested on ballads alone. He was a celebrated singer in his own right, touring as a baritone under his real name of Michael Maybrick and appearing in all the leading London and provincial concerts. He was born in Liverpool, and, having shown great musical promise as a youngster (he became an organist of St Peter's at fourteen), he followed the usual route abroad, studying at Milan and Leipzig. In later life he established himself as a respectable member of the Isle of Wight community: he became Chairman of the Isle of Wight County Hospital, a member of the Royal Yacht Club (he was probably the only famous composer of sailors' songs who could actually sail himself), and he was elected five times as Mayor of Ryde.

Stephen Adams' first really successful ballad was introduced by himself (as Maybrick) at a Stratford Bow subscription concert in 1876. Notwithstanding a text by the ubiquitous Weatherly, it had been rejected by Adams' publisher, Chappell. Along with others, Boosey & Co. had also rejected it, so Adams introduced the song from manuscript. Its title was 'Nancy Lee' and its audience reception persuaded Boosey to rush it into his catalogue. From now on Adams wrote exclusively for Boosey, introducing most of his subsequent ballads (and several of Molloy's) in his own rich baritone voice from the stage of St James's Hall. It is perhaps an indication of how far Boosey's ballad concerts had begun to limit perspectives on what constituted a successful song that no publisher was willing to risk putting into print a ballad which looked like a throwback to

Dibdin's 'jolly Jack Tar' songs. It is bracing and vigorous throughout, full of cries of 'Yeo ho!' from Jack (was there a possibility that these might be thought to ring out in rather too vulgar a manner in the drawing room?) and, what is more, his Nancy remains healthy throughout, surviving the generally fatal third verse. Probably nothing seemed more out of fashion in the mid-70s than this kind of ebullient sailor song.[6] *HMS Pinafore* had not yet arrived; in fact, Sullivan had seemed to sound the death knell for sailors' songs in 1872 with his solemn 'The Sailor's Grave' (words by H. F. Lyte, published by Cramer). It now appeared as if Adams was destined to become another Dibdin. His next nautical success, 'The Midshipmite' (1879), a setting of a Weatherly poem calculated to revive memories of Lord Raglan's body being returned home after the Crimean War, was one Charles Dibdin would have been proud of. In 'The Tar's Farewell' (words by F. C. Burnard) Adams tries to repeat the dramatic turn into triple time which had lent an added attraction to the refrain of 'The Midshipmite' (see Examples 38 and 39).

Example 38

'The Midshipmite'

Example 39

'The Tar's Farewell'

Unfortunately in 'The Tar's Farewell' the triple-time section overpowers the song, leaving the impression that Adams really wished to write a waltz. It did seem a possibility that he might turn to composing waltz songs at this time, as 'The Blue Alsatian Mountains' (words by Claribel) and 'Good Company' (words by Dr C. Mackay) demonstrate.

In 'The Little Hero' (words by Arthur Matthison) of 1881, Adams' customary strophic treatment undergoes modification: the song contains a passage which shows one of his later favourite dramatic devices in embryonic form, a quiet atmospheric section of fragmented melody and recitativelike accompaniment at the start of the third verse. The music in this particular case is a slowed-down variation of the expected verse tune, but the potential was obvious: here was a place where elements of the *gran scena* might be employed.

Example 40

In Example 40 there is a hymnlike motion to the accompanying chords, an octave sounded in the depths of the piano to emphasize the word 'low', a trumpet effect in bar 8, a chant-like monotone and a plagal cadence to underline the conclusion of the Lord's Prayer; the rest of the ballad contains very little in the way of musical effects like these. Adams had similar problems to Molloy when writing music for a narrative poem, difficulties which he had encountered as early as 1871 when the hero of 'A Warrior Bold' (words by E. Thomas, published by Chappell & Co.) was forced to meet his gory death to the same jolly tune as for verse 1. 'The Viking's Song' (words by his publisher's son, William Boosey) written in the same year as 'The Little Hero' also shows formal experimentation; but its wealth of themes, variety of accompaniment textures, and sudden piano outbursts create a mood of incoherent bluster which is reinforced by the lack of an organized narrative. Nevertheless the song shows Adams' growing command of the sonorous possibilities of the late nineteenth-century piano.

Adams began to incorporate quasi-operatic sections effectively into his ballads when he moved away from nautical subjects to elevated religious themes where the addition of dramatic musical devices was a much more novel proposition. Though it may be argued that Handel never stinted at using operatic techniques in his oratorios, there was an overt theatricality about Adams' religious ballads which caused Maurice Disher to remark later that they 'tremble on the brink of blasphemy'.[7] His first attempt to provide a rival to 'The Lost Chord' and 'The Better Land' was 'The Star of Bethlehem' (words by Weatherly). It was written for the tenor Edward Lloyd in 1887 and, like 'The Lost Chord', included a harmonium in its accompaniment. It was not in verse and refrain form, although a lyrical melody which appears at the end of each stanza has a function similar to a refrain. The opening bars of the first two stanzas are treated in a recitativelike fashion but with steady rhythm. The singer is asked to deliver these passages *quasi parlando* (as if speaking).

Example 41

Surging arpeggios soon follow.

Example 42

A crescendo then leads to the aforementioned lyrical theme, marked *cantabile* (singing).

Example 43

Adams spends more time on the first six lines of Weatherly's final stanza than he had previously spent on all eight lines. He lengthens the singer's note values, providing new melodic material against an increasingly agitated piano accompaniment. Before the climactic return of the quasi-refrain theme, impetus is provided by throbbing triplets and shifting chromatic harmonies as the singer ecstatically contemplates the movements of the star.

Example 44

The effect is more erotic than religious, the rolling back of the heavenly gates positively orgasmic! A sublimation, perhaps, of sex into religion.

From a comparison of the analysis above with the one to follow, it will be seen that 'The Star of Bethlehem' is Adams' prototype for his famous song of 1892, 'The Holy City'. The pattern of the first two stanzas is similar: a narrative beginning excitedly in short note values;

Example 45

a gathering of tension as the accompanying chords break into arpeggios;

Example 46

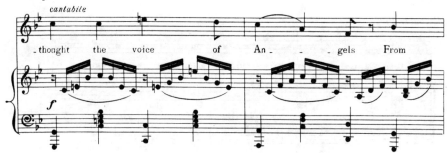

and then an appealing and memorable melody to follow.

Example 47

Weatherly this time provides a longer third stanza specifically to suit Adams' purpose; but, even so, Adams decides he needs still more space and repeats a line. The section begins with a dramatic key change, emphasizing that 'the scene was chang'd'.

Example 48

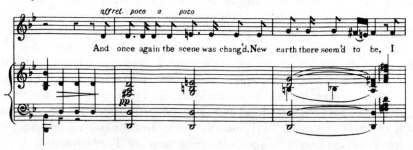

A further dramatic shift of harmony occurs at the mention of the holy gates.

Example 49

Adams' harmony was 'advancing' over the years: he makes plentiful use of dominant extensions in this ballad and uses the chord of the augmented sixth in a major rather the conventional minor context. Having followed the plan of 'The Star of Bethlehem' to the point reached in Example 49, Adams now faces a problem. How is he to increase the tension and drive the song towards the final cries of 'Jerusalem!' without resorting to triplets and thereby spoiling the impact of the triplets which accompany those cries? His only solution is to pile on more and more surging arpeggios, trusting in the excitement of passing modulations and rising motion to propel the music forward. Adams still has one novelty in store, however: the final climax of the refrain comes on an unusual dissonance created by a suspension instead of on a predictable dominant seventh.

The texts of 'The Holy City' and 'The Star of Bethlehem' show great similarity in their joint concern with the magical transformations occurring in a visionary dream which allows the sleeper the privilege of a trip 'beyond the starry skies'. Each song stresses the egalitarian nature of heaven: in 'The Star of Bethlehem' homeless wanderers 'see a home at last' and 'The Holy City' carries an assurance that 'all who would might enter'. Although 'The Holy City' is a clear case of the duplication of a formula, it provided Edward Lloyd with his most successful song. In 1899 he told the *Musical Times*, 'In Montreal I was engaged to sing four times in one month at a fee of 250 guineas each concert, *on condition* that I sang "The Holy City" on each occasion.'[8] The average annual sales of 50,000 copies must have also pleased Adams and Weatherly. It is understandable that, after a few years, they should want to try out the same formula again.

'The Light of the World' was written for Lloyd in 1896.[9] The tempo marking is now *Andante Religioso* rather than *Andante Moderato*, and the refrain bears the instruction 'With fervour.' Some modification of the formula has taken place: it is verse 2 which is lengthened and contains the atmospheric effects. The song is a curious mixture of the stale and the new. Adams continues to develop his harmony, making use of the dominant seventh with augmented fifth (a chord of which he became increasingly fond in later songs); yet he returns to his earlier penchant for mediant modulations at the fourth line of verse. After producing an 'entirely new edition' in 1898, it still remained a short-breathed and patchy work which could not be saved by Weatherly's new dream narrative or a refrain constructed on the lines of the passionate imperatives of 'The Holy City'.

No 1 in E FLAT   No 2 in F   No 3 in G   No 4 in A FLAT

Sung by MR EDWARD LLOYD.

THE

STAR OF BETHLEHEM

SONG

The Words by

F. E. WEATHERLY

The Music by

STEPHEN ADAMS.

PRICE 2/ NET

ORGAN OR HARMONIUM ACCOMPANIMENT (AD LIB) PRICE 3⁄

"THE STAR OF BETHLEHEM" ARRANGED FOR THE PIANOFORTE BY BOYTON SMYTH. 2/ NET
ALSO AS A VIOLIN SOLO WITH PIANOFORTE ACCOMPANIMENT BY WILLIAM HENLEY. 2/ NET
THE STAR OF BETHLEHEM ARRANGED FOR VIOLIN AND PIANO BY W.HENLEY. 2/ NET
ORCHESTRAL ACCOMPANIMENTS (IN THE KEY OF F) CAN BE HAD. 4/ NET

BOOSEY & C⁰
295, REGENT STREET, LONDON. W.
AND
9, EAST SEVENTEENTH STREET, NEW YORK

THIS SONG MAY BE SUNG IN PUBLIC WITHOUT FEE OR LICENSE

No 1 IN A♭   No 2 IN B♭   No 3 IN C   No 4 IN D♭

SUNG BY
MR. EDWARD LLOYD.

THE HOLY CITY

SONG

THE WORDS BY

F. E. WEATHERLY

THE MUSIC COMPOSED AND DEDICATED TO

Mrs Philip H. Waterlow

by

STEPHEN ADAMS.

PRICE 2/ NET

A SPECIAL EDITION OF THIS SONG IS PUBLISHED IN B♭ WITH GERMAN WORDS

ORGAN OR HARMONIUM ACCOMPANIMENT (AD LIB) PRICE 3⁄
CHORUS PARTS (IN C ONLY) PRICE 3⁄ OR IN TONIC SOLFA. PRICE 3⁄
AN ORCHESTRAL ACCOMPANIMENT IS PUBLISHED IN B♭

TRANSCRIPTION FOR THE PIANOFORTE BY CHARLES GODFREY. JUNR PRICE 2/ NET
TRANSCRIPTION FOR THE ORGAN ...... BY MYLES B. FOSTER ...... PRICE 2/ NET
THE HOLY CITY ARRANGED FOR VIOLIN AND PIANO BY W.HENLEY ...... PRICE 2/ NET

BOOSEY & C⁰
295, REGENT STREET, LONDON. W.
AND
9, EAST SEVENTEENTH STREET. NEW YORK.

THIS SONG MAY BE SUNG IN PUBLIC WITHOUT FEE OR LICENSE.
THE PUBLIC PERFORMANCE OF ANY PARODIED VERSION HOWEVER IS STRICTLY PROHIBITED.

COPYRIGHT 1892 BY BOOSEY & C⁰ LONDON ENG

Example 50

Adams and Weatherly were not, of course, collaborating only on religious ballads in the 1880s and 90s; they were also having some success with love songs. The first to gain popularity was 'The Romany Lass' of 1883: a familiar tale of a poor girl who stubbornly tries to improve her economic status, and who pays the price for failing to recognize that her bright eyes are worth more than gems. A later favourite was 'Mona' (1888), sung by a lover who has been exiled for an unspecified disgrace, a theme returned to in 'Thora' (1905). Perhaps the most imaginative is 'Nirvana' (1900), though it lacks the melodic appeal of 'Thora'. This largely results from Adams' experimental treatment of the third stanza. It begins in his usual recitative manner, with striking diminished sevenths whose disintegrating effect on the tonality parallels the decay of the lotus flower.

Example 51

It proceeds, again in his usual manner, to become increasingly animated, but then thwarts expectations by neatly dovetailing into an elongated and varied return of the thematic material which concluded the earlier stanzas. Buddhism is only present in the song as an exotic element, helped along by token *chinoiserie* in the piano part. See example 52. The concept of Nirvana attracts nothing but patronizing scorn in an age of imperialist expansion: verse 2, for example, ends 'I only know Nirvana / Within thy loving arms.' Weatherly clearly sees the Buddha as the 'Bloomin' idol made o' mud' described by Kipling's soldier in 'On the Road to Mandalay'.

To conclude the chapter, some biographical details are necessary to flesh out the character of Frederic Edward Weatherly (1848–1929). He was, himself, frequently peeved to find that the composers who set his verse received the whole

Example 52

credit for the song, even though the concern for words of a singer like Sterling was notorious (she refused to sing any song whose words she found unconvincing). Weatherly was born in Portishead, Somersetshire, and educated at Brasenose College, Oxford. He was called to the bar in 1887 when he was already well known as a songwriter and had published two books on logic. He wrote English versions of Italian opera that are still used today: 'On with the Motley' is Weatherly (from his translation of Leoncavallo's *I Pagliacci*). The idea that Weatherly revamped formulas, as in the religious ballads or in 'Mona' and 'Thora', in order cynically to manipulate the market is contradicted sharply by Eric Coates' memories of him reading aloud to friends: 'If the words were particularly moving he would frequently break down with emotion and have to wait until he could compose himself sufficiently to continue.'[10] Weatherly needed to feel sympathy with the subject matter of a song. Once the forces of labour began to organize, he could no longer create characters like the lad in 'The First Letter' (music by Molloy) who knows he is hard, rough, and lowly, but is proud to own a true heart. Writing in 1910, Weatherly states, 'the poor have become so haughty they are no longer sympathetic subjects for songs'.[11] His solution was to turn in the direction of 'rustic songs' and 'the old English folk-song'.[12] His most famous effort in the new direction was 'Danny Boy' (1913). Weatherly was not untypical in suddenly discovering the merit of 'rustic songs'; Clara Butt, who inherited all Antoinette Sterling's ballad classics, had taken to singing 'The Keys of Heaven'.

The temptation to interpret the design of a successful song as the magical embodiment of a best-selling formula was not confined to the mighty amongst ballad composers. Piccolomini favoured narratives on a religious theme which included a refrain requesting divine intervention, set to an accompaniment of pulsating quavers or triplets. 'Ora Pro Nobis' of 1889 obviously builds upon the design of 'The Toilers' of the previous year. John Behrend's 'Daddy' is a transparent attempt to duplicate the success of 'Auntie'. Paolo Tosti, settling in Britain in 1880 and appointed singing teacher to the royal family, produced in 'Goodbye!' (1881) a model for impassioned songs of separation ('For Ever and For Ever!', 'Parted', 'Never!').

Composers did not merely try to repeat their own successes; they were quite ready to try to repeat each other's as well. Trotère's 'The Deathless Army' is a flattering tribute to Barri's 'The Old Brigade'. Jude's 'The Skipper' shows his immense admiration for Adams's 'Nancy Lee'. Other composers tried setting the same poem as that of a well-known ballad; but this seldom met with much success and seemed to endorse the notion that the secret of a song's appeal lay in the musical form at least as much as the text.

Publishers were eagerly on the look out for composers who might have lit upon a formula for commercial success. J. H. Larway signed up Hamilton Gray (real name William Jones) on an exclusive contract as a result of his talent for imitating Adams in 'Holy City' vein in ballads like 'The Heavenly Song' and 'A Dream of Paradise'. John Blockley thought to save his ailing firm by paying an unprecedented sum when he handed over £1212. 15*s*. for the copyright of Michael Watson's 'Anchored'.[13] Everything seemed propitious about this ballad: it was in an elevated style containing elements of *gran scena* as the happy sailor lad's boat is wrecked amidst thunder and lightning, and as his soul rises to heaven while the stars twinkle sympathetically in triplets. It had a tuneful refrain and a text by Samuel Cowen which played on a favourite ambiguity: the sailor thinks he is going home to his father, and indeed he is, but not the home or father he has in mind. Watson had a good ballad pedigree which included previously admired work on nautical themes, such as 'Afloat'. To add to the good omens, he had recently died. It seemed that the ballad could not fail; yet it was only a modest success, and by 1897 Blockley's catalogue had been acquired by Ascherberg, Hopwood & Crew. It seemed that the secret of the successful song formula was to remain elusive.

8   Nationalism and Imperialism

For the larger part of the nineteenth century, a much narrower meaning was generally implied by describing an English song as a 'national song' than might be presumed from an acquaintance with Boosey's *National Song Book* of 1906. Although the title 'national songs' or 'national airs' was commonly given to a collection containing a varied selection of songs of a single country (for example, Moore's Irish *National Airs* of 1818–28), when applied to English songs, the description 'national' tended to signify songs of patriotic sentiment rather than songs sharing the same ethnic quality. The notion of there being an Englishness in the musical character of a song which could be labelled 'national' did not gain wide currency until the 1890s. The English 'national song' and the search for an English national musical identity in song must be seen in the context of British imperialism.

If imperialism were to be defined solely as the formal annexation of territory, there would be an argument for regarding 1815–70 as an anti-imperialist era. Annexation did not altogether cease (the Falkland Islands, for example, were annexed in 1833), but mercantilism and colonialism were being challenged and forced to give way to *laissez-faire* and free trade. Lenin, however, who defined imperialism as a particular stage in the development of capitalism, argued that the enthusiasm for liberating the colonies (shown by some bourgeois politicians) sprang from thriving capitalist competition; but, as capitalism passed into the monopoly stage – as other countries industrialized, as companies became larger, and as the big banks increased their control as agents of finance capital – there came about an 'intensification of the struggle for the partitioning of the world'.[1] Fear of losing markets was a stimulus to the 'conscious imperialism'[2] or 'new imperialism' which was being articulated in the 1880s. Behind the 'scramble for Africa' lay a European economic crisis, though Conservative politicians talked of a 'civilizing mission' and 'imperial responsibility',[3] and criticized Gladstone for not upholding British interests abroad (the death of General Gordon was constantly flung at him). With an air of inevitability, the Liberal Party itself witnessed its imperialist wing rapidly growing in strength during the later years of the century.

It is noticeable that songs written in the period of 'new imperialism' lay greater stress on Britain and things British than had been the norm earlier in the century, when a title like 'Britain's Glory', which was given to a 'National Song' of 1845, was unusual. In later years, however, there appeared such songs as 'The Glory of Britain' (1876), 'Britain's Flag' (1888), and 'Britannia's Sons' (1893). These were followed by many others after the turn of the century which demonstrated an increasing fondness for waving the British flag and invoking Britannia. After the Napoleonic Wars and before the 1890s, patriotic songs were almost entirely concerned with England: examples are 'England, Europe's Glory' (*c.* 1859), 'England's Strength' (1860), 'England's Greatness Still Endures' (1864), and 'England's Heroes' (1880). All of these songs could have used 'Britain' in their titles with little change of meaning; England *was* Britain at this time. In the 1890s and later, however, the word 'England' tended to be preferred as part of a personal emotional appeal: this is epitomized by W. E. Henley's poem 'England, My England', which was set to music often in the early twentieth century. As part of a broad patriotic appeal, the word 'British' was better suited to the age of 'new imperialism' since it acted as a claim upon the loyalty of the Empire's subjects in its suggestion of a homogeneous British imperial unity.

The crown of the United Kingdom became the symbol of imperial unity, particularly during and after the Jubilee of 1887 (though the idea may be traced to Disraeli and the conferring of the title 'Empress of India' upon Victoria in 1876). E. P. Thompson sees the Golden Jubilee as the inauguration of a 'modern' concept of royalty as a distracting pageant (1887 was a year of depression), with the monarchy as a focal point for orthodox herding instincts, jingoism, circuses, 'respectability', and guff.[4] Even a music-hall publisher, Francis Bros. & Day, turned out a 'Song of Jubilee'. It was a sign of things to come; by 1900 another music-hall publisher, Hopwood & Crew, was offering a whole *Navy and Army Patriotic Album*. Songs in praise of Victoria were nothing new to the drawing-room ballad market, of course; and the idea of Victoria as Empress had been foreshadowed in song almost twenty years before she received that title – following the suppression of the Indian Mutiny in 1857, a 'new national anthem' was written by Edward Clare, entitled 'Victoria! Empress of the East'. In fact, there is much in the songs written at the time of Crimea and the Indian Mutiny to add weight to Gallagher and Robinson's 'continuity thesis',[5] which holds that there was no aversion to empire building during this period, but that it lacked the strategic planning which came in the depression-dogged years of 1873–96.[6] Gallagher and Robinson coined the phrase 'imperialism of free trade' and suggested that there was an 'informal empire' of places not formally ruled by Britain, yet dominated by Britain in some way. Colonial 'responsible governments', for example, may have enjoyed local autonomy but were still economically dependent on Britain; it was an idea hatched after the Canadian rebellions which successfully served to forestall a repetition of the American Revolution. If necessary, force was always ready to be used to protect the interests of free trade.

There were contradictions in the way formal and informal control was exercised: while internal self-government was being introduced in British North America in 1846, India was still being developed in a mercantilist way; only after the Mutiny did the British government rely on class collaboration from princes and magnates (the 'natural leaders' of the people) to ensure control. Gilbert and Sullivan's operetta *Utopia Limited* (1893) could be seen as a comic fantasy on the free trader's faded dream of informal control of a country by market forces; in this work, Utopia becomes the first country to be floated as a limited company. Before the dawn of the 'new imperialism', many songs shared the perspective of the free trader. Here is verse 3 of 'The Men of Merry England' (1858), a song written and composed by J. B. Geoghegan, published in an arrangement by J. Blockley. The occasionally eccentric punctuation of the original has been maintained.

> Oh! the men of merry, merry England,
> Where'er Jove's thunders are hurled;
> Bright monuments rise, of their enterprise,
> And their commerce gives wealth to the world.
> Still, may it increase, whilst the fair hands of peace
> Shed plenty and blessings so free,
> Should war call again, our rights we'll maintain,
> Then gaily my burthen shall be.
>
> The men of merry, merry England, etc.

Sympathy can also be found for the pacifist wing of the Manchester School, led by Richard Cobden, which opposed the use of power in foreign policy. Here is the first verse of Henry Frank Lott's 'Song for the Peace Movement' (1849).

> God knows with what a trumpet tongue we've boasted of our wars,
> And set our Soldier-idols up and lauded gallant Tars,
> And blown a loud defiant blast across each purple sea
> But men of Peace have risen, and said, 'This shall no longer be,'
> For that fierce Lion carnage-clawed we'll from our flag remove,
> And straight inscribe with olive branch a gentle milk-white Dove.

There is a clear distinction between the demand that the British flag be respected, which is voiced in a great number of songs during the period of 'imperialism of free trade', and the transparent aggression and covetousness found in eighteenth-century songs espousing the mercantilist cause, or late nineteenth- and early twentieth-century songs committed to the 'new imperialism'. Arthur Benson's well-known words, fitted to Elgar's music, in the refrain of 'Land of Hope and Glory' (1902), 'Wider still and wider shall thy bounds be set; / God, who made thee mighty, make thee mightier yet.', show a return to the aspirations articulated in verse 5 of 'Rule, Britannia':

> To thee belongs the rural reign,
> Thy cities shall with commerce shine,
> All thine shall be the subject main
> And ev'ry shore it circles thine.

There were times when enthusiasm for new patriotic songs waned (noticeably 1825–30, 1845–50, and 1865–70), but they were always ready to roll off the presses when the possibility of international hostility loomed on the horizon. Then, not only were new songs produced, but 'traditional' patriotic songs were dug out and revitalized: in 1851 'The British Grenadiers' was published in London as an individual sheet-music item, labelled 'National Song'; and at the outbreak of the Crimean War the publisher C. Jeffreys issued a new version to which had been added extra verses of his own. Yet there is no record of this song having received the distinction of being published on its own since the 1770s.

When the Crimean War began in 1854, songs were being produced such as 'England! Empress of the Sea!', 'England's Queen to England's Heroes', and 'England's patriotic appeal to her sons against the Russian despot, To Arms!' The difference between the warmongering at the time of Crimea (1854–6) and that at the time of the Russo-Turkish War (1877–9) was that the Conservatives made a conscious effort to involve the working class in imperialist sentiment during the latter.[7] They wished to intervene in this war and, as part of their effort to whip up popular support, may have paid for the services of the music-hall entertainer, the 'Great Macdermott'.[8] It was 'Macdermott's War Song',[9] with its refrain beginning 'We don't want to fight, but by jingo if we do', which gave the word 'jingoism' to the English language. The success of this approach was evident when demonstrators smashed Gladstone's windows, and a previously vacillating Parliament was moved to vote £6,000,000 for military use.[10] With few exceptions, the songs published at the time of Crimea adopted a style more suited to the drawing room than the battlefield; even Captain J. Wilson's parody of 'Kelvin Grove' in 'Crimea's Battlefield' (1854), which begins, 'Oh! campaigning's no for you, bonnie lassie. Oh!', probably owes more to the fashionable enthusiasm for 'Scotch songs' in the 1850s than to any desire to acknowledge the part played by Scottish soldiers. A large number of men recruited to fight were actually Irish, and one of their songs which is still sung today is 'The Kerry Recruit';[11] its gory detail and stoical humour are in strong contrast to the elevated patriotic sentiment favoured by the bourgeoisie.

Until Gerard F. Cobb's settings of Kipling's *Barrack-Room Ballads* in the early 1890s, there was an immense gulf between the fighting man as depicted in drawing-room ballads and the British Army soldier (for whom, in reality, there was widespread contempt both among the bourgeoisie and his own commanding officers). After Dibdin, vernacular speech was less commonly used, even in sailors' songs; that Cobb became known as 'the Dibdin of the Army' probably owed as much to the use of the vernacular in Kipling's verse as to the tunefulness of the music. Kipling's men speak in a markedly different manner from the eloquent belligerance of the soldiers and sailors of the early nineteenth century, such as were encountered in 'The Death of Nelson' (1811) and 'The Soldier' (1815) in Chapter 1. In the years following the Napoleonic Wars, these characters developed a tender side, as revealed in 'The Soldier's Tear' of *c.* 1830 (words by T. H. Bayly, music by A. Lee), but not at the sacrifice of an ounce of courage, as is confirmed by 'Yes, Let Me Like a Soldier Fall', a favourite air from Wallace's *Maritana* (1845). The Dragoons of Gilbert and Sullivan's *Patience* (1881) are not an unfair caricature of the type of martial characters met with in the drawing room up to that time. The growing interest in the thoughts and words of the ordinary fighting man, as mediated by middle-class poets and composers, may be related to the search for English identity during the age of 'new imperialism'. There was also, of course, a feeling that this sort of song would win cross-class appeal. The following are press comments concerning some of Cobb's settings of *Barrack-Room Ballads*: 'Sure to gain popularity, both in the mess-room and in the barrack-room' (*Madras Times*, 28 September 1892). 'We have no hesitation in saying that these songs are bound to become popular throughout the entire British Army' (*United Services Gazette*, 13 August 1892).[12] Nevertheless, their perceived market is middle class. It was the music-hall which remained the prime vehicle for winning workers over to the imperialist cause, right up to the outbreak of the First World War when recruiting was helped by Vesta Tilley singing 'The Army of To-Day's All Right'. Jingoism did not, however, find its base in any working-class movement, but, according to the Liberal critics of imperialism in the 1890s, J. A. Hobson and L. T. Hobhouse, in the 'villa Toryism' of the suburban middle and lower middle class.[13] Suburbanization in the late nineteenth century was not unconnected to the construction of an English rural mythology which helped to build a new kind of nationalism, both aggressive and sentimental. England becomes the land of thatched cottages, red roses, and ripe corn. Although it lacks the rural images in its verse, 'Land of Hope and Glory' establishes the new musical style for patriotic songs. The nineteenth-century variety called for a booming masculine voice; the newer type aims to fill the heart with pride and the eyes with tears and, for that reason, allowing for gender stereotyping, is eminently suited to the female voice. Dame Clara Butt must have seemed to many the voice of the motherland personified. The last gasp of British imperialism as a 'popular' cause came with a song clothed in all the garments of English national identity which had been stitched up in the present century. Written in 1939, 'There'll Always Be an England' gives an assurance that England will always exist while there is a 'country lane' and a 'cottage small beside a field of grain'. Here is the pastoral ideal, not to be confused with the farm labourer's cottage and its tin bath and earth closet (living conditions still occasionally found in Yorkshire in the 1980s, let alone the 1930s). When the stirring call to action comes, Englishness is typically replaced by Britishness:

Red, white and blue, what does it mean to you?
Surely you're proud, shout it aloud, Britons awake!
The Empire too, we can depend on you,
Freedom remains, these are the chains nothing can break.

One way of asserting English identity was to project as imperial virtues such English bourgeois values as 'character' and 'duty'. In Kipling's 'The White Man's Burden', imperialism itself has become invested with a sense of duty. The ideology of the home was similarly magnified: England begins by offering shelter to a bourgeois conception of freedom, as in 'England, Freedom's Home' of 1848; then it stretches out in a global embrace, as in 'England, the Home of the World' (1872), a 'national song'. The word 'men', with its connotations of courage and firmness, also began to appear in titles of increasing grandeur: in 1877 came 'Men of England', a 'national song'; in 1894 came 'Men of Britain'; then, in 1915, came 'Men of Empire', written to the tune of 'Scots Wha Ha'e'. Songs in the later nineteenth century came to acknowledge that men were dying overseas. Verse 2 of 'The Old Brigade' of 1881 (words by F. E. Weatherly, music by O. Barri) begins, 'Over the sea far away they lie, / Far from the land of their love;' and Weatherly pursues a similar vein of thought in verse 3 of 'The Deathless Army' of 1891 (music by H. Trotère):

> Their bones may bleach 'neath an alien sky,
> But their souls, I know, will never die,
> They march in a deathless army.

The formal design of 'The Deathless Army', with its middle section pondering the subject of death, and a triumphant apotheosis for its conclusion, was a prototype for many later ballads concerning the armed forces, well-known examples being 'The Trumpeter' (1904) and 'Shipmates o' Mine' (1913).

In the 1890s the image of the patriotic Englishman was built into the character that was being constructed of the 'typical' or 'traditional' Englishman. The threat posed by imperial federation to English national identity was met by attempts to recapture some imagined rural ideal, included in which was the belief that unadulterated English qualities could be found in songs collected in the country-side. These songs, like patriotic songs, were given the label 'national', and, helped by the mediations of bourgeois folksong collectors, an idea of a homogeneous nation was formed which obscured the class divisions within British society. In a paper delivered to the Royal Musical Association in 1891, F. Gilbert Webb defines 'nation' as 'a number of people having certain things in common, such as language, one form of government, etc.'[14] and argues that 'Folk-song may fairly claim to be the vital principle in the music of all nations.'[15] Having referred (in the next sentence) to folksongs as 'national songs', he later proclaims that 'the origin of all folk-music is the endeavour to perpetuate by forcible and picturesque means the glories of love and war'.[16] Behind much of Webb's article lies the pseudo-science of race. Darwinian anthropology had reinforced the notion of there being distinct races, and the pseudo-science of phrenology also related to racial questions (the 'long-headed man' and the 'broad-headed man' who anciently inhabited the British Isles). Theories of race should be distinguished from those of ethnicity: the former allude to unchanging, hereditary factors, while the latter allude to cultural factors; members of the same ethnic group may or may not be members of the same race, yet still be bound by the same cultural ties. Webb uses folksong to confirm racial stereotyping. He notes with regard to the rhythmic device known as the 'Scotch snap' which is so commonly found in Scottish song:

> (it) is the musical expression of great muscular strength allied with highly-developed nervous force – I mean rapidity of nervous action, or transmission of thought to the muscular mechanism, which proceeds from great determination of mind and quick decision. It is the language of relentless resolution, of a mind which once fixed on the acquisition of an object cares not what consequences may result to itself or others so long as the end in view is attained. These, I need hardly say, are the chief elements which form the characters of successful warriors and conquerors, such as the Kelts.[17]

A grand claim for a rhythm which may simply derive from the greater ease with which the Highland bagpipe plays uneven quavers (♫ is always liable to turn into ♪. or ♫.). Even Webb's example of a song whose 'petulant, wayward character' derives from use of the 'Scotch snap' is ''Twas Within a Mile of Edinboro' Town', which, as has been noted in Chapter 1, happens to be by an Englishman, James Hook (from Norwich). Webb then discusses what he calls the 'English style of music' (meaning, presumably, a white Anglo-Saxon style):

What is the character of the majority of ordinary Englishmen? A well-balanced mind which regards everything in an intensely practical light and which submits everything to the question: 'What good will that do to my pecuniary or social position?' We hate display. All extravagance of language, dress, and gesture; we look upon the impulsive man with suspicion and upon the exaggerator with disgust, and regard enthusiasm as dangerous; we fear to let ourselves 'go' lest we should excite ridicule; in a word, we lack 'passion'. On the other hand, we are magnanimous and chivalrous, whether the object be worthy or no; emotional on social subjects, patriotic, and home-loving. What should be the music of such a people? Just what it is; good, honest, bold, straightforward strains, rich in melody, and breathing strong, healthy, human affection or simple-hearted gaiety, but innocent alike of exaggerated sentimentality, intellectual subtleties, or maddening mysticism.[18]

The novelty of Webb's application of racial theory to music in 1891 is shown by someone remarking in the course of the discussion which followed Webb's paper, 'I am very glad that someone has had the courage to stand up and assert the claims of national music to be regarded as the outcome of a people's feelings . . . The matter has never been thoroughly gone into.'[19] Webb's views occasionally reveal the influence of racist ideas which grew apace as an adjunct of the 'new imperialism', when 'the ideology of Anglo-Saxon supremacy more than ever served as a guide and comfort to the colonizers and as a rationale for coercion of their troublesome subjects'.[20] Those ideas were reinforced by the theory of the inevitability of human evolution and progress associated with Herbert Spencer, 'survival of the fittest',[21] and Social Darwinism, which allowed an 'advanced' nation to see itself as saving a 'backward' nation from savagery, offering a helping hand to 'races struggling to emerge into civilization'[22] in return for their country's riches. The English soldier's patronizing contempt for the cultural and religious differences of other countries is caught in Kipling's 'On the Road to Mandalay':

An' I seed her first a-smokin' of a whackin' white cheroot,
An' a-wastin' Christian kisses on an 'eathen idol's foot:
Bloomin' idol made o' mud –
What they called the great Gawd Budd –
Plucky lot she cared for idols when I kissed her where she stood!

This attitude clearly stems from the above-mentioned ideas which, in combination with late nineteenth-century imperial expansion, 'tended to exacerbate more racist notions of black and brown inferiority'.[23]

Before the development of Darwinian anthropology (*The Origin of the Species* was published in 1859), and while ethnology was in its infancy, the quality of 'Englishness' was deemed to lie largely in the possession of certain virtues. Indeed, in *English Traits*, published in 1854, Ralph Waldo Emerson fails to find anything particularly English about the rural population at all; his main concern is with the urban bourgeoisie. In 'The Englishman', a song published about 1840 which was very well known in the mid-century (it reached its twentieth edition by 1870), the Englishman is defined geographically by reference to his island home, his vast domain, and the symbol of his territorial possessions, his flag. In 'The Men of Merry England', Englishmen are defined by their freedom, bravery, and enterprising spirit; but these are the same aspects of Englishness with which the eighteenth-century bourgeoisie would have identified, and which had already been celebrated in songs like 'Heart of Oak' (1759). Indeed, in a major new contribution to a neglected area of historiography, Gerald Newman locates the rise of English nationalism in the second half of the eighteenth century.[24] He sees it emerging from anti-aristocratic and anti-French feelings: the 'real' Englishman is therefore projected as one who loathes foppishness and who lays claim to virtues the French are presumed to lack, such as sincerity, honesty, and independence. Roast beef becomes a symbol of Englishness because the French eat fancy ragouts; 'The Roast Beef of Old England' (1734) makes reference to 'effeminate France' and the 'vain complaisance' of the French. This song became part of the ritual of grand military banquets throughout the nineteenth century, being used as the announcement of dinner.

Even if an image of English national character was being assembled well before the nationalist enthusiasm of the late nineteenth century, the issue of whether or not there was a distinctly national character to the musical side of English songs, as opposed to their literary content, had been largely ignored. It was not even vital for the music of a 'national song' to be of English origin; Braham's 'The Death of Nelson' was rumoured to be founded on a French air.[25] The use of the description 'national' as a reference to words rather than music allows for a seemingly paradoxical situation in which 'God Bless The Prince of Wales' can be viewed as a 'truly national song',[26] and the Orange Lodge song 'Derry's Walls' which borrows the same Brinley Richards melody can also be called a 'National Song'.[27] William Chappell published two volumes entitled *National English Airs* in 1838 and 1840, but though by 'national air' he was avoiding some of the restrictive connotations pertaining to 'national song', he was apparently dissatisfied with that description, for when he issued a much larger collection to subscribers in 1855–9, which used the previous publications as its basis, he called it *Popular Music of the Olden Time*. There is no analysis of musical style in Chappell's work, and no sense of musico-sociological endeavour, nor is there any acknowledgement of the respective musical contributions of different social groups. He seems to have been primarily motivated by the desire to trace the music mentioned in literary sources, such as Shakespeare plays, and the 'olden time' refers mainly to the sixteenth and seventeenth centuries. Chappell was the founder of the Musical Antiquarian Society and saw his publication as 'not only a repertory of English popular music, but also a continuation of the literary work of Percy and Ritson'.[28] After Chappell's death, and during the folksong-collecting craze of the 1890s, his work was republished, but now its title, *Old English Popular Music*, carried a specific reference to nationality. It was also in the 1890s that Frank Kidson published his *English Peasant Songs*, which parts company with Chappell in two ways: first, Kidson claimed that he was originally driven to collect songs in order to demonstrate the absurdity of the accusation that the English had no national music, thus implying that Chappell had failed to counter that accusation;[29] second, Kidson locates this English national musical style in the music of a distinct social group. Kidson, like other folksong collectors, was interested in finding a rural population who had remained unaffected by the commercially oriented music of the cities; his use of the word 'peasant', till then rarely used in the nineteenth century, is an indication of his wishful thinking. Before the interventions of people like Kidson and Sabine Baring-Gould, the musical traditions of the 'lower orders' were 'regarded with scorn'.[30] In fact, it was only very late on in the century that folksong gained entry to the drawing room, and then in a mediated form. Rather than learn about Englishness from rustic labourers, who, as has been noted, were for most of the century not necessarily thought of as being typically English anyway, the bourgeoisie were more concerned to win these people over to an appreciation of morally elevating drawing-room ballads and blackface minstrel songs performed in village halls and the like. Ironically, the early folksong field-collectors were partly motivated by contempt for the sentimentality of bourgeois music-making, seeking instead an honest, healthy and spontaneous alternative in the English countryside.

The Folksong Movement had two noticeable effects on the drawing-room ballad at the close of the century and during the early years of the next: an exotic spicing was now almost always added to music intended to evoke other lands (pointing to the contrast with Englishness), and it became fashionable to write ballads containing regional vernacular speech. The new exoticism is evident if music concerning India composed in the middle of the century is compared with that composed at the end of the century. 'Jessie's Dream' (1857), a story of the Relief of Lucknow, makes no attempt whatsoever to introduce any music remotely Indian in character, though it manages to include snatches of 'The Campbells Are Coming', 'Auld Lang Syne', and 'God Save the Queen'. Adolphe Schubert's descriptive fantasia 'The Battle of Sobraon', published in London in 1846, has the Sikhs marching to their entrenchments to the missionary strains of 'There Is a Happy Land'. In John Pridham's plagiarized version, 'The Battle March of Delhi' (1857), this section is labelled 'Indian Air (at a distance)'.

Although reputedly Indian in origin, the tune above suggests nothing of the exotic atmosphere conveyed by the introduction to the 'Kashmiri Song' (words by L. Hope, music by A. Woodforde-Finden) from *Four Indian Love Lyrics* of 1902. See the musical example on page 178.

Exotic elements can, in fact, be found in songs earlier in the nineteenth century (for example, Norton's 'No More Sea'), but they are a rarity and, even in 1892, Cobb's 'Mandalay' (a setting of Kipling) has nothing exotic about it; indeed, it is a waltz which, in the shape of an arrangement by Bewick Beverley, became one of

Moderato assai, con molto sentimento.

the most fashionable dances of the season. In contrast, Oley Speaks in his famous 'On the Road to Mandalay' of 1907 uses an insistent rhythm joined to ominous harmonies for the verse sections and exotically colours the references to palmtrees and temple bells. In the 1890s an exotic turn of musical phrase came to be used to indicate non-European countries in general; Florence Turner's highly flavoured music for the 'Egyptian Boat Song' of 1898 owes, in reality, no more to any alternative musical culture than did Frederic Clay's 'I'll Sing Thee Songs of Araby' of 1877. Franklin Clive illustrated the late Victorian all-embracing image of the far-off land in 1899, when he discovered that he could sing Kipling's 'On the Road to Mandalay' not to any pseudo-Burmese music, but to Walter Hedgcock's 'Japanese' music composed in 1893 for 'The Mousmee'.

It was probably a conjunction of imperialist sentiment, the Folksong Movement, and enthusiasm for Kipling's verse which lay behind the upsurge in the use of vernacular speech in drawing-room ballads. Devon and Drake were favourite subjects, a well-known example being Newbolt's poem 'Drake's Drum', set by Hedgcock in 1897, but most familiar in C. V. Stanford's setting of 1904. Imperialist sentiment is relevant here because imperialist endeavour and 'chivalric aspects of colonial adventure'[31] could be related to the Elizabethan merchant adventurers like Raleigh and Drake (the message 'Sail overseas and conquer!' might easily have been inferred from Millais' painting *The Boyhood of Raleigh*). In 'army ballads' the rugged sergeant figure is probably a Kipling bequest; the humorous as well as intimidating aspects of his character are exploited in later ballads like 'A Sergeant of the Line' (1908), 'The Company Sergeant-Major' (1918), and 'When the Sergeant Major's on Parade' (1925).

In spite of all the activity surrounding the search for a specifically English musical style, there was no consensus about what that style consisted of in the late nineteenth century. In the 1890s some writers on music were still pointing to the bourgeois patriotic song as the 'national song', but claiming a national character for the music as well as the words. 'Rule, Britannia' is described in one song collection of this period as 'one of the finest national tunes we have, thoroughly expressive not only of the words, but embodying in its bold, ringing, martial-like strains, the very character and spirit of the British nation'.[32] Whether a 'bold, ringing, martial-like strain' springs from the 'character and spirit of the British nation' or from the use of certain well-trodden Western compositional techniques is a matter which can be disputed. The opening of the first verse of 'Rule, Britannia' will serve as an illustration.

When Bri - tain first____ at Heav'n's com - mand,

The use of a march metre and the construction of a tune around the tonic arpeggio, suggestive of a fanfare, undoubtedly conveys a martial mood (the bugle, for example, can play only notes of the tonic arpeggio, so all bugle calls share this character). If this is typically English, it obviously follows that so, too, is the tune of 'The Englishman',

There's a land   that bears   a   world - known name,

and also that of 'The Men of Merry England'.

Oh! the men   of mer- ry, mer - ry Eng   -   land,

There are, of course, countless other nineteenth-century English 'national songs' of this character; but perhaps this melodic and rhythmic device ought to be considered first and foremost as a feature of songs signifying a militaristic rather than a national character. Compare the refrain of 'The Old Brigade', which begins as follows:

Then   stea- di- ly____ shoul - der to shoul - der,

The refrain of 'The Deathless Army' begins in similar fashion.

March-ing for the dear old   coun   -   try,

Again, it need hardly be added that other examples are legion. It may be noted that the 'Marseillaise' is a tune of this type; one then needs to ponder why military bands in England were prohibited from playing it till 1879,[33] and why the writer quoted above, who was so enthusiastic on the subject of 'Rule, Britannia', found that in the case of the 'Marseillaise', 'there is an element of danger in a song of this kind.'[34]

If Britishness or Englishness implies unquestioning devotion to the concept of a homogeneous nation, there can be no danger for the bourgeoisie in a song like 'Rule, Britannia'. Nor was any danger perceived in the new pastoral image of Englishness which gained ground rapidly in the early twentieth century and took its idea of the typical expression of English character in music from folksongs like 'Searching for Lambs'.[35]

As   I walked out ___ one   May morn-ing,   One   May morn- ing ___ be - times

Here, the rolling irregularity of the English landscape finds its melodic counterpart, and the modality and lack of clearly implied harmony (there is no obvious choice of chord for bar two, for example) suggest an Eden undefiled by the commercial music industry. Yet folksongs, as the new 'national songs', soon became part of that industry. Whether 'Searching for Lambs' in any better served by the label 'national' than is 'Rule, Britannia', is once more a matter for ideological debate.

9   Hegemony

It may seem at first contradictory that, alongside songs of a loyal and patriotic nature, it should have been quite acceptable to sing ballads about outlaws and bandits in middle-class homes. Reasons for the need to rehabilitate an outlaw hero like Robin Hood may be easily conjectured, but the negotiations and compromises involved in doing so are complex. A major area of negotiation concerns what crime the outlaw has committed, and against whom. If outlaws are perceived to be fighting local injustices in an age of feudalism (now rectified by capitalism), all is well; these people belong to the band of noble robbers Hobsbaum calls 'social bandits'. When outlaws fall into this category, he notes a 'tendency of "official" culture to upgrade them socially as the price of assimilating them, i.e. to turn Robin Hood into a wronged Earl of Huntingdon'.[1] Contradictions remain, however, revealing that a compromise has been reached: for example, Robin Hood continues to use a peasant weapon, the longbow.

The key characteristics of the noble robber are that he is a *male* victim of injustice, kills only in self-defence, rights local wrongs, and ends by being betrayed. This kind of social bandit had not been seen in England since the early seventeenth century,[2] but in the United States an example was furnished after the Civil War in the shape of Jesse James (1847–82). As part of Jesse James's assimilation into the dominant culture, he was projected as a man who never robbed widows, preachers, or ex-Confederates, and who commanded respect as a devout Baptist and a teacher of church singing. In Billy Ganshade's song 'Jesse James', written 'As soon as the news [of his death] did arrive,' he is already depicted as 'a friend to the poor', and as one who 'never would see a man suffer pain'. Even so, he was too uncomfortably close in time to be sung about in North American or British drawing rooms, where preference was given to the kind of romantic bandolero made familiar in the writings of John Haynes Williams (1836–1908). The street ballad, on the other hand, was always ready to forge links between the idea of the noble robber and contemporary criminals, as is demonstrated in the following lines, which supposedly issued from the lips of Leopold Redpath before his transportation:

> I procured for the widow and orphan their bread,
> The naked I clothed, and the hungry I fed;
> But still I am sentenced, you must understand,
> Because I had broken the laws of the land.

The reaction of the bourgeoisie to these ballads was one of outrage: 'Some of these songs are indecent; almost all of them have a morbid sympathy with criminals.'[3] It is obvious, therefore, that criminals or outlaws were only assimilated on certain conditions and after fierce struggle.

For an outlaw to be acceptable to the bourgeoisie, he had to be, in political terms, a reformer not a revolutionary. Robin Hood emerges from his assimilation as a true patriot; he has no wish to abolish the monarchy and is ready to swear allegiance to a just king. In some ways, the enthusiasm shown for Garibaldi (albeit a republican) in the 1860s is related to the enthusiasm for the outlaw patriot. A million people turned out to welcome him in London on his visit in 1864. There were Garibaldi blouses, Garibaldi Staffordshire figures, Garibaldi biscuits, and Garibaldi songs. Besides Olivieri's Italian 'National Hymn' which had become well known in J. Oxenford's translation as 'Garibaldi's Hymn' (1861), the latter included a 'Garibaldi' of 1860 and a 'Garibaldi' of 1864; moreover, after Italian unity in 1870 interest continued for some time yet, as is shown by 'Garibaldi the True' of 1874.

Another type of outlaw ballad, already met with in Chapter 1 ('The Wolf'), worked in a different way. Here the protagonist boasts of his villainy but keeps his identity anonymous; thus, an important distinction is drawn between this kind of song and unacceptable 'low' ballads such as 'Sam Hall'. In 'A Bandit's Life Is the Life for Me!' of 1872, the singer adopts the persona of a roguish brigand who dwells in the mountains with his brave comrades. The appeal of the song would appear to lie in its offering the singer opportunity for a melodramatic performance calculated to inspire just the right degree of fear to stimulate excitement but not alarm on the part of listeners. The drawing-room audience is shielded from anxiety by two distancing devices: the musical accompaniment is based on a typical guitar-strumming pattern, and the bandit sings only of robbing monks and pilgrims. A clear hint is therefore given in both words and music that this is not Britain. Finally, the century which gave the world Frankenstein's monster and Count Dracula also produced the drawing-room ballad for a demonic outcast. 'Will-o'-the-Wisp' of 1860 comes complete with ghoulish laughter and a delight in evil:

> To mark their shriek as they sink and die,
> Is merry sport for me,
> I dance, I dance, I'm here, I'm there,
> Who tries to catch me catches but air;
> The mortal who follows me follows in vain,
> For I laugh, ha! ha! I laugh, ho! ho!
> I laugh at their folly and pain.

Where songs of outcasts were concerned, a working-class vernacular culture existed which rejected the ethics and morality of the bourgeois drawing room. A mid-century writer, commenting on the public house 'free-and-easy' entertainment, notes 'how alien the costermonger race is in sympathy and life from the respectable and well-to-do. Their songs are not ours, nor their aims nor conventional observances'.[4] This cultural activity flourished in the pub, which was so

markedly working class as to be unavailable as an arena for hegemonic negotiation. The music-hall, on the other hand, frequently functioned as such. In the
previous chapter it was seen how the music-hall played a part in winning over a
large portion of the working class to imperialist sentiment; but the music-hall also
provided a vehicle for bourgeois morality and values in the songs of 'respectable'
entertainers like Harry Clifton in its early years, and Felix McGlennon in the
later century. Clifton specialized in motto songs (for example, 'Bear It Like a
Man', 'Work, Boys, Work', and 'Paddle Your Own Canoe'), though the only
song of his well known today is 'Pretty Polly Perkins of Paddington Green'
(parodied as 'Cushie Butterfield'). Felix McGlennon's 'That Is Love' was quoted
from in Chapter 3; but the song of his most familiar now, and one which follows an
equally elevated plane of thought, is 'Comrades' (1890). Some music-halls, like
Wilton's in London's East End, went in for regular doses of uplifting culture;
there, 'an entirely local audience of sailors, tradesmen and worse' were regularly
treated to a half-hour's 'drawing-room entertainment' given by 'a small troupe in
evening dress, with a piano, who recited and sang operatic and ballad numbers'.[5]

Blackface minstrel troupes, who often appeared at music-halls as well as more
'respectable' establishments, also included ballads (and parodies of ballads) in
their entertainments (see Chapter 4). Minstrels, perhaps more than any other
group of performers, helped to disseminate bourgeois song among the working
class, since they performed in a wide variety of venues – large public halls,
theatres, and pleasure gardens. Harry Hunter, the interlocutor of Moore's
minstrels, shared Clifton's passion for earnest motto songs (for example, 'Keep a
Good Heart', and 'There's Danger in Delay'). The influence of the minstrels was
spread far and wide by their being imitated in villages and by urban street
performers.

Street singers of all kinds – glee singers, ballad singers, blackface 'Ethiopians' –
who had bourgeois songs in their repertoire, provided another source of access to
this material for the working class. The street singers themselves, according to
one of their number, picked up tunes 'mostly . . . from the street bands, and
sometimes from the cheap concerts, or from the gallery of the theatre, where the
street ballad-singers very often go, for the express purpose of learning the airs'.[6]
Some of these singers, of course, learned songs to earn money in middle-class
neighbourhoods rather than their own.[7] Nevertheless, the printing of drawing-
room ballads as broadsides shows that an interest existed in working-class
environs.[8] Other street entertainment was provided by the variety of mechanical
instruments which had begun to appear at the end of the eighteenth century. On a
recent recording of nineteenth-century mechanical instruments,[9] a *Cabinetto*
paper-roll organ can be heard playing blackface minstrel songs, a *Celestine*
paper-roll organ playing nonconformist hymns, and a street piano (commonly
known as a 'barrel organ') playing music-hall songs. These instruments, particularly the street pianos (which were developed in the 1870s from the cylinder
piano), were mostly made by Italian immigrants living in London. They were
pushed around by itinerant street 'musicians' who often had no knowledge of
music and cared little for their maintenance and tuning. Legislation was introduced in 1864 to combat what was being declared a public nuisance. However,

care is needed in defining the class nature of the public to whom they had supposedly become such a nuisance. Consider, for example, the following contemporary words of caution:

> Let not those who write abusive letters to the newspapers, and bring in bills to abolish street music, think they will be able to loosen the firm hold which the barrel-organist has over the British public. Your cook is his friend, your housemaid is his admirer; the policeman and the baker's young man look on him in the light of a formidable rival.[10]

The 'players' of mechanical instruments did take pains, all the same, to appeal to both a middle-class and a working-class audience, for obvious economic reasons. As one of them explains to Mayhew, 'You must have some opera tunes for the gentlemen, and some for the poor people, and they like the dancing tune.'[11] In concluding this brief survey of street music, a mention must be given to the German Bands; these other groups of immigrant musicians constituted '*the second great fact* of street music'[12] according to Haweis (he gave priority to the barrel-organists). They, too, had a varied repertoire which included Italian arias, occasional movements of symphonies, ballads, music-hall songs, and dances.

The working class found further access to performances of bourgeois music in parks (military bandstands[13]), spas (spa orchestras), and fairgrounds (especially after the perfection of the steam organ in the 1870s). There were also the cheap concerts, already briefly mentioned, such as those begun in the Crystal Palace by August Manns in 1855, which took place in a hall holding so many people that 'only a small charge was made for admission'.[14] The pleasure gardens are usually referred to as being in decline in the nineteenth century. Part of this decline has been attributed to the need for land for housing and industry, but that fails to account for the opening of new pleasure gardens like the Eagle Tavern in 1822 and Cremorne in 1836; the latter replaced Ranelagh (closed 1803) as Chelsea's pleasure garden. It would seem reasonable to suppose that the meaning of the word 'decline' is in no small measure related to the hostile bourgeois reaction to the pleasure gardens being increasingly invaded by the petit bourgeoisie and wealthier working class (together with what they saw as a consequent increase in vulgarity and rowdiness). The bourgeoisie were beginning to feel alarmed at the 'thousands of idle pleasure-seekers'[15] in the gardens in the 1850s. The wages boom of the 1860s and expansion of leisure time encouraged further working-class interest in pleasure gardens. During this decade the wealthy residents of Chelsea complained that the value of their property was falling on account of its propinquity to Cremorne. When the garden closed in 1877, its 'open air dissipation' was compared to the 'indoor dissipation of the music hall'.[16]

Having seen how the working class found access to bourgeois song, the next thing to consider is the question of intention and reception involving this cultural material; for, if a relative autonomy exists, allowing meaning to be made in the process of consumption, then the meaning constructed by the working class during the consumption of bourgeois art may differ from that intended by its bourgeois creator. Tennyson, for example, might write of 'Airy Fairy Lilian', but the working class might make a new meaning of this epithet.[17] The dialectic between intention and reception emerges in examinations made by the Select Committee on Dramatic Literature in 1832. Thomas Morton, answering questions, remarks that there is 'a tendency in the audience to force passages never meant by the author into political meanings'.[18] As an illustration, he recalls that when the king commanded a performance of *Massaniello* during the time of the revolution in France,

> handbills were printed about the town to induce the public to assemble in the theatre, not to partake with His Majesty in the social enjoyment of the drama, but to teach him, through the story of Massaniello the Fisherman, the danger to his throne if he disobeyed the wish of his people, and the King was advised to change the play in consequence of that.[19]

The author of the play, James Kenney, was later brought before the Committee, and he explained with bewildered irritation,

> there is no question, if I may be allowed the expression, that it has a Tory moral. The revolutionary fisherman is humiliated, and a lesson is taught very opposite to a revolutionary one.[20]

Some of the songs of Tom Moore provide a musical parallel to the above. 'The Minstrel Boy', for example, as performed by a celebrated singer in the Crystal Palace, may have been considered a purely uplifting aesthetic experience for the huge audience, and an occasion for winning wider appreciation of bourgeois art:

> I shall never forget Grisi's rendering of 'The Minstrel Boy' at the Crystal Palace. She refused to sing again after three encores. The audience who had listened to her singing spellbound, rose in a mass, and the applause was like thunder.[21]

Yet 'The Minstrel Boy' also came to be appropriated as an Irish rebel song.[22] The Anglo-Irish bourgeoisie, too, in struggling to shake off English political and economic restraints, lighted upon Moore's songs; 'The Shan Van Vocht', a rewritten 'Love's Young Dream', was published in *The Nation*, 29 October 1842, Dublin. The 'Shan Van Vocht' is the 'Poor Old Woman' who had come to symbolize a distressed Ireland. It is doubtful, however, that any Moore song held the same popularity as the songs born out of the people's own struggles, like Caroll Malone's ballad of 1798, 'The Croppy Boy' (cropped hair was the style of French revolutionaries). The *Westminster Review* in 1855 notes that this song 'has even now, in that unhappy isle, a fatal attraction and dread significance'.[23] 'The Croppy Boy' was not absorbed by bourgeois culture until the present century, when it was recorded by the concert tenor John McCormack and also featured prominently in the 'sirens' chapter of James Joyce's landmark of literary modernism, *Ulysses*.

There were a variety of ways in which the working class could respond to bourgeois song. It could be accepted without conscious alteration, any changes to words and tune being attributable to oral transmission. Thus the present-day 'Jingle Bells' is a simplified version of James Pierpont's 'The One Horse Open Sleigh' of 1857, published by Oliver Ditson & Co., Boston.[24] The bourgeois song becomes, in cases like this, a sort of 'folksong', although one to be weeded out by mediators who have felt able to define what true folksong is.[25] Fred Jordan, for example, a Shropshire farmer 'discovered' by Peter Kennedy in 1952 whilst on a field trip recording for the BBC Folksong Archive, had bourgeois songs like Henry Clay Work's 'Grandfather's Clock' in his repertoire which earlier collectors would have rejected. A common method of working-class appropriation of bourgeois song was deliberately to change the words, but to model the new text around the original text. A nineteenth-century broadside ballad published by Pitts, 'The Chartist Song', uses Burns' 'For A' That, an' A' That' as its basis. The first stanza runs,

> Art thou poor but honest man
> Sorely oppressed and a' that.
> Attention give to Chartist plan
> 'Twill cheer they heart for a' that.
> For a' that and a' that,
> Though landlords gripe and a' that,
> I'll show thee friend before we part
> The rights of men and a' that.[26]

The Burns original begins,

> Is there, for honest poverty,
> That hangs his head, an' a' that?
> The coward slave, we pass him by,
> We dare be puir for a' that!

Throughout 'The Chartist Song', Burns' emphasis on moral victory is transformed into the desire for political victory.

Sometimes the new text, while loosely based on the original, is changed in order to make the song more relevant to the social circumstances of the singer. Henry Clay Work's 'The Ship That Never Return'd' (1865) was transformed into the railroad song 'The Wreck of the Old '97', in which appropriated form it has survived today while the original has been forgotten.[27] Sometimes the new text parodies the original in an attempt to ridicule its sentiments, a technique Joe Hill uses in 'The Preacher and the Slave', a parody of 'Sweet By and By'.[28] A new text may show the influence of the bourgeois original but depart from it so radically as to require a new tune. 'The Spinner's Ship', a union song of the Preston strike of 1854, shows the influence of Charles Mackay's text to Henry Russell's song 'Cheer, Boys! Cheer!' (1852) but has dispensed with the latter's tune.[29] Conversely, the tune may be retained but the original text completely ignored. This was, of course, common practice when the tune was a traditional air but also happened when the tune was of recent bourgeois origin: 'Strike for Better Wages', a song of the London Dock Strike of 1889, used the tune of Root's 'Tramp! Tramp! Tramp!' of 1864.[30] It most often occurred with blackface minstrel songs, a well-known example being Joe Wilson's 'Keep Yor Feet Still!'[31] which used the tune of Handby's 'Darling Nelly Gray'. Occasionally the tune survived more or less intact as a dance and the words disappeared altogether, as happened with 'The Dashing White Sergeant' in Britain and 'Turkey in the Straw' in the United States.

What also must be considered is the collision between bourgeois and working-class musical practice. It should not be assumed that bourgeois song was automatically simplified when adopted by a working-class singer. The author recollects hearing an archive recording of a 'folksinger'[32] performing 'The Mistletoe Bough' with decorations not in the original. Here, for example, is one of his concluding phrases, followed by Bishop's melody.

Embellishments found in vernacular musical practice (for example, slides and decorative two-note runs up or down to a main melody note) often derive from traditional methods of enhancing an unaccompanied tune, whereas the ornamentation in bourgeois music is frequently designed to exploit the tensions of a harmonic background. Another difference between bourgeois and working-class song performance is that of *timbre*, the colour of the sound. The timbre of the 'untrained' voice lends a more natural emphasis to words, since the tone is produced as in speech, forward in the mouth, with a considerable volume of air passing down the nose; the classical singer employs artifices like the chest register and consciously avoids a nasal tone. The appropriation of bourgeois song had its effects on working-class song, however, most noticeably in the increasing fondness shown for the major key rather than the old modes. Furthermore, there was a growing assumption of accompanying harmony to tunes, and a tendency for them to imply the characteristic chord progressions of bourgeois songs. Examples can be found today in American country music, which of all twentieth-century popular musical culture relates most closely to nineteenth-century bourgeois domestic music. To take but one example, a turn to subdominant harmony for the first half only of the second bar of melody – a move much favoured by Joseph Skelly (as in 'A Boy's Best Friend Is His Mother', 'The Picture with Its Face Turned to the Wall', and 'The Old Rustic Bridge') – finds an echo in Bill Monroe's 'Little Cabin Home on the Hill' and Hank Williams' 'Why Should We Try Anymore?', among others. The primary link is probably the blackface minstrel show; indeed, the first country star, Jimmie Rodgers ('the singing brakeman'), sometimes performed in blackface in his early days. Some nineteenth-century minstrel songs, such as 'Buffalo Girls' and 'When You and I Were Young, Maggie', have become bluegrass standards. Outside the world of 'pure' country, Mitch Miller had a million-selling record in 1955 with 'The Yellow Rose of Texas', a minstrel song written almost a hundred years before, in

1858. However, it was country music which did most to absorb and revitalize bourgeois song, and not just minstrel song: Johnny Cash had a hit record in 1959 with 'Lorena', a ballad aimed directly at the domestic market in 1857.[33]

The explanation for the appeal of bourgeois song to working-class people and the meanings they were able to make of it are complex and, to a degree, impenetrable issues. Bourgeois music was part of the dominant culture, which in the nineteenth century gave it an exclusive claim to the label 'culture'. Drawing-room music may, therefore, have signified certain social aspirations, perhaps not simply economic, but moral and intellectual, too. The attraction of its 'refine-ment' may have lain in the realm of fantasy or escapism. A Balfe aria, like 'The Dream', may have suggested a world outside the squalor of working-class slums, and signified the hope of a higher quality of life.[34] The reason for the connection between nineteenth-century bourgeois domestic music and modern country music may lie in the fact that the latter so often serves to articulate the aspirations of the American lower middle class.

Those who failed to be won over to bourgeois values or pursued their own 'unofficial' culture posed the biggest challenge to nineteenth-century bourgeois society. Here, a breakdown in hegemony inevitably resulted in its replacement by coercion: it would have required considerable daring, for example, to sing 'The Wearing of the Green' in England while the Fenian struggle raged, though whether it was an actual criminal offence or not has now been debated.[35] In the last chapter it was noted that military bands were not allowed to play the 'Marseillaise' for much of the century; but, what is more, *all* public performances of the song were long proscribed.[36] In addition to the attempt to eradicate songs of a highly political nature, there were constant moves to censor on moral grounds. Sometimes, however, an unexpected construction of meaning in the consumption of even the most impeccable bourgeois song could cause havoc. As Buddy Bolden's band played 'Home, Sweet Home!' during the embarkation of troops for the Spanish-American War (1898), many soldiers jumped overboard and swam ashore, an incident which prompted the US Army to prohibit its performance at all future departures. The best kind of censorship, of course, is achieved when people censor themselves. Tennyson's 'The Charge of the Light Brigade', written in hot-blooded mood at the news from Balaclava and printed shortly after in a newspaper, became popular with the Crimean troops, who relished the un-precedented suggestion of blunder:

> Forward the Light Brigade!
> Was there a man dismayed?
> Not though the soldier knew
> Someone had blundered.

After Tennyson's friends pointed out to him the offence given to the War Office, he removed the lines from his next published collection of poems (they remain excised from a recent Penguin anthology of Victorian verse). In this case the censorship was only temporary, probably because the 'monumental mismanage-ment' of the war was laid at the feet of the old aristocracy.[37] John Blockley's setting of 1860, the only one to enjoy any measure of drawing-room success, is based on the original text.

Bourgeois song was also consciously employed as a medium of persuasion by various fractional interests within the hegemonic bloc. At times the persuasion was aimed at encouraging the working class to embrace bourgeois values, at others it was targeted at the 'better nature' of the bourgeoisie themselves, by depicting working-class misery. Temperance groups were especially fond of harnessing the power of music to their cause. The favourite method was to promote songs which portrayed the devastating effects of drunkenness on the home and family life, such as Henry Clay Work's 'Come Home, Father' of 1864. Mrs Parkhurst, a friend of Stephen Foster in his alcohol-sodden latter days, performed temperance songs in public with her daughter, 'little Effie', adding thereby an extra poignancy to compositions like 'Father's a Drunkard and Mother Is Dead' of 1868. Sometimes the fervour of the gospel hymn was joined to temperance ideals, as in the Rev. Ufford's 'Throw Out the Life-Line!', which makes typical metaphorical use of men needing to be saved from drowning at sea. Sometimes a stern admonition is given, as in 'Don't Marry a Man If He Drinks'. Temperance songs were published by 'respectable' firms in Britain, usually on the cheaper side of the market, suggesting the lower middle class as a target; the last-mentioned song was No. 4444 of the Musical Bouquet (1874), but an even cheaper publisher, Davidson, had earlier issued a *Temperance Melodist*. The in some ways radical Salvation Army was willing to parody any kind of songs which were already popular, in order to spread the word; other groups tended to use parodies only of 'respectable' songs, choosing those they thought had widest appeal. Whatever diffidence there may have been concerning the original material, the message of the temperance song was forthright. Here is the beginning of Emmet Coleman's parody of 'The Last Rose of Summer':

> There's no hope for the drunkard,
> Left dying alone.[38]

It will be noted that most of the temperance songs, like the gospel hymns, came to Britain from the United States.

Examples of bourgeois songs designed to persuade in a direct manner are legion. Where the young were concerned, the Sunday School provided an opportunity to drive home bourgeois ideology, at times with military-style drilling: Sabine Baring-Gould's 'Onward Christian Soldiers' (1864) was written for his Sunday School scholars to march to (it was originally written to a tune by Haydn; Sullivan composed his well-known tune later). In her efforts to smother egalitarian sentiments, Mrs Alexander verges on feudal absolutism in one frequently omitted verse from 'All Things Bright and Beautiful' (from *Hymns for Little Children* of 1848):

> The rich man in his castle,
> The poor man at his gate,
> GOD made them, high or lowly,
> And order'd their estate.

Besides promoting the dominant ideology, bourgeois song strongly attacked alternative ideologies, like Jacobinism. Dibdin's efforts have already been noted (in Chapter 1), but a hundred years later W. S. Gilbert can still be found attacking republicanism in *The Gondoliers* (1889), particularly in Don Alhambra's song 'There Lived a King', with its message,

> When every one is somebodee
> Then no one's anybody.

The song has an almost identical message to the one Capt. Marryat tries to put over in *Mr Midshipman Easy* (1836), when Jack Easy rebels against his father's views on the rights of man, and exclaims,

> Were we all equal in beauty, there would be no beauty, for beauty is only by comparison . . . Were we all equal in ability, there would be no instruction, no talent, no genius.[39]

Marryat no doubt hoped to signify in young Jack's rejection of his father's opinions that Paine's ideas were outmoded; indeed, the nineteenth-century bourgeoisie were as keen to dismiss Paine as out of date as today's Conservative politicians are to write off Marx.

There were, in addition to the myriad songs of an openly didactic nature, the more subtle variety which fostered an imaginary relationship on the part of the working class to the real social conditions in which they lived. 'Home, Sweet Home!', with its apparent praise of the humble dwelling, has already been mentioned in this connection in Chapter 1, and the 'coincidence' of Weiss's setting of Longfellow's 'The Village Blacksmith' (that famous tribute to the poor, honest, hard-working individual) appearing in the same year as the great strike in Preston has been noted in Chapter 7. To give one more example, the favourite drawing-room song in the early nineteenth century about farm life was the anonymous 'To Be a Farmer's Boy', which scarcely seems to belong to the same world as that of the Tolpuddle Martyrs of 1834, and the farmers' boys who, throughout the land, were being forced to accept cuts in wages.

Perhaps the effect most desired by the bourgeoisie was that their songs would persuade the working class of the rightness of bourgeois morality. The 1851 ecclesiastical census had disturbingly found an 'unconscious secularism' in big towns, where funerals were the only important religious ceremony. Outside the church the Utilitarians' scientific approach to morality ran into difficulties when measuring the moral priorities of certain needs against the preference of the majority. Soon the music-hall seemed set to overtake Christian teaching in guiding social morality, and the first example of what would now be called a 'moral panic' occurred over the *lions comiques*. As 'sources of social morality', the halls and music-hall songs became 'as important as the modern media'.[40] Gazing into this moral void, the bourgeoisie seized upon the supposed ability of music to influence behaviour: Haweis advised, 'Let no one say the moral effects of music are small or insignificant.'[41] As will be seen a little later, the most powerful apparatus of the hegemonic bloc proved to be state education.

Before turning to the efforts made to teach the working class how to appreciate 'good music', some thought must be given to those who saw in the drawing-room ballad an opportunity to prick the consciences of the bourgeoisie and campaign for social reform. An early example of a songwriter frequently engaged along these lines was Henry Russell (as was noted in Chapter 1) in songs like 'The Maniac' and 'The Song of the Shirt'. Bourgeois disapproval of this kind of socially concerned art was usually couched in terms of a circumscribing definition about the purpose of art: for instance, a favourite argument was that this was an area for charity work, not art; art should show that suffering enobles, not degrades. Nevertheless, a part of the bourgeoisie could not shake off their fear that a lack of social reform might prompt the working class to violence. Christian Socialism, for example, began in response to the 1848 revolutions abroad and to Chartism at home. It was a movement without a coherent manifesto, and its key figures, Ludlow, Maurice, and Kingsley, seem to have been largely ignorant of socialist thought; their paramount considerations were education and moral improvement. From 1849 the publication of Mayhew's articles entitled *London Labour and the London Poor* was a spur to action. The Rev. Charles Kingsley's attitudes were sometimes contradictory: he despised the industrial bourgeoisie, but said, 'it was God who taught us to conceive, build and arrange that Great Exhibition' of 1851.[42] He also had periodic losses of religious faith; his poem 'Three Fishers Went Sailing', which later in the century proved an outstanding success when sung by Antoinette Sterling in the musical educator John Hullah's setting of 1857, contains, surprisingly, no angels or other heavenly consolation in its final desolate stanza:

> Three corpses lay out on the shining sands
> In the morning gleam as the tide went down,
> And the women are weeping and wringing their hands
> For those who will never come back to the town;
> For men must work and women must weep,
> And the sooner it's over, the sooner to sleep,
> And goodbye to the bar and its moaning.

Unfortunately, the fate of the poor fishermen arrives in an all too predictable manner for the song to convince today; and, indeed, the familiar tragic sea-song structure of embarkation, storm, and disaster never required more than an acquaintance with drawing-room ballad conventions to respond to its emotional content. Any knowledge of the class of people the song concerned was purely incidental; a point made by Sterling herself, who claimed that 'although she had never been to sea in a storm nor had even seen fishermen, she understood the piece by instinct'.[43] Kingsley, himself, became ever more suspicious of attempts by working people to take control of their own destinies and finally moved to condemning the activities of trades unions in the 1860s.

Another problem existed with this kind of socially concerned ballad; it may throw light on the plight of an oppressed class, but it was addressed to the oppressing class, as its elegant diction and musical refinement make clear. Hood's 'The Song of the Shirt' was published in *Punch* (1843), not *The Poor Man's Guardian*. Failure to recognize this, creates an apparent contradiction:

> The greatest song-writer for the people was, beyond all question, Thomas Hood: he felt their wrongs and sorrows most keenly . . . but, nevertheless, the great majority of his countrymen have never heard of either Hood or his songs.[44]

The above writer, however, acknowledges Hood's efforts 'in rousing the sympathies of the higher classes for their suffering brothers'.[45] When Hood, in fact, was sent a collection of poems by Ebenezer Jones, a poet with Chartist connections, whose verse, in spite of its consciously poetic diction, made no appeal in its sentiments to the bourgeoisie, he reacted with outrage.[46] It may seem ironic that some Chartist songs resembled the style of bourgeois domestic music, an example being 'Song of the Lower Classes' of *c*.1856 (words by Ernest Jones, music by John Lowry). The relationship, it must be stressed, is one of style and not content, but it does show the strength of the dominant culture, in that protest or complaint was thought to be given greater dignity or status in this way. The bourgeois, socially concerned ballad continued to reverberate around drawing rooms (to little practical effect) throughout the century. A later example is Piccolomini's 'The Toilers' of 1888; in this song two orphans relate how their respective fathers died toiling for bread (one was a miner, the other a fisherman), and the appeal goes out:

> O happy ones of this fair earth,
> While gather'd round your glowing hearth,
> Think of the toilers' load of care,
> And pray for all, in God's own pray'r:
> 'Give us, this day, our daily bread!'

The 'hearth', of course, is a talismanic word conjuring up bourgeois family values and given added significance here by the song's being about orphans. Typically, however, the call is not for action, but for prayers.

It may be wise to pause, before moving to educational questions, and consider the dominant culture's claim to the 'best' values in the arts. A fruitful comparison would be Beethoven's arrangement of 'Johnnie Cope' and Ewan MacColl's 'folk-style' performance of the song accompanied by Peggy Seeger, as recorded on the album *The Jacobite Rebellions*.[47] A striking difference is found in the musical accompaniment to each version: Beethoven has provided a carefully written out score for tenor, violin, cello, and piano to be followed precisely, whereas MacColl has Seeger's semi-improvisational guitar for support. Furthermore, Beethoven interrupts the stanzas of the song with musical interludes which hamper the dramatic pace of the narrative and necessitate cuts so that the piece does not become over long. The cuts are also necessary to avoid monotony, since the singer can bring little variation to his part on account of its being doubled throughout by the violin, whereas MacColl can not only make spontaneous changes, but also indulge in the metrical irregularity of beginning a fresh verse half way through a bar of accompaniment. In short, Beethoven's compositional efforts serve only to cramp the song in ways which cannot be redeemed by invoking the 'best' values of high art. One might ask, too, what the choice of instruments signifies: do the violin, cello, and piano represent an ideal *timbre* for the song, or are they chosen because they are instruments of the drawing room, in other words instruments representative of the taste of a particular class? The inappropriateness of Beethoven's version may not be contested now, but it must be remembered that Thomson's purpose in commissioning it from one whose own work carried the authority of high culture was to raise the song's status as art. Therefore Beethoven's failure provides grounds for arguing that the cultural practices of subordinate social groups are not necessarily improved by applying the values of the dominant culture. Now, if culture bears a class character, then educationalists and those intent on 'culturing' the working class must be seen as performing a hegemonic function in promoting the dominant culture. To an early cultural theorist like Matthew Arnold there was no working-class culture, there was only one culture embracing the 'best' values, 'the best knowledge, the best ideas';[48] Arnold wastes no time in *Culture and Anarchy* on the music hall.

The state was rather late in coming round to the opinion that 'culturing' the lower orders was desirable. Steps to promote 'good' music were taken first by religious groups and moralists wishing to create an appetite for 'rational amusement' among the working class. Moreover, it was hoped that an interest in music might lead to the substitution of wholesome recreation for that principal and notorious working-class recreation, drinking. The method most commonly chosen was to involve them in a choir. Here was the first snag; bourgeois music was based on a literate tradition requiring an ability to read musical notation, yet a musical skill like that had to be formally taught. Before the 1840s what little instruction in music was given in such places as Sunday Schools tended to rely on rote learning. In some areas, for example, Derbyshire, Lancashire, and the West Riding of Yorkshire, whole oratorios had been learnt in this manner. These northern manufacturing districts were held up as a model:

> Almost every town has its choral society, supported by the amateurs of the place and its neighbourhood, where the sacred works of Handel and the more modern masters are performed, with precision and effect, by a vocal and instrumental orchestra, consisting of mechanics and workpeople; and every village church has its occasional oratorio, where a well-chosen and well-performed selection of sacred music is listened to by a decent and attentive audience, of the same class as the performers, mingled with their employers and their families. Hence the practice of this music is an ordinary domestic and social recreation among the working classes of these districts, and its influence is of the most salutary kind.[49]

There were, of course, those on whom the salutary influence of music was thought to be wasted: for example, Huddersfield Choral Society (founded in 1836) had a rule prohibiting socialists from joining.[50]

Brass bands are also associated with the North and were seen by many of the industrial bourgeoisie as another way of providing 'rational amusement' for their workforce. In 1855 John Foster and Sons of Queensbury sponsored the band renowned today as the Black Dyke Mills Band. The growth of the railways created an opportunity to travel to competitions which were often very well attended: at Hull's Zoological Gardens (now no more) in 1856, 12,000 people paid to hear a contest in which first prize was awarded to the Leeds Railway Band.[51] The repertoire of brass bands relied heavily on bourgeois taste:

The correspondent of a London paper, while visiting Merthyr was exceedingly puzzled by hearing boys in the Cyfarthfa works whistling airs rarely heard except in the fashionable ball-room, opera-house, or drawing-room. He afterwards discovered that the proprietor of the works, Mr Robert Crawshay, had established among his men a brass band, which practises once a week throughout the year.[52]

It is interesting to note that the above, written in 1850, refers to a band being sponsored in Merthyr Tydfil, a hotbed of Welsh Chartism less than a decade earlier.

During 1840–50 the bourgeoisie began to place increasing trust in the power of music to win the working class over to their values; the following two quotations from this period show typical opinions on music: 'a means of softening the manners, refining the taste, and raising the character of the great body of the people'.[53] and 'a means of refining the tastes, softening the manners, diffusing true pleasure, and humanizing the great mass of the people'.[54] These quotations are separated by an interval of ten years, which helps to illustrate that the phrases 'softening the manners' and 'refining the tastes' were truisms. The breakthrough in bringing 'good' music to 'the great mass of the people' had come with the development of new methods designed to facilitate sight-singing. The key figures were Joseph Mainzer (1801–51), whose book *Singing for the Million* was produced shortly after his arrival in Britain in 1841; John Hullah (1812–84), whose text book *Wilhelm's Method of Singing Adapted to English Use* was also published in 1841; and John Curwen (1816–80), whose *Grammar of Vocal Music* of 1845 sowed the seeds of the system which finally won out. Mainzer embarked upon a lecture tour, spreading his method of teaching to the provinces (particularly Bristol, Newcastle upon Tyne, and Manchester) and to Scotland. His efforts were supported by the temperance movement and various educational establishments, including mechanics' institutes. The latter, dating from the early 1820s, had turned into places of rational recreation for the lower middle class by the 1840s and were eagerly starting up singing classes for members and their families.[55] One of Mainzer's most notable achievements was founding *Mainzer's Musical Times and Singing Circular* in 1842; it was taken over by Novello two years later and survives today as the *Musical Times*.

Hullah began his classes at about the same time as Mainzer, but the second edition of Hullah's text book had the advantage of being able to refer to its having been produced 'Under the Superintendence of the Committee of Council on Education', thereby indicating government approval. The government may have been swayed in so doing by the French government's formal sanction of the Wilhelm method (the basis of Hullah's own). Nevertheless, encouragement was all that was given: an article in 1850 pointed out, 'the Government has never contributed a shilling to the support of any of Mr Hullah's classes.'[56] Hullah's success was seen in 1847 to be of a limited kind, however; it was 'almost wholly confined to the preparatory adult classes of choral societies and normal institutions [places for teacher training]' and he had 'failed generally to connect music with the primary instruction of elementary schools'.[57] In 1849 the *Westminster Review* remarked that Hullah's classes, 'instead of spreading over the country, as was intended, are chiefly confined to the training of recruits for one or more of the London Sacred Harmonic Societies'.[58] It should be pointed out, though, that many of the members of these choirs were of the working class.[59]

It was the nonconformist clergyman and non-musician Curwen who produced the tonic sol-fa system which eventually overtook all else. He had been commissioned, at a Sunday School conference in Hull, to find the simplest way of teaching children to sing by note. His inspiration was the Norwich Sol-fa Ladder of Sarah Glover (1785–1867), which had a movable doh, in contrast to the fixed doh of the Hullah and Mainzer systems; it meant, in effect, that there was only one key, doh being the name given to the first note of any key (there are obvious similarities to the use of a capo on a guitar). So successful was Curwen that from the mid-1870s enormous Tonic Sol-fa Festivals became an annual event at the Crystal Palace, tonic sol-fa choirs having by then spread to almost every town in Britain.[60]

Despite government approval for the use of Hullah's method in schools, by 1860 tonic sol-fa dominated. Schools began to play an important role in disseminating bourgeois musical values among the working class, particularly after the Elementary Education Act of 1870, in which the government made provision for a system of 'National Education' controlled locally by 'School Boards'. The school is a crucial part of the hegemonic cultural apparatus; indeed Althusser once saw the school as the dominant ideological state apparatus of capitalist society.[61] Althusser argued that the school became the dominant ideological state apparatus not as the result of simple choice on the part of the bourgeoisie, but as the result of class struggle; otherwise the church could have continued to function as the dominant ideological state apparatus, as it did in feudal society. Hence, even in 1885 one can find the complaint that 'our Government . . . literally does next to nothing for an art that has the power of making better citizens by its refining influences',[62] and a plea put forward for 'a central Metropolitan Institution, aided by Government grants and subject to Government inspection'[63] to develop a system of musical elementary education. Music was, in fact, designated a grant-earning subject in the rate-aided elementary schools:

> music is acknowledged and supported by the State in the form of payment on results. In England and Wales, and also in Scotland, where the same code applies, a payment of 1s. per head of the average school attendance is made where the children can give some evidence of understanding written musical characters, and can sing from sight to a small extent. Where music from note is not taught a payment of 6d. is made for singing by ear three or four songs previously learned.[64]

The money given by the state was in recognition of music's importance 'from a trade point of view' and its well-recognized claims 'from a social standpoint'.[65] The 'payment by results' system helped the cause of tonic sol-fa since there was an understandable tendency for schools to opt for the system which most easily produced the results the inspectors were looking for. Nearly all board schools (rate-aided schools) opted for tonic sol-fa; other methods, including ordinary notation, survived almost exclusively in public schools and voluntary schools (schools supported by voluntary contributions, as well as a fee paid by each child).[66] The Committee of Council on Education expressed no opinion on the merits of tonic sol-fa, 'but merely recognized it as having been adopted on a sufficient scale to justify official sanction'.[67] As musical education was increasingly perceived to be important to working-class children in the 1870s, the public schools also found it necessary to remedy their previous neglect of music and ensure that their pupils were taught 'the difference between good music and bad',[68] since many of these pupils had succumbed to the attraction of the very music which board schools were trying to eradicate from the minds of working-class pupils.

> To the musician nothing is more pathetic than to find a nice clean cherub-faced youngster, hailing from the wilds of Scotland or Wales, the possessor, perchance of an angelic voice, knows nothing of 'Auld Lang Syne' or the 'March of the Men of Harlech', but can howl the latest London music hall vulgarity.[69]

Although 'Slap, Bang, Here We Are Again' and 'Champagne Charlie' would not have been considered appropriate for music lessons in any school, some of the contemporary blackface minstrel songs were. In a list of songs taught to children attending the National School in the small Yorkshire village of Pocklington in the late 1860s and early 70s,[70] minstrel songs of the 'improving' variety can be found, such as 'I'd Choose To Be a Daisy' and 'I'm Lonely Since My Mother Died' (both referred to in Chapter 4). The children there also sang hymns, such as H. F. Lyte's 'Far from My Heavenly Home', and simple arias, like 'O Forest Deep and Gloomy' ('Bois épais' from Lully's *Amadis*). This school seems to have used tonic sol-fa, because several of the songs used appear in the *Tonic Sol-fa Times*, which ran from 1864 to 1873. In some elementary schools a remarkable degree of accomplishment was attained, with glee-singing in two or three parts and even the mounting of large-scale works, as the description below from 1885 tells:

> There is a school in the neighbourhood of Gray's Inn Road and Clerkenwell – not a cultured or aristocratic region – a school where fees are a difficulty, and boots a ceaseless care – where boys, girls, and teachers united in studying Mendelssohn's 'Athalie' ... The performance was listened to, and heartily appreciated, by a crowded audience of children, parents, school managers, and a few members of the board.[71]

The school performed this oratorio from a tonic sol-fa edition. It will be noted that music in schools meant vocal music; very few schools (including public schools) offered any other kind of musical instruction. It is thus clear that music which acted as a vehicle for text was deliberately privileged, partly no doubt because singing was the cheapest form of music-making and the most amenable to class teaching, but also perhaps because the dominant ideology can function more actively through the medium of song than through the abstract medium of instrumental music. To conclude with one among countless examples which illustrate this hegemonic function, a new version of 'Onward, Christian Soldiers' was composed by J. Tilleard (who was heavily involved in compiling school music for Novello) and 'intended to be sung by Schools' in commemoration of the passing of the Elementary Education Act'.[72]

Having been given an understanding and maybe an appetite for bourgeois music as working-class children, greater access to concerts and recitals then needed to be provided in order to keep up the good work. An example in London was the People's Concert Society (formed in 1878) designed to cater for the poorer parts of London.[73] In the provinces, concerts were also promoted for their 'humanizing' influence on the working class. The chief constable of Chester states, in his report for the year ending 29 September 1870, that with the opening of Saturday evening concerts 'a considerable decrease in the amount of drunkenness takes place'.[74] In Glasgow the Abstainers' Union established Saturday evening concerts at the City Hall, which the magistrates recognized as 'a most valuable auxiliary in keeping the streets quiet on a Saturday night, in the prevention of drunkenness and brawls, and in the improvement of a healthy and moral tone'.[75] Further stimulus to active participation in various forms of music-making (choirs, brass bands, etc.) was created by the ever growing number of competitions and competitive festivals from the 1880s onward. The last words go to Henry Leslie, a prominent judge in such competitions; his sentiments epitomize bourgeois hopes and desires regarding music as a means of promoting social order and family values among the working class:

> If there exists any rational mental employment that can be given to the masses after their hours of daily work, no one will deny that a humanizing, elevating, and refining influence will be obtained, that must be productive of increased strength to the ties of social and family life, and consequently of powerful good to the national life.[76]

10 Continuity and Change

In the mid-1890s the possibilities of the drawing-room ballad seemed to have been exhausted. Efforts to ensure its future led British ballad composers along the path of greater complexity, particularly with respect to harmony and the technical demands made on singer and accompanist. Composers in the United States, on the other hand, were moving in a different direction, producing ballads in a new and simple sentimental style. These flowed in abundance from an area surrounding Union Square, New York, known as 'Tin Pan Alley'. The origin of the name is attributed to Harry Von Tilzer (best known for 'A Bird in a Gilded Cage' of 1900), who said that the clatter of pianos sounding from open windows in every direction reminded him of tin pans.[1] Among the many influential figures who set up business there was Charles K. Harris, the 'father of Tin Pan Alley', who wrote and composed the famous song 'After the Ball' (1892) and was author of the standard text *How To Write a Popular Song*. The emphasis in Tin Pan Alley was on speed of production, followed by aggressive marketing using bribes and 'plants' (planted supporters in an audience), and, at the close of the century, employing professional 'pluggers' whose job was to advertise their firm's wares to suitable artistes. Pluggers also sang their publishing house's songs in music shops, restaurants, on street corners, and anywhere else they could command attention. The stimulus to all this activity was the new mass market which had been created by the US industrial revolution (*c*.1860–1900). The population of cities swelled dramatically as the economy changed from rural to industrial; New York grew from 800,000 in 1860 to 2,500,000 in 1900,[2] and had become the centre of music publishing in the United States in the 1880s.

Vaudeville theatres were the main shop window for Tin Pan Alley songs. Vaudeville was the new and respectable family entertainment begun in New York by Tony Pastor after the Civil War. The respectable character of this entertainment was important because it meant that middle-class women could attend, thereby guaranteeing sheet-music sales. Blackface minstrelsy gradually lost its pre-eminence and gave way to vaudeville in the 1890s. Minstrelsy had become more and more overblown and reliant on spectacle from the late 1870s when J. H. Haverly's Mastodon Minstrels were all the rage because of the size of the troupe (they were an unheard of forty strong) and their lavish productions. In the 1880s minstrelsy in Britain was exhibiting the same tendency towards opulent and spectacular shows, till the final stage was reached in which the troupes started to adopt the attire of the old courtly aristocracy, such as kneebreeches and powdered wigs. The traditional kind of minstrelsy was soon to be represented only by nostalgia shows. At the seaside resorts Pierrot shows were rapidly replacing the minstrels in the late nineteenth and early twentieth centuries.

Apart from minstrelsy the strongest influences on the initial style of Tin Pan Alley were British music-hall and the New York entertainments of Harrigan and Hart. Dave Braham, who composed the music to Ned Harrigan's words, was, in fact, a Londoner. The Harrigan and Hart shows were light comedies, usually based on an Irish theme: their first big success was *The Mulligan Guard* (1873), and one of the best-known of the Harrigan–Braham songs is 'Maggie Murphy's Home'.[3] The Tin Pan Alley style developed as a result of a dialectical interplay between publishers and consumers. The industry was never sure it knew the formula for success and therefore engaged in constant market research (to discover which songs sold best) and product testing (to gauge the reactions of performers and audience, and to weigh the risks of publication).

The first successful composer connected with the birth of Tin Pan Alley is Paul Dresser. His ballads 'On the Banks of the Wabash' and 'The Pardon Came Too Late' (both written and composed by him in 1891) sowed the seeds of the early style: two rather than three verses, and with each line being set syllabically in short and regular musical phrases; the structure is verse and refrain, with a generous amount of melodic and rhythmic repetition, though the chorus has an independent, almost detachable, quality not found in minstrel song.[4] Dresser's influence can be detected in Harry Armstrong's songs of the next century, such as 'Sweet Adeline' (1903) and 'Nellie Dean' (1905).[5] In early Tin Pan Alley songs the verse (which told the story) was always longer than the chorus; the latter was most frequently 16 bars long (32 if triple time), constructed on the typical British music-hall plan ABAC (where each letter denotes a musical phrase). The 16-bar ABAC structure was overtaken by the 32-bar AABA format later, as in 'Ain't She Sweet?' of 1927. Even if the singer and accompanist enjoyed some musical independence in the verse section, the piano invariably reinforced the tune of the chorus.[6] The weight of the song's appeal moved more pronouncedly to the chorus when it became conventional to end the verse in the dominant key in order to create expectation. This shift of emphasis (which eventually led to choruses becoming the only memorable parts of songs) is evident in 'Sweet Rosie O'Grady' of 1896, and is made markedly so by the contrast between duple time verse and triple time chorus.[7] Triple time was common in Tin Pan Alley songs and stands as testimony to the continuing attraction of the *valse boston* (the forerunner of the 'modern waltz'). Sometimes the lilting movement seems singularly at odds with the words, as in G. L. Davis's 'In the Baggage Coach Ahead' (1896), the tale of a man escorting his dead wife in her coffin by rail, accompanied by their crying child.[8] Nevertheless, this kind of song caught on in Britain, as is shown by 'Give Me a Ticket to Heaven' of 1903.[9]

One of the striking features of Tin Pan Alley songs is their use of musical clichés. This is generally taken to be symptomatic of the application of formula in their construction. Yet, although the songwriters of Tin Pan Alley were indeed keen to discover an archetypal successful song formula which could then be put into production with minimal changes over and over again, they were no more able to achieve this than were the songwriters for Boosey's ballad concerts. The musical clichés are more likely to be a reflection of the speed of production: clichés are ubiquitous in improvised music, for example, usually passing under such names as 'licks' (stereotyped accompaniment patterns) and 'ending tags' (stereotyped patterns at the close of a musical phrase). Typical Tin Pan Alley 'ending tags' are given below; the first might come half-way through a chorus, the second at the end.

The number of clichés which entered the songs increased when the influence of the improvized 'jig piano' of black musicians began to be felt. The decline of the minstrel show had also affected black musicians, who were now returning to performing for mainly black audiences and developing new black styles (black vaudeville for whites did not arrive until the 1930s). The term 'ragtime' was first coined for this music by a Chicago journalist in 1897, but by then it was becoming a non-improvisational form (the Scott Joplin rags contain no improvisation). Ragtime swept Tin Pan Alley in two waves, the most successful ragtime song of the early period being 'Hello! Ma Baby' of 1899, and the most successful song of the ragtime revival being 'Alexander's Ragtime Band' of 1911, which actually only had its verse written in ragtime. Of course, singers went back to earlier songs and gave them a ragtime treatment: a notable example was 'Bill Bailey, Won't You Please Come Home', which in its 1902 edition contained no ragtime rhythms. The first wave of ragtime from the United States had little obvious impact in Britain; yet the infectious rhythmic character of some of Leslie Stuart's songs, like 'Lily of Laguna' (1898), is undoubtedly indebted to the new style.

Tin Pan Alley triumphantly reversed the direction of traffic in music, which till then, with the exception of minstrelsy, had flowed from Britain to the United States. Previously, British music-hall had offered opportunities for American composers (like Alfred Lee, who supplied the music to Leybourne's songs 'Champagne Charlie' and 'The Man on the Flying Trapeze'); now vaudeville enticed British composers to cross the Atlantic. Harry Dacre, well known for 'Daisy Bell' (1892), was one who succumbed to this temptation ('I'll Be Your Sweetheart' was written in the United States in 1899) and Felix McGlennon was another. Songs written for the US market were found to be serviceable for the UK market. Even songs written specifically for the Spanish-American War of 1898 (a conflict which was short-lived and represented a poor investment for music publishers) were recycled for the Boer War; an example is 'Dolly Gray'. A problem arose only with regard to place names (though, strangely, not one affecting Stuart's references to Laguna and Idaho): songs which vaunted a prominent foreign name, like 'On the Banks of the Wabash' were under a handicap. All the same, this difficulty could be felicitously overcome, as when Harry Von Tilzer's 'Under the Anheuser Busch' was transformed into 'Down at the Old Bull and Bush' (the name of a Hampstead pub).

At the turn of the century the United States, not Britain, was the leading force in the commercial music industry. Even what might be termed the British style of ballad had found rivals in the compositions of Reginald De Koven, Ethelbert Nevin, and Carrie Jacobs Bond. As mentioned at the beginning of this chapter, the British ballad was becoming more complex, taking on in a watered-down fashion some of the innovations, especially harmonic, of composers like Brahms, Wagner, and Liszt. British composers still looked to Germany for their training, as singers looked to Italy. There was conviction in the progress of musical art: John Barnett felt able to say categorically in 1891, 'I think there has been a great improvement in the smaller compositions as compared with those of a hundred years ago.'[10] At the same time there was a feeling that music in Europe was approaching a turning point when people would 'tire of this constant striving after effect' and revert to simplicity.[11] Simplicity was restored to ballad composition by Tin Pan Alley and it would be tempting to see this alone as the reason for the decline of the British ballad.

There are other factors to consider, however, not the least of which concerns the improvements made to the comfort and safety of bicycles. The attraction bicycling held for young women in the 1890s created growing resentment in the music trades, culminating in a welter of anti-cycling propaganda in 1896. Here is an example taken from the *Musical Times* of May of that year:

> We may point out that a new and most formidable enemy of the pianoforte has arisen of late in the bicycle . . . there are literally thousands of young ladies whose leisure hours, formerly passed in large part on the music-stool, are now spent in the saddle of the 'iron bird' . . . proof positive is afforded by advertisements which announce the sale of pianofortes by individuals at great sacrifice on the ground that their owners are 'going in for cycling'.[12]

Attempts were made to dissuade women from cycling by appealing to their concern for health – 'the rapid passage through the air may be a positive source of danger'[13] – or by appealing to their vanity – 'the bicycle hand . . . becomes flattened, bulges out at the sides, gets lumpy and out of shape, and the fingers all become crooked'.[14] The last bit of 'expert' advice issued from the United States where cycling was also turning women away from music during their leisure hours. It would be wrong, therefore, to see the bicycle as something only threatening the profits of the British music trade. The situation was obviously being exaggerated, since there still remained an enormous demand for teachers of music (particularly piano teachers), the number of 'music masters' almost doubling between 1881 and 1911, according to census figures.[15] These teachers were forced to compete in a 'payment by results' environment when the Associated Board of the Royal Schools of Music developed a system of graded examinations (which could be taken only on 'respectable' instruments). However, their pupils were now able to gain good passes in all of the exams by restricting their learning to a few pieces a year. In 1899 the *British Medical Journal* voiced their concern not against cycling but against too much piano practice, suggesting it was responsible for 'the chloroses [green sickness – a form of anaemia] and neuroses from which so many young girls suffer', and adding, 'All – except perhaps teachers of music – will agree that at the present day the piano is too much with us.'[16]

Since the Diamond Jubilee of 1897 prompted so much summing up of achievements during the Queen's reign, it is a convenient date to choose for assessing the continuity and discontinuity between the music-making of the late nineteenth and early twentieth centuries. One of the comments made with pride during the Jubilee year was 'we get more music now in one month than they had in the whole of the year 1839'.[17] The years that followed, up to 1914, continued to see a spread of choirs and orchestras, opera companies, brass bands, and recitals of various kinds. Yet some of the long-established concerts were on the wane in the 1890s: the Monday 'Pops' closed down in 1893, the Saturday 'Pops' closing, too, in 1903, and there was diminishing interest in the triennial Crystal Palace Handel Festival, the audience dropping by a quarter between 1888 and 1897. Enthusiasm for tonic sol-fa had also passed its peak, for, although it was a 'great cause for congratulation' that music had 'come within the grasp of the horny-handed sons of toil', it was now hoped that the tonic sol-faists would 'soon recognize the drag which the letter notation imposes on the progress of school singing and musical education generally'.[18]

The drawing-room ballad, as already remarked at the beginning of this chapter, was at a turning point; two years before the Jubilee a writer pronounced, 'The old drawing-room ballad is as dead as Thomas Haynes Bayly.'[19] Nevertheless, in the twentieth century the ballad made a temporary recovery: 1919 was one of Boosey's best years for ballad sales, and the Ballad Concerts were not terminated until 1936. There were certain broad changes in the Edwardian ballad which set it apart from the Victorian variety. The 'moral fibre' was different; either Victorian solemnity gave way to Edwardian forced gaiety, or sentimentality was employed for its own sake rather than to reinforce a moral message (hence the use of narrative was not so necessary). The richer harmonies of the later ballad might be interpreted as cloying and decadent in the 1890s, but sophisticated in the 1900s. Moreover, a new artistic ambitiousness was evident in the production of ballad cycles, prompted by the great success of Liza Lehmann's *In a Persian Garden* of 1896 (words selected from Fitzgerald's translation of the *Rubáiyát of Omar Khayyám*).

Several new directions were taken in early twentieth-century ballads. The emergence of a new kind of imperialist song has been noted in Chapter 8. Emotional but 'stiff upper-lipped' appeals to patriotism took the place of boastful threats to the enemy set in vigorous strains. It is this, the sentiment of ballads like 'Land of Hope and Glory', which still moves many today, while Felix McGlennon's 'Sons of the Sea' (1897) is found ludicrous. Though the latter remained well known for the first half of this century (made famous by Arthur Reece), the second line of the chorus came to be changed from 'All British born!' to 'Bobbing up and down like this' (accompanied by actions), thus deflating the jingoism. The historical pageantry so favoured in Edwardian ballads may be traced back to the Diamond Jubilee which exceeded the 1887 Golden Jubilee in every respect. Among the ritualistic musical offerings were Cowen's *All Hail the Glorious Reign* (words by C. Bingham) and Elgar's *The Banner of St George* (words by S. Wensley). Jubilee commemorations and memorabilia were everywhere: trees were planted, medals awarded, villages had new water pumps, and innumerable other ways were found to mark the occasion. The monarchy was now firmly entrenched as a symbol of Britain and all things British; one of the ballad 'hits' of the 1897 Jubilee, Leslie Stuart's 'The Soldiers of the Queen', demonstrates this in its title (the words of the song were later rewritten to aid recruiting for the Boer War). The period of the Queen's reign was already being openly referred to as 'the Victorian age' during the previous Jubilee[20] and it is no surprise that comparisons with the long reign of Elizabeth I would increase. This left its mark in the fascination with 'merrie England' and characters like Drake so often encountered in Edwardian ballads.

Love songs, especially of an exotic nature, were far more prevalent than before. Musical comedies from the United States, like Kerker's *The Belle of New York*, had pioneered a new boldness in the expression of male and female relationships (see, for example, Fifi's song 'Oh, Teach Me How To Kiss'), and a few years later Viennese operettas, like Lehár's *The Merry Widow*, introduced a new sensuous manner. The passionate and seductive sensuality found in 'Come, Come I Love You Only' from Oscar Straus's *The Chocolate Soldier* is on a different plane from the melancholy, if equally passionate, yearning of Woodforde-Finden's 'Kashmiri Song'. Viennese operetta for a while blocked the flow of stage works from the United States which looked set to swamp British theatres after the tremendously successful run of *The Belle of New York* at London's Shaftesbury Theatre from 1898 to 1901.

Songs in vernacular speech or dialect form another prominent type of Edwardian ballad. These songs fall into two categories, those purporting to be the expression of the common soldier or sailor, and those sporting a rustic character. The former have their origin in Kipling's *Barrack-Room Ballads* (Newbolt doing for the Navy what Kipling did for the Army), while the latter show the influence of the Folksong Movement. They may have original music, like Vaughan Williams' 'Linden Lea', or only the words may be fresh, as in Weatherly's 'Danny Boy'; there again, they may contain a mixture of traditional and new, as in 'The Floral Dance' by Katie Moss. In the last-mentioned ballad the tale of refreshment afforded to a tired urban soul by a traditional Cornish dance can be read as a metaphor for the condition of the drawing-room ballad at that time. Folksong research began to have an impact on the drawing-room ballad about the time of the Diamond Jubilee, when Boosey published Arthur Grimshaw's ballad 'The Songs My Mother Sang', described as a 'Come-all-ye' and making use of traditional words and tunes. The Folk-Song Society was itself founded the year after the Jubilee.

It was not just the drawing-room ballad into which the Folksong Movement helped breathe new life; this movement and that of musical antiquarianism, rather than the much lauded German music and German musical instruction, proved to be the means of kindling an English musical renaissance. In the nineteenth century British composers were sent to study in Germany; music of the German school was then synonymous with the term 'classical music' and carried no suggestion of national style. Only when the subject of national styles started to intrigue composers was there much thought given to the question of the appropriateness of German musical practices to British composers. The search for national character, as noted in Chapter 8, led composers towards an elusive and largely mythical category of music given the label 'folk music'. One of the remarkable achievements of Sullivan was that, having mastered both German and Italian compositional techniques, he moved away to create a style dominated by neither. Thus he anticipated later developments in British music, particularly when he reverted to a manner evocative of an old English air, as in 'I Have a Song To Sing, O!' from *Yeomen of the Guard* (1888). The attractive and imaginative musical idiom Sullivan developed from *Trial by Jury* (1875) onward precipitated the two-way split of burlesque into operetta and variety entertainment. It is an accepted notion now that Vaughan Williams and company rid English concert life of the stifling effect of poorly imitated German music, but in the year of Sullivan's death it had seemed a valid claim that his *Golden Legend* of 1886 'finally drove Mendelssohnianism off the concert platform'.[21] However, forward-looking as Sullivan may have appeared in some ways, by the end of the century his reliance on literal descriptive effects was beginning to be thought outmoded. Even in 1893 *The Golden Legend* came in for criticism on these grounds.[22]

Sullivan provides one line of continuity between the ballad of the early twentieth century and that of the nineteenth; but it is the songs of his operettas which proved more enduring and influential in this respect (Edward German can clearly be seen assuming Sullivan's mantle). Another unbroken line links the big sacred ballads of the 1890s with those which came later. Sacred songs continued to sell steadily, including those written for a combination of piano and harmonium accompaniment, like Teresa Del Riego's 'The Perfect Prayer' of 1908. It would be mistaken, too, to assume that Victorian ballads were merely forgotten; there was a stream of publications offering selections of these.

A boost for ballads came with the birth of the gramophone industry. At first, the cost of records automatically restricted their purchase to the wealthy, ensuring that middle-class taste was well served. A record of Patti singing 'Home, Sweet Home!' retailed at £1 in 1906.[23] Eventually, of course, records would begin to outsell sheet music, but that was a long way ahead. When another Patti, Patti Page, had a hit in 1950 with 'Tennessee Waltz' it proved to be the last time a song had sheet music sales exceeding one million; subsequently disc sales displaced sheet music sales (and even this disc overtook its sheet music sales six times over by 1967).[24] All the big Tin Pan Alley hits, from 'After the Ball' onwards, had sold well over a million copies of sheet music.

The drawing-room ballad lingered on for many years, promoted by singers like Peter Dawson (a pupil of Charles Santley and a prolific recorder for the gramophone). In variety shows the description 'ballad vocalist' on the bill denoted a singer who specialized in this kind of repertoire. The ballad still thrived in seaside pavilions, though Tin Pan Alley may have occupied the beach. The music of blackface minstrelsy continued to resonate too: Paul Robeson inherited the drawing-room leanings of minstrel song, while G. H. Elliot and Al Jolson took over the vaudeville side (now blended with ragtime). It must be said, however, that Robeson moved from the transparent racism of songs such as 'Honey (Dat's All)' which contained the lines 'Angels brought yo' in da night, Done forgot to make yo' white' to a version of 'Ol' Man River' rewritten from a socialist perspective. The great Victorian institution of the 'musical evening' also continued into the twentieth century, although in the words of Maurice Disher, 'the sense of tribal duty was lacking'.[25]

Conclusion

Here I must end what has been a book devoted very much to a general survey of this music and historical period. I emphasize again that there was no actual end to British ballad production in 1897 or 98; it was merely the end of a boom, and therefore a convenient point to conclude this survey, since the ballad in the twentieth century demands a book to itself. Some types of ballad, as I have already mentioned, continued to flourish at the turn of the century, unaffected by Tin Pan Alley, Viennese operetta, or musical comedy from the United States – prominent among these were the sacred ballad and what might loosely be termed the 'imperialist' ballad and the 'rustic' ballad. The drawing-room ballad enjoyed another boom immediately after the Great War. Yet it is interesting to note that in a recent collection of original recordings of songs and music of the First World War (Saydisc CSDL 358, 1986) about a third of the musical items date from the nineteenth century; nothing has supplanted 'old favourites' like 'The Deathless Army' and 'Boys of the Old Brigade'.

Virtually every aspect of nineteenth-century bourgeois 'popular song' needs further research, together with a detailed study of the domestic instrumental music. There is a lot more work to be done on the early market (pre-1870), but even my account of the later, rapidly expanding market is sketchy. The Boosey

Ballad Concerts would make an excellent centre piece for a deeper analysis of the 'ballad boom'. More evidence is required and more research needed on the reception and use of bourgeois song; indeed the whole question of nineteenth-century bourgeois song and hegemony needs to be tackled in greater detail. On the subject of cheap concerts, choirs and bands, broached in Chapter 9, I should draw the reader's attention to Dave Russell's new book (published as this work was going to press) for a wealth of information of which I was unaware when writing my own account (see bibliography). Among other matters, those which spring first to mind in calling for particular exploration are the ideological side of the growth of the music market, the class basis of revivalism, and its relation to gospel song, and the way bourgeois domestic music has been mediated (perhaps it could be argued that its removal from the 'art music' canon was an attempt to disguise the conflicts in bourgeois music). To end on a musical matter, the way in which the music itself articulates meaning in drawing-room ballads also deserves to be investigated.

Notes

Introduction

1 See Harker 1985: 198–210.
2 Lamb, A. 1980, 'Popular music, §1', in Sadie 1980, vol. 15: 89.
3 For a short historical account of the several uses of the word 'popular', including its shift in sense to mean 'well-liked' in the nineteenth century, see Williams, R. 1976, *Keywords*, London: Fontana, rev. and expanded edn 1983: 236–38.
4 Eagleton, T. 1983, *Literary Theory*, Oxford: Blackwell: 11.
5 '. . . musical reformers like Palestrina, Bach, Gluck, Beethoven, Berlioz and Liszt have shown the art its laws.' Einstein, A. 1947, *Music in the Romantic Era*, London: Dent: 314.
6 Ibid., 296.
7 Longyear, R. M. 1969, *Nineteenth Century Romanticism in Music*, London: Prentice Hall: 180.
8 Gramsci, A. 1971, *Selections from the Prison Notebooks*, ed. and trans. Hoare, Q. and Nowell-Smith, G., London: Lawrence and Wishart: 57.
9 Marx, K. and Engels, F. 1964, *The German Ideology*, Moscow: Progress Publishers: 61.
10 Padover, S. K. (ed.), 1979 *The Essential Marx*, New York: Mentor Books: 241.
11 Letter to J. Bloch, 21 September 1890, quoted in Williams, R., 1963 *Culture and Society*, Harmondsworth: Penguin.
12 Barthes, R., 1977 'Musica Practica', Heath, S. (ed.), *Image–Music–Text*, Glasgow: Fontana.
13 For a full-length study of British punk rock, see Laing, D., 1985 *One Chord Wonders*, Milton Keynes: Open University Press.

Chapter 1

1 Quoted in Birnie, A., 1935 *An Economic History of the British Isles*, London: Methuen: 245.
2 Marx and Engels 1975: 28.
3 'The line from 1832 to Chartism is not a haphazard pendulum alteration of "political" and "economic" agitations but a direct progression' Thompson 1968; 1982 reprint: 909.
4 Disraeli, B., 1844 *Coningsby* chapter 7 (reprinted Heron Books, 1978, and Oxford University Press, 1982).

5   Durfey, T., *Wit and Mirth: or Pills to Purge Melancholy*, final edn of 6 vols., London, 1719–20.

6   Thomson, W., *Orpheus Caledonius*, London, 1725–6.

7   Burney, C., 1776 *A General History of Music*, reprint of 1789 edn, New York: Dover, 1957: 1016.

8   See No. 17, Air with Chorus, Thomas and Sailors.

9   See No. 23, Recit., Thomas, Sally and Squire.

10 See No. 14, Duetto, Sally and Squire.

11 For information, see Fiske, R., 1973.

12 Buck, P. C., 1931 *The Oxford Song Book*, Oxford: Oxford University Press: vol. 1, 52.

13 The original song may be found in Turner and Miall 1972: 296–303.

14 Corder, F., 1918 'The Works of Sir Henry Bishop', *Musical Quarterly*, vol. 4: 78.

15 Bratton 1975: 90–1.

16 Quoted in Turner and Miall 1972: 143.

17 For further information, see White 1951.

18 Max Miradin has reconstructed the lost libretto of this work, and a modern score has been published, edited by Nicholas Temperley.

19 This aria may be found in Turner and Miall 1972: 32–4.

20 See Cherubino's aria *Non so più*, from Act 2 of *The Marriage of Figaro*.

21 See the Countess's aria *Dove sono*, from Act 3 of the above.

22 See Rosina and Figaro's duet *Dunque io son*, from Act 2 of *The Barber of Seville*.

23 See Percy's aria *Vivi tu, tu ne scongiuro*, from Act 2 of *Anna Bolena*.

24 See Rodolfo's cavatina *Vi ravviso*, from *La Sonnambula*.

25 Disher 1955: 22.

26 Quoted in Fiske 1983: 67.

27 See Boydell 1979: 15.

28 J. W. Glover's *Preface* in 1859 Dublin edition of the *Irish Melodies*.

29 The song may be found in Turner and Miall 1972: 214–16.

30 Kalischer, A. C., (trans. Shedlock, J. S.), 1972 *Beethoven's Letters*, New York: Dover: 140.

31 Hogarth 1842: xxv.

32 Dibdin 1803: xxii.

33 Dibdin, C., 1807 *The Public Undeceived*, London: 10. Note that the adjective 'democratic' is used pejoratively at this date.

34 Dibdin 1807: 21.

35 Dibdin 1807: 24.

36 The song may be found in Turner and Miall 1972: 94–6.

37 A sheer-hulk was a dismasted ship used as a floating crane-platform.

38 Hogarth 1842: xxv–xxvi.

39 Dibdin 1803: xxiii.

40 Lest it be thought that Bayly and his wife furnish a typical example of absentee landlordism, it should be mentioned that Bayly attacked neglectful absentee landlords in his poem 'The Absentee' (from *Erin and Other Poems*, 1822). Bayly donated the profits from this publication to the fund for the relief of distressed peasantry in the South of Ireland.

41 Quoted in Hanchant 1932: xxix.

42 Russell 1895: 12.

43 Lee 1970: 99–100.

44 Russell 1895: 67.

45 Russell 1895: 177.

46 Russell 1895: 193.

47 Russell 1895: 188.

48 The song may be found in Turner and Miall 1972: 101–5.

49 Russell 1895: 253.

50 Hogarth 1842: xxii. Burns offers a similar illustration of this maxim; for, though considerably lax in his own 'moral standards' (especially concerning drink and women), he endorses bourgeois respectability in his poetry:

> But Nelly's looks are blithe and sweet,
> And what is best of a' –
> Her reputation is complete,
> And fair without a flaw.

(from 'My Handsome Nell')

51 The typical glee was in three-part harmony for male voices. Perhaps the best-known example is John Callcott's 'Ye Gentlemen of England' (an updated early nineteenth-century version of a song which first appeared in *180 Loyal Songs*, printed in 1686).

Chapter 2

1 Price lists given in Harding 1933: 381–2.

2 See Best 1979: 110.

3 See Ehrlich 1976: 38.

4 Quoted Ehrlich 1976: 44.

5 H. F. C., 1838–9 'The pianoforte', *Westminster Review*, vol. 32: 306.

6 Haweis 1871: 409.

7 Smiles, S., 1851–2 'Music in the house', *Eliza Cook's Journal*, vol. 6: 210.

8 Smiles 1851–2: 209.

9 Quoted in Stratton, S. S., 1882–3 'Women in relation to musical art', *Royal Musical Association Proceedings*, vol. 9: 125.

10 M., 1859–60 'Classical music and British musical taste', *Macmillan's Magazine*, vol. 1: 389.

11 Haweis 1871: 515–16.

12 Lake, E., 1891–2 'Some thoughts on the social appreciation of music', *RMA Proceedings*, vol. 18: 98.

13 E. C., 1852 'Our musical corner', *Eliza Cook's Journal*, vol. 7: 270.

14 E. C., 1852–3 'Our musical corner', *Eliza Cook's Journal*, vol. 8: 76.

15 Ibid., p. 76.

16 Ibid., p. 76.

17 Ibid., p. 76.

18 H. F. C., 'The Pianoforte', op. cit.: 309.

19 Haweis 1871: 112.

20 Sutherland Edwards, H., 1875–6 'The literary maltreatment of music', *Macmillan's Magazine*, vol. 33: 555.

21 M., 'Classical Music and British Musical Taste', op. cit.: 383.

22 Quoted in Poole, H. E., 1980 'Printing and publishing of music, I', in Sadie 1980, vol. 15: 247.

23 In 1849 the *Morning Herald* reported that over 20,000 copies had been sold. See Hurd, M., 1981 *Vincent Novello and Company*, London: Granada: 55.

24 Cummings, W. H., 1884–5 'Music printing', *RMA Proceedings*, vol. II: 111.

25   King, A. H., 1949–50 'English pictorial music title-pages 1820–1885', *The Library*, 5th series, Oxford, Oxford University Press vol. 4: 263.
26   ·Lunn, H. C., 'Music of society', Lunn 1854.
27   See Traies, J., 1986 'Jones and the working girl: class marginality in music-hall song 1860–1900', in Bratton 1986: 23–48.
28   These comments are reprinted on the back page of Mrs Streatfeild's 'The Golden Gate', a religious ballad published by Robert Cocks & Co., London, 1864.
29   Ibid., advertising 'The Bridge', a setting of Longfellow's poem by Miss Lindsay.
30   *Westminster Review*, vol. 42, 1844: 263.
31   Wood, A., 1964 *The Physics of Music*, London: Methuen: 237.
32   Crawford 1977: v.
33   Confusingly, 'melodeon' is also the name given to the button accordion; an instrument which differs from the ordinary accordion in that it produces different notes from the same button, depending on whether the bellows are drawn or squeezed. This particular melodeon became a favourite instrument in Germany from the mid-nineteenth century onwards.
34   Wiley Hitchcock, H., notes accompanying the recording *Songs by Stephen Foster*, Nonesuch Records, H-71268, 1972.

Chapter 3

1   Thompson 1968: 454.
2   *Westminster Review*, January 1884: 153.
3   Stedman, J. W., 1980 'From dame to woman', in Vicinus 1980: 37.
4   *Westminster Review*, October 1856: 443–4.
5   *Dictionary of National Biography*, vol. XXI: 32.
6   Dunbar 1953: 89.
7   *Englishwoman's Review*, 15 October 1888: 446–7.
8   *Englishwoman's Review*, 15 January 1900: 47.
9   Wood, E., 1980 'Women in music', in *SIGNS, Journal of Women in Culture and Society*, University of Chicago, vol. 6, no. 2, Winter 1980: 295.
10   'Prefatory memoir' (anon.), no date (*c.* 1880) *The Poetical Works of Mrs Hemans*, London: Frederick Warne: xxiv.
11   *Englishwoman's Review*, 14 December 1889: 540.
12   Ibid., 539.
13   The song may be found in Turner and Miall 1975: 27–30.
14   Acland 1948: 93.
15   Peters, M., 1972 *Jean Ingelow, Victorian Poetess*, Ipswich: Boydell Press: 77.
16   The song may be found in Turner and Miall 1972: 51–3.

Chapter 4

1   See Wittke 1930: 21 and 23–4.
2   Toll 1974: 25.
3   Evidence provided by his brother, Morrison Foster, in Foster 1896: 20.
4   See Seeger, P., 1961 *How To Play the 5-String Banjo*, Beacon, NY: author publisher, 3rd Edition: 5 and 68–9.

5   Letter printed in Chase 1966: 293.
6   Advertisement quoted in Wittke 1930: 51.
7   Pickering, M., 1986 'White skin, black masks', in Bratton 1986: 84.
8   For a discussion of the significance of the mask, see Bratton 1986: 78–80.
9   Bratton 1986: 79.
10 Printed on the back cover of 'The Doctor Says I'm Not To Be Worried', and other Hunter songs published by J. Turner, London.
11 Advertisement on the back cover of 'Driven from Home' (Will S. Hays), another lachrymose ballad sung by Horace Norman.
12 Advertisement on the back cover of 'Sammy Stammers' (words by J. F. McArdle, music by Vincent Davies), a 'great stuttering song' sung by James Francis of the Mohawk Minstrels.
13 Anon., 1852 'The songs of Scotland', *Eliza Cook's Journal*, vol. 7: 278.
14 Ibid., 276.
15 Allibone, S. A., 1858 *Dictionary of English Literature*, Philadelphia: Lippincott, 1858, republished Detroit: Gale Research Company, 1965: 123.
16 Quoted in the *Dictionary of National Biography*, vol. 1: 1157.
17 For the original tune, see Beethoven's *12 Scottish Songs*, No. 9.
18 The two versions are printed in Ross, A. (ed.), 1910 *Thirty Songs by Lady John Scott*, Edinburgh: Paterson.
19 Anon., 1852 'The songs of Scotland', *Eliza Cook's Journal*, vol. 7: 277.
20 Blackie, J. S., 1885 'Popular songs of the Scottish Highlanders', *Macmillan's Magazine*, vol. 52: 304.
21 Blackie, op. cit., constantly speaks of *volkslied* or of 'popular song'; E. J. Breakspeare, in 'Songs and song-writers' (*RMA Proceedings*, vol. 8, 1882: 59), speaks of *volkslied* or of 'folk's-song'.
22 Quoted in Paterson, A. W., 1897 'The characteristic traits of Irish music', *RMA Proceedings*, vol. 23: 96.
23 St John Lacy, F., 1890 'Notes on Irish music', *RMA Proceedings*, vol. 16: 180.
24 The song may be found in *49 Irish Songs*, London: Bayley & Ferguson (n.d.): 28, in an arrangement by Alfred Moffat.
25 See Turner and Miall 1975: 202. The song itself is given on pp. 196–201 (it contains one or two printing errors).
26 The song may be found in Turner and Miall 1972: 116–19.
27 In *Welsh Melodies*, c. 1865 published by Lamborn Cock, Addison & Co., London.
28 See Gill, W. H., 1895 'Manx Music', *RMA Proceedings*, vol. 22, 115.
29 The early English field-collectors are discussed in Harker, D., *Fakesong*, Milton Keynes: Open University Press, 1985, pp. 146–69.

Chapter 5

1   Disher 1955: 140.
2   See Mackerness 1964: 191–3.
3   Trevelyan, G. M., 1946 *English Social History*, London: Longmans, Green, 3rd edition: 517.
4   See Palisca, C. V., 1968 *Baroque Music*, New Jersey: Prentice Hall: 196.
5   Buckley, R. J., 1909 'Preface' in Stein, J. (ed.), *The Nation's Music*, London: Cassell, vol. 5, *Sacred*.
6   Spencer Curwen, J., 1886–7 'The musical form of the hymn tune', *RMA Proceedings*, vol. 13: 41.

7   Ibid., 55.

8   Buckley, op. cit.: 10.

9   See Best 1979: 74–5.

10 Unattributed quotation advertising Miss M. Lindsay's sacred songs, on the back cover of 'The Golden Gate', words by Miss Proctor (*sic*), music by Mrs Charles N. Streatfeild, published by R. Cocks & Co., London, 1864.

11 The song may be found in Turner and Miall, 1972: 98–9. This version does, however, omit the plentiful use of trills which decorate other copies, and avoids the dramatic *tremolando* effects in verse 2.

12 The duet may be found in Turner and Miall 1975: 254–62.

13 See Ward, T. R., 1980 'The modern English hymn' in Sadie 1980, vol. 8: 850.

14 No. 139 of Sankey, I. D. (ed.), 1873 *Sacred Songs and Solos*, London: Morgan & Scott.

15 For information on Lorenzo Dow in England, see Jackson 1943: 89–98.

16 Cravath, E. M., 1899 'Fisk University's Great Necessity', preliminary note in Marsh: 1899.

17 Marsh 1899: 73.

18 Marsh 1899: 84.

19 See Burleigh, H. T. (arranger), 1917 *Negro Spirituals*, London: G. Ricordi. This collection consists entirely of arrangements for solo voice plus piano, whereas *Jubilee Songs: As Sung by the Jubilee Singers* (New York: Biglow & Main, *c.* 1872) contained vocal parts only, for soloists and chorus.

20 The *First Vocal Album* of Schubert songs published as part of Schirmer's *Library of Musical Classics*, for example, makes no mention of Scott's authorship of the 'Ave Maria'.

21 This song may be found in Turner and Miall 1972: 189–95.

22 A selection of Christmas piano music, songs, and musical games can be found in Graves 1980.

Chapter 6

1   Young 1968: 127.

2   Pearce 1924: 219.

3   Scholes 1947, vol. 1: 197.

4   *British Parliamentary Papers, Stage and Theatre*, vol. 2, 1866, Irish University Press, 1968: 321.

5   *Dictionary of National Biography*, vol. VII: 108.

6   Boosey 1931: 23–4.

7   *The Monthly Musical Record*, 1 February 1871: 24.

8   Boosey 1931: 89.

9   Advertisement on the back of 'Wouldn't You Like To Know?' (words by J. P. Hutchinson, music by E. Reyloff), published in Davidson's *Musical Treasury*. The phrase 'music for the million' had been made famous by Mainzler.

10 Mair 1961: 10.

11 See Saul, S. B., 1969 *The Myth of the Great Depression, 1873–1896*, London: Macmillan: 13–14.

12 Advertisement in *The Graphic*, 22 January 1887: 88.

13 Advertisement used by Hopwood & Crew in the late 1860s to recommend their complete repertoire of the Christy Minstrels (Moore & Burgess props.). Their list contains some four hundred songs.

14 Meadows White, F., 1880–1 'A concise view of the law of copyright as affecting composers of music', *RMA Proceedings*, vol. 7: 153.

15 Ibid., 158; a contribution by W. H. Cummings to the discussion which followed Meadows White's paper. The ballad in question was written by T. H. Bayly and composed by J. P. Knight.

16 Mair 1961: 33.

17 Simpson 1910: 145.

18 Russell 1895: 198. Russell is prone to exaggeration, so it is not advisable to accept his remarks verbatim. It is difficult to locate anywhere near the eight hundred publications he mentions, for example.

19 *The Songs of Charles Dibdin*, London: Davidson, 1842: xx.

20 A photograph of the contract appears in Garrett 1976 (no page numbers).

21 The letter is reproduced in Young 1971: 108.

22 Boosey 1931: 17.

23 Comments by Mr Praeger in the discussion following Charles Santley's paper, 'The Vocal Art', in *RMA Proceedings*, vol. II, 1884–85: 58–9.

24 Santley, op. cit.: 56.

25 See Scholes 1947, vol. I: 296.

26 Pearsall 1973: 95.

27 Scholes 1947, vol. I: 293.

28 Scholes 1947, vol. I: 295.

29 Boosey 1931: 22. Mentioning songs and solos is not tautology; ballad concerts contained instrumental pieces as well as songs: the great violinist Kreisler, for example, gave performances at ballad concerts.

30 Pearsall 1973: 222.

31 Pearce 1924: 256.

32 Pearce 1924: 306–7.

33 Laurence 1981, vol. I: 176.

34 Laurence 1981, vol. I: 176–7.

35 W. B. S., 'Braham, John', entry in *Dictionary of National Biography*, vol. II: 1104.

36 Scholes 1947, vol. I: 281.

37 Scholes 1947, vol. I, quoted on p. 203.

38 Daly, W., jnr, n.d. (1890s) 'Modern singers and Modern "Methods"', *British Minstrelsie*, London: Blackwood, Le Bas, vol. 2: vii.

39 See *The Graphic*, 30 July 1887: 123.

40 Scholes 1947: 287.

Chapter 7

1 For example, see Pearce 1924: 196.

2 Thomas's elder brother, William, was particularly interested in what he termed 'old English ditties'; his main work was the publication *Popular Music of the Olden Time*, 2 vols., 1855–9.

3 The story originates in Arthur Lawrence's volume of Sullivan's memoirs, and is quoted at length in Simpson 1910: 150.

4 Simpson 1910: 151.

5 *New York Herald*, 23 October 1879, quoted in Young 1971: 122.

6 Since writing this I have come across the claim by William Boosey that it was *he* who told Maybrick, 'it *must* be a sea song' (Boosey 1931: 18) and that originally it had

sentimental words. Which version of the song was rejected 'by several publishers' (according to Simpson 1910: 193) it is impossible to now say without further evidence.

7   Disher 1955: 212.
8   Quoted in Turner and Miall 1975: 189.
9   The British Library Catalogue of Printed Music gives 1898 which was actually the date of the 'entirely new' edition.
10 Quoted in Nettel 1956: 220.
11 A contribution by Weatherly to Simpson 1910.
12 This sort of behaviour is discussed in Harker 1985. See, for example, pp. 169–71.
13 He advertised the amount paid, quoting a report in *The Times*, 26 April 1894, on the front cover of copies of the sheet music. It read as follows: '*Anchored!*, by the late Michael Watson, realized £1212..15..0: the largest price, we believe, that has ever been given for a song.' (The song had first been published in London in 1883, and a little later republished by the firm of B. Williams.)

Chapter 8

1   Lenin, V. I., 1917 *Imperialism: the Highest Stage of Capitalism*, Moscow: Progress Publishers, 1968: 73.
2   The phrase 'conscious imperialism' was coined by J. A. Hobson in *Imperialism: A Study*, London, 1902.
3   See Sturgis, J., 1984 'Britain and the new imperialism', in Eldridge, C. C. (ed.), 1984 *British Imperialism in the Nineteenth Century*, London: Macmillan: 88.
4   See Thompson, E. P., 1976 *William Morris*, New York: Pantheon: 479–81.
5   Gallagher, J. and Robinson, R., 1953 'The imperialism of free trade', *Economic History Review*.
6   Some historians now argue over the extent of the 'Great Depression' – see, for example, Bèdarida, F., 1979 *A Social History of England 1851–1975*, London: Methuen, chapter 4 – but though the depression may not have been universal (the ballad market thrived), it was of such concern to the government that they agreed to set up a Royal Commission to investigate the 'Depression of Trade and Industry' in 1885.
7   See Cunningham, H., 1971 'Jingoism in 1877–78', *Victorian Studies*, vol. 14: 429–53.
8   Pearsall cites (without evidence) the belief 'that Macdermott was in the pay of the Conservative Party, which was interested in meddling in that war.' See Pearsall 1973: 48.
9   A modern reprint of this song appears in Waites and Hunter 1984: 180.
10 See Lee 1970: 101.
11 The song may be found in Silber, I. (ed.), 1964 *Reprints from Sing Out!*, vol. 6, London: Music Sales Ltd: 8–9.
12 These comments appear on the back of 'Danny Deever', words by R. Kipling, music by W. Ward-Higgs, published by C. Sheard & Co., London and Boston, 1906.
13 See also Porter 1975: 136–7.
14 Gilbert Webb, F., 1890–1 'The foundations of national music', *RMA Proceedings*, vol. 17: 114.
15 Ibid., 121.
16 Ibid., 122.
17 Ibid., 122.
18 Ibid., 125.
19 Ibid., 133.

20 Bolt, C., 1984 'Race and the Victorians', in Eldridge, C. C. (ed.), 1984 *British Imperialism in the Nineteenth Century*, London: Macmillan: 147.

21 It was Spencer, not Darwin, who coined this phrase, in *Principles of Biology*, 1872, part 6, chapter 12, section 363.

22 The phrase used by the Earl of Carnarvon, addressing the Philosophical Institution in Edinburgh. An extract from his speech is given in Eldridge, C. C., 'Sinews of empire: changing perspectives', in Eldridge, op. cit., 185.

23 Rich, P., 1987 'The quest for Englishness', *History Today*, vol. 37, June: 29.

24 Newman, G., 1987 *The Rise of English Nationalism: a Cultural History 1740–1830*, London: Weidenfeld.

25 Stein, J. (ed.), 1909 *The Nation's Music*, London: Cassell. Preface and notes by R. J. Buckley, vol. I, *English*: 10.

26 Ibid., 12.

27 Anon., n.d. 'Foreword', *Orange Standard*, Glasgow: Mozart Allan.

28 Chappell, W., 1893 *Old English Popular Music*, ed. H. Ellis Wooldridge, New York: Jack Brussell, 1961: vi.

29 See Harker 1985: 155–6. Carl Engel is also relevant in this connection, too: see pp. 142–6.

30 Baring-Gould, S., 1925 *Further Reminiscences*, quoted in Mackerness 1964: 216.

31 Rich, P., op. cit., 25.

32 Hadden, J. C., n.d. (1890s) 'Our patriotic songs', *British Minstrelsie*, vol. 5, London: Blackwood, Le Bas: iv.

33 Ibid., v.

34 Ibid., v.

35 'A very perfect example of a folk-song', Sharp, C. J., 1919 *English Folk Songs*, London: Novello: xxii.

Chapter 9

1 Hobsbaum, E. J., 1969 *Bandits*, London: Weidenfeld and Nicolson: 30, footnote.

2 See ibid., 15. It is worth noting, too, that highwaymen had disappeared when the train replaced the coach as a means of transporting the Royal Mail in the late 1840s.

3 Ritchie 1858: 205.

4 Ibid., 207.

5 Bratton 1975: 30.

6 Mayhew 1861–2, vol. 3: 196.

7 Ibid., 196.

8 See Bratton 1975: 27. She mentions that ballads by Moore (especially 'The Last Rose of Summer') and arias by Balfe are found as broadsides.

9 *Music of the Streets*, Gloucester: Saydisc Records, 1983.

10 Haweis, H. R., *Music and Morals*, London: Longmans, Green and Co., 1871, reprinted 1912, p. 535.

11 Mayhew, op. cit., p. 175.

12 Haweis 1871: 538.

13 Military bands began to flourish after the founding of the Royal Military School of Music, Kneller Hall, in 1857.

14 Raynor, R., 1980 'London, §VI, 5: concert life – halls', in Sadie 1980, vol. II: 205.

15 Ritchie 1858: 198.

16 Taken from a quotation from the *Standard*, given in Lee 1970: 92.

17   The phrase may have gained currency via the 'cockney ballad' 'She Ain't No Airy Fairy', referred to in Disher 1955: 120.

18   Minutes of Evidence before the Select Committee on Dramatic Literature, 1832, *British Parliamentary Papers*, Irish University Press, 1977, *Stage and Theatre*, vol. I, 219, minute 3945.

19   Ibid., minute 3946.

20   Ibid., minute 4081.

21   Pearsall 1972: 74.

22   See sleeve notes to the album *Irish Songs of Rebellion*, The Clancy Brothers, Everest Tradition, 2070.

23   Unattrib., 1855 'Ballads of the people', *Westminster Review*, vol. 7 (N.S.): 37.

24   The original song, in its second edition of 1859, may be found in Jackson 1976: 93–6.

25   See Harker 1985: 193.

26   The song may be found in Richards, R. and Stubbs, T., 1979 *The English Folksinger*, Glasgow and London: Collins: 178–9.

27   The original song may be found in Wiley Hitchcock 1974: 91–4.

28   Joe Hill's song, published in the 3rd edn of the *IWW Songbook*, may be found in Collins, M., Harker, D., and White, G. (compilers), 1981 *The Big Red Songbook*, London: Pluto Press (enlarged ed.): 55 and 108.

29   The words of 'The Spinner's Ship' may be found in 'Ballads of the People', *Westminster Review*, vol. 7 (N.S.), 1855, 47–8.

30   'Strike for Better Wages' may be found in Richards and Stubbs, op. cit., 174–5; 'Tramp! Tramp! Tramp!' is fairly easily located, but a reprint of the original sheet music is in Jackson 1976: 214–17. The tune was also used by Clifton for *Work, Boys Work*.

31   The image of Joe Wilson as 'working-class hero' has taken a battering recently, however, in Harker, D., 'Joe Wilson: "Comic Dialectical Singer" or Class Traitor?' in Bratton 1986.

32   I have been unable to trace either the recording or the name of this singer whom I heard on the radio.

33   He recorded the song, slightly adapted from the original, on 8 August 1959; it was released on Columbia B-2155.

34   Manny Shinwell recollected that during his childhood in London's East End his mother's favourite song of optimism was this Balfe aria (BBC 1 Tribute, 8 May 1986, the day of his death).

35   See Fuld 1971: 630 and footnote.

36   See Hadden, J. C., n.d. (1890s) 'Our Patriotic Songs', in *British Minstrelsie*, vol. 5, London: Blackwood, Le Bas: v.

37   See Best 1979: 261.

38   Coleman, E. G., 1907: *The Temperance Songbook*, republished by Wolfe Publishing Ltd., London, 1972.

39   Marryat, Capt. F., *Mr. Midshipman Easy*, Chapter 36.

40   Rutherford, L., 1986 ' "Harmless nonesense": the comic sketch and the development of music-hall entertainment', in Bratton 1986.

41   Haweis 1871: 112.

42   Kingsley, C., 1852 *Sermons on National Subjects*, quoted in Norman, E. 1987 *The Victorian Christian Socialists*, Cambridge: Cambridge University Press: 38.

43   Quoted in Turner 1975: 73; the complete song is on pp. 71–3.

44   'Ballads of the People' op. cit., 44.

45   Ibid., 44.

46 See Ashraf, P. M., 1978 *Introduction to Working Class Literature in Great Britain*, Berlin: Humbolt University, Part I, *Poetry*: 153–4. Publication of enlarged edn. in US forthcoming.

47 *The Jacobite Rebellions*, London: Topic Records Ltd., 12T79, 1962, side I, band 8.

48 Arnold, M., 1869 *Culture and Anarchy*, chapter I, §25.

49 Unattrib., 1849 'On Musical Taste', *Eliza Cook's Journal*, vol. I: 278.

50 See Mackerness 1964: 148.

51 Ibid., 168.

52 Jullian, L., Hogarth, G., and Wills, W. H., 1850 'Music in humble life', in Dickens, C. (ed.), 1850 *Household Words*, vol. I: 161.

53 *Westminster Review*, vol. 35, 1841, 249–50.

54 Smiles, S., 1851–2 'Music in the home', *Eliza Cook's Journal*, vol. 6; 211.

55 See Mackerness 1964: 147–50.

56 Jullien, Hogarth, and Wills, op. cit., 163.

57 *Westminster Review*, vol. 46, 1847, 311.

58 H., 1849 'Notation of music', *Westminster Review*, vol. 50: 463.

59 For more information on the Sacred Harmonic Society, see Raynor, H., 'London, §VI, 3: concert life – choirs', in Sadie 1980: vol. II.

60 For more information on sight-singing in the nineteenth century, see Scholes 1947: vol. I, 1–19.

61 See 'Ideology and ideological state apparatuses', in Althusser, L., 1971 *Lenin and Philosophy and Other Essays*, London: New Left Books.

62 Leslie, H., 1885 'Music in England', *Macmillan's Magazine*, vol. 52: 250.

63 Ibid., 250.

64 Hill, A., 1888–9 'Rate-aided schools of music', *RMA Proceedings*, vol. 15: 134.

65 Ibid., 137.

66 See Browne, M. E., 1885–6 'Music in elementary schools', *RMA Proceedings*, vol. 12: 1 and 4.

67 Hadden, J. C., 1890–1 'The jubilee of tonic sol-fa', *Macmillan's Magazine*, vol. 63: 205.

68 Parker, L. N., 1893–4 'Music in our public schools', *RMA Proceedings*, vol. 20: 98.

69 Ibid., 101.

70 I am indebted for a list of song titles to Janet H. Bateson, a local historian working for the Workers' Educational Association in Yorkshire.

71 Browne, op. cit., 9.

72 Scholes 1947, vol. 2: 861.

73 Lee, 1970: 87.

74 Leslie, op. cit., 248.

75 Ibid., 248.

76 Ibid., 245.

Chapter 10

1 Shepherd 1982: 2.

2 Ibid., 23.

3 This song may be found in Turner and Miall 1972: 174–7.

4 'On the Banks of the Wabash' may be found in Turner and Miall 1975: 119–22, and 'The Pardon Came Too Late' may be found in Turner and Miall 1972: 322–4.

5 These songs may be found in Gammond 1983: 110–12 and 123–5.

6 A notable exception is 'The Volunteer Organist' of 1893 (words by W. B. Gray, music

by H. Lamb), where the tune of the 'Old Hundredth' serves as an accompaniment in the refrain.

7   This song is in Gammond 1983: 72–3, and Turner and Miall 1975: 214–17.

8   This song may be found in Turner and Miall 1975: 157–61.

9   This song may be found in Gammond 1983: 99–102.

10 J. F. Barnett speaking in the discussion following William H. Cummings' paper, 'Some observations on music in London in 1791 and 1891', *RMA Proceedings*, vol. 17, 1890–91, 173.

11 Cummings, op. cit., 170.

12 Quoted in Scholes 1947, vol. 2: 876.

13 Ibid., 876.

14 Ibid., 876.

15 See Mackerness 1964: 233.

16 Quoted in Ehrlich 1976: 92.

17 Cummings, W. H., 1896–7 'Music during the Queen's reign', *RMA Proceedings*, vol. 23: 144.

18 Ibid., 147–8.

19 Anon., 1895 'Poetry and music', *Macmillan's Magazine*, vol. 72: 102.

20 In 1887 J. L. Roeckel composed a cantata to words by F. E. Weatherly entitled 'The Victorian Age'.

21 Maclean, C., 1901–2 'Sullivan as a national style-builder', *RMA Proceedings*, vol. 28: 99.

22 See W. H. T., 1893 'On descriptive music (as illustrated by "The Golden Legend")', *Macmillan's Magazine*, vol. 68: 109–14.

23 Scholes 1947, vol. 2: 790.

24 See Murrells, J., 1984 *Million Selling Records*, London: Batsford Ltd: 64.

25 Disher, M. W., 1955 *Victorian Song*, London: Phoenix House: 239.

Glossary of Musical Terms
Used in the Text

Alberti bass	a stereotyped accompaniment taking its name from Domenico Alberti.
appoggiatura	a note dissonant with the chord (made consonant by moving up or down one step).
aria	a solo vocal air in opera, oratorio, or cantata.
arpeggio	a group of chord notes sounded in succession rather than simultaneously.
augmented chord	one containing a chromatic alteration (enlarging one of the chord's intervals by a semitone).
bar	a musical rhythmic measure (shown by a vertical line).
bel canto	the nineteenth-century Italian operatic style of singing.
blue note	a flattened 3rd, 7th, or even 5th note of the major scale (common in Afro-American music).
broken chord	see *arpeggio*.
call and response	musical phrases given by a soloist answered by a scrap of tune (usually unchanging) given by an ensemble (vocal or instrumental).
cantata	a short (often religious) piece for soloist(s) and (usually) chorus, with instrumental accompaniment.
canzonet	a 'little song' (from the Italian, *canzonetta*).
cell	a short, distinctive melodic and/or rhythmic grouping (like a motive).
chromaticism	the use of notes additional to those in the major or minor key in which the piece is set.
coda	a concluding section.
contrapuntal	two or more melodic lines woven together.
crescendo	growing louder.
diminished 7th	a chromatic chord not belonging to a specific key (often used for dramatic disorientating effect).
discord	a combination of notes which seem to clash and require resolution.
dissonance	the effect created by notes which seem to clash together.
dominant	the fifth note of a major or minor scale, the most important note in the tonal hierarchy after the tonic.
dominant extension	a chord formed on the fifth note of the major or minor scale which is given increased tension by adding dissonant notes (7th, 9th, etc.).

drone bass	an unchanging bass note or notes.
duple time/metre	two main beats per bar.
dynamic	the level of softness or loudness.
expression	'expressive' playing (Italian = *espressivo*) usually means adopting a certain amount of flexibility in relation to dynamics and rhythm; the tension created by the resulting unpredictability is felt to convey the player's personal emotion.
figure/figuration	a pattern of notes used repeatedly (generally as an accompaniment).
grace notes	musical ornaments which lend emphasis to the note they decorate.
gran scena	operatic set piece, usually for anguished *prima donna*.
grandioso	to be performed in a grand and dignified fashion.
hammered-on note	a note sounded on the guitar by hammering-on a finger of the left hand after the string has been picked by the right hand.
harmonic rhythm	the rate of change of harmonies (chords).
key (major/minor)	a concept reliant upon a hierarchy of notes (as in a major or minor scale). The first note of a major or minor scale gives its name to the key.
leading-note	the seventh note of a major or minor scale which leads back to the tonic.
major and minor	see key. The two important tonal scales.
mediant	the third note of a major or minor scale, or the key based on that note.
metre	the musical equivalent of the 'foot' in poetry.
modes	the old system of scales ousted by the 'invention' of keys in the seventeenth century.
modulation	a change from one key to another.
monotone	an unchanging pitch.
motive	a short, distinctive rhythmic and/or melodic pattern, offering possibilities for development.
musical phrase	a melodic unit which a singer would take in one breath.
octave	the interval stretching from first to eighth note of a major or minor scale (the notes being the same except for pitch).
opera seria	'serious opera' carrying high artistic status, established in the seventeenth century, and mostly filled with recitatives and arias sung by gods, goddesses, mythological heroes, etc.
oratorio	a large-scale work (usually religious) for soloists, chorus, and orchestra.
pasticcio	a freshly written stage work making use of pre-existing music by different composers.
pedal	a note (usually in the bass) sustained throughout changing harmonies.
pentatonic	music based on a scale of five notes (such as found in many traditional musical cultures).
phrase	see musical phrase.
pitch	the height or depth of a note.
recitative	a declamatory style of word-setting.
refrain	a recurring combination of words and tune.

relative minor	a minor key sharing the same key signature (i.e. having the same number of sharps or flats) as the major key being used.
rondo form	the use of a recurring tune, separated by contrasting musical episodes.
scale	a stepwise succession of notes.
semitone	the smallest interval between notes in western 'art music'.
'Scotch snap'	an accented short note followed by a longer note.
sonata form	a musical form based on a conflict of keys; since the nineteenth century its sections have been labelled 'exposition', 'development', and 'recapitulation'.
stops	devices to alter the sound of an organ or harmonium.
strophic setting	each verse set to the same tune.
style galant	a highly embellished 'courtly' style of eighteenth-century music.
syncopation	transference of musical accent from strong to weak beats.
tempo	overall speed
ternary form	a three-part form in which the third part repeats the first.
texture	the thinness or thickness of the sound.
through-composed	in the case of a song, different music for each verse; in the case of an opera, no spoken dialogue.
timbre	the 'colour' of the sound (e.g. a guitar playing the same note as a piano sounds different).
tonality	another word for key.
tonic	the first note of a major or minor scale, the key note.
transpose	change the overall pitch up or down.
tremolando	rapid repetitions of the same note (often used for dramatic effect).
triple time/metre	three beats per bar.
turn	a particular kind of musical ornament.

Select Discography

The World of Favourite Ballads, 1984 (Decca 411 642–1)
The Dicky Bird and the Owl, 1973 (EMI EMD 5509)
Give Me a Ticket to Heaven, 1976 (Argo ZFB 95–6)
Parlour Song Book, 1973 (Charisma CAS 1078)
Love's Old Sweet Song, 1978 (Argo ZK 45)
Songs by Stephen Foster, 1972 (Nonesuch H-71268)
Songs by Stephen Foster, vol. 2, 1976 (Nonesuch H-71333)
Music of the Streets, 1983 (Saydisc CSDL 340)
Beethoven: Irish & Scottish Folk Songs, 1970 (DG 2535 241)
Beethoven: Folksong Settings, 1977 (Nonesuch H-71340)
Songs of the Civil War Era (H. C. Work) 1975 (Nonesuch H-71317)
Keep the Home Fires Burning, 1986 (Saydisc CSDL 358)
The Golden Age of Ballads, 1987 (EMI TC-GX 2554)
A102 Summer School Cassette, 1988 (Open University)
Victorian Vocal Gems, 1985 (Available from Derek B. Scott)
Celebrated Victorian and Edwardian Ballads, 1988 (Available from Derek B. Scott)
Angels' Visits, 1977 (New World Recds NW 220)
The Jacobite Rebellions, 1962 (Topic 12T 79)
The Floral Dance, n.d., *c*.1983 (EMI ONCM 506)
The Great John McCormack, 1966 (EMI MFP 1090)
John McCormack, A Legendary Performer, 1977 (RCA RL 12472)
Love Songs (Stuart Burrows), 1971 (Decca SOL 324)

In addition, the lyric tenor Robert White has made several recordings of this material (e.g. RCA RL 01698).

Select Bibliography

Acland, A., 1948 *Caroline Norton*, London: Constable.

Best, G., 1979 *Mid-Victorian Britain 1851–75*, London: Fontana.

Boosey, W., 1931 *Fifty Years of Music*, London: Ernest Benn.

Boydell, B., 1979 *Four Centuries of Music in Ireland*, BBC Publications.

Bratton, J. S., 1975 *The Victorian Popular Ballad*, London: Macmillan.

Bratton, J. S. (ed.), 1986 *Music Hall: Performance and Style*, Milton Keynes: Open University Press.

Burney, C., 1789 *A General History of Music*, reprint of 1789 edition, New York: Dover Publications, 1957.

Bush, G. and Temperley, N., 1979 *English Songs 1800–1860, Musica Britannica*, Vol. 43, London: Stainer and Bell.

Chase, G., 1966 *American Music, from the Pilgrims to the Present*, New York: McGraw-Hill.

Coover, J. (ed.), 1985 *Music Publishing Copyright and Piracy in Victorian England*, London: Mansell Publishing.

Crawford, R. (ed.), 1977 *The Civil War Songbook*, New York: Dover Publications.

Dibdin, C., 1803 *The Professional Life of Mr Dibdin*, London.

Dictionary of National Biography, 1921–2, Oxford: Oxford University Press.

Disher, M. W., 1955 *Victorian Song*, London: Phoenix House.

Dunbar, J., 1953 *The Early Victorian Woman*, London: Harrap.

Ehrlich, C., 1976 *The Piano: A History*, London: Dent.

Fiske, R., 1973 *English Theatre Music in the Eighteenth Century*, Oxford: Oxford University Press.

Fiske, R., 1983 *Scotland in Music*, Cambridge: Cambridge University Press.

Foster, M., 1896 *Biography, Songs and Musical Compositions of Stephen C. Foster*, Pittsburgh.

Fuld, J. J., 1971 *The Book of World-Famous Music*, New York: Crown.

Gammond, P. (ed.), 1983 *The Good Old Days Songbook*, EMI Music Publishing.

Garrett, J. M. (ed.), 1976 *Sixty Years of British Music Hall*, London: Chappell.

Graves, R. (ed.), 1980 *A Victorian Christmas Song Book*, London: Macmillan.

Hanchant, W. L. (ed.), 1932 *Songs of the Affections by Thomas Haynes Bayly*, London: Desmond Harmsworth.

Harding, R. E. M., 1933 *The Pianoforte: Its History Traced to the Great Exhibition of 1851*, reprinted New York: Da Capo Press, 1973.

Harker, D., 1985 *Fakesong*, Milton Keynes: Open University Press.

Haweis, H. R., 1871 *Music and Morals*, reprint of 1871 edn, London: Longmans, Green, 1912.

Hogarth, G. (ed.), 1842 *The Songs of Charles Dibdin*, London: Davidson.

Jackson, G. P., 1943 *White and Negro Spirituals*, reprint of 1943 edn, New York: Da Capo Press, 1975.

Jackson, R. (ed.), 1974 *Stephen Foster Song Book*, New York: Dover Publications.

Jackson, R. (ed.), 1976 *Popular Songs of Nineteenth-Century America*, New York: Dover Publications.

Laurence, D. H. (ed.), 1981 *Shaw's Music*, 3 vols., London: Bodley Head.

Lee, E., 1970 *Music of the People*, London: Barrie and Jenkins.

Lunn, H. C., 1854 *Musings of a Musician*, London: Robert Cocks.

Mackerness, E. D., 1964 *A Social History of English Music*, London: Routledge & Kegan Paul.

Mair, C., 1961 *The Chappell Story*, London: Chappell.

Marsh, J. B. T., 1899 *The Story of the Jubilee Singers*, London: Hodder and Stoughton.

Marx, K. and Engels, F., 1975 *Articles on Britain*, Moscow: Progress Publishers.

Mayhew, H., 1861–2 *London Labour and the London Poor*, reprint of enlarged edn of 1861–2, London: Frank Cass, 1967.

Nettel, R., 1956 *Seven Centuries of Popular Song*, London: Phoenix House.

Pearce, C. E., 1924 *Sims Reeves*, London: Stanley Paul.

Pearsall, R., 1972 *Victorian Sheet Music Covers*, Newton Abbot: David & Charles.

Pearsall, R., 1973 *Victorian Popular Music*, Newton Abbot: David & Charles.

Porter, B., 1975 *The Lion's Share*, London: Longman.

Ritchie, J. E., 1858 *The Night Side of London*, London: William Tweedie (2nd edn).

Russell, D., 1987 *Popular Music in England 1840–1914*, Manchester: University of Manchester Press.

Russell, H., 1895 *Cheer, Boys, Cheer!*, London: John Macqueen.

Sadie, S. (ed.), 1980 *The New Grove Dictionary of Music and Musicians*, London: Macmillan.

Scholes, P. A., 1947 *The Mirror of Music*, 2 vols., London: Novello and Oxford University Press.

Shepherd, J., 1982 *Tin Pan Alley*, London: Routledge & Kegan Paul.

Simpson, H., 1910 *A Century of Ballads*, London: Mills & Boon.

Temperley, N. (ed.), 1981 *The Romantic Age 1800–1914*, London: The Athlone Press.

Temperley, N. (ed.), 1986 'Music in Victorian society and culture', *Victorian Studies*, special issue Autumn, Indiana University.

Thompson, E. P., 1968 *The Making of the English Working Class*, Harmondsworth: Penguin Books, new edn 1980.

Toll, R. C., 1974 *Blacking Up: The Minstrel Show in Nineteenth-Century America*, New York: Oxford University Press.

Turner, M. R. and Miall, A. (eds.), 1972 *The Parlour Song Book*, London: Michael Joseph.

Turner, M. R. and Miall, A. (eds.), 1975 *Just a Song at Twilight*, London: Michael Joseph.

Vicinus, M. (ed.), 1980 *Suffer and Be Still*, London: Methuen.

Waites, A. and Hunter, R., 1984 *The Illustrated Victorian Songbook*, London: Michael Joseph.

Wallace, I. (compiler), 1981 *The EMI Book of Parlour Songs*, London: EMI Publishing.

White, E. W., 1951 *The Rise of English Opera*, London: John Lehmann.

Wiley Hitchcock, H. (ed.), 1974 *Songs of Henry Clay Work*, Earlier American Music, 19, New York: Da Capo Press.

Williams, R., 1963 *Culture and Society*, Harmondsworth: Penguin.

Wittke, C., 1930 *Tambo and Bones*, reprint of 1930 edn, Westport, Connecticut: Greenwood Press, 1968.

Young, K., 1968 *Music's Great Days in the Spas*, London: Macmillan.

Young, P. M., 1971 *Sir Arthur Sullivan*, London: Dent.

Song Index

a = arranged *m* = music *p* = published *w* = words
NB Dates of hymns refer to words only, since several settings are common. Where there is a well-known musical setting to which the words are almost always sung, the information concerning it is given in brackets. Elsewhere, the date which follows the song title refers to its musical composition or first publication.

Abide with Me (1847), *w* H. Lyte (*p* 1850) (*m* W. Monk, *p* 1861), 110
Absalom (1868), *w* Bible, *m* M. Lindsay, 79, 108
Afloat (1886), *w* & *m* M. Watson, 168
After the Ball (1892), *w* & *m* C. Harris, 198, 205
Ah! Sim Papilio (*c.* 1830), *w* T. Bayly, *trans.* Archdeacon Wrangham, *m* T. Bayly, 37
Ain't She Sweet (1927), *w* J. Yellen, *m* M. Ager, 199
Alas! Those Chimes So Sweetly Stealing (1845), *w* E. Fitzball, *m* W. Wallace, 18
Alexander's Ragtime Band (1911), *w* & *m* I. Berlin, 200
Alice, Where Art Thou? (1861), *w* W. Guernsey, *m* J. Ascher, 78, 134, 141
All People That on Earth Do Dwell, see *The Old Hundredth*
All Things Bright and Beautiful (1848), *w* C. Alexander (*m* W. Monk, *p* 1887), 189
All Through the Night, see *Ar Hyd y Nos*
All's Well (1803), *w* T. Dibdin, *m* J. Braham, 8
Alone (?), *w* unattributed, *m* V. Gabriel, 71, 79
Am I a Soldier of the Cross? (1724), *w* I. Watts (hymn), 113
Anchored (1883), *w* S. Cowan, *m* M. Watson, 117, 168
Anchored Soul, The (1873), *w* W. Cushing, *m* R. Lowry, 117
Anchor's Weigh'd, The (1811), *w* S. J. Arnold, *m* J. Braham, 8
Anchorsmiths, The (1798), *w* & *m* C. Dibdin, 34
Angels Ever Bright and Fair (1750), *w* T. Morell, *m* G. Handel, 106
Annie Laurie (1838), *w* & *m* A. Scott, *a* F. Dun, 96–7
An-t-Eilean Muileach (?), *w* D. MacPhail, *m* anon., 97
Ar Hyd y Nos (?), *w* & *m* anon., 101
Arab's Farewell to His Favourite Steed, The (*c.* 1865), *w* C. Norton, *m* J. Blockley, 66
Army of To-Day's All Right, The (1914), *w* F. Leigh, *m* K. Lyle, 173
Arrow and the Song, The (1856), *w* H. Longfellow, *m* M. Balfe, 22
As Slow Our Ship (*c.* 1815), *w* T. Moore, *m* anon., *a* J. Stevenson, 25
At the Mid Hour of Night (1813), *w* T. Moore, *m* anon., *a* J. Stevenson, 25
Auld Lang Syne (1796), *w* R. Burns (*after* A. Ramsay), *modern tune adapted from* W. Shield, 7, 23, 177, 196
Auld Robin Gray (1812), *w* A. Lindsay (1771), *m* W. Leeves, 32, 95–6
Auntie (*c.* 1880), *w* F. Weatherly, *m* A. Behrend, 78, 167
Ave Maria (*c.* 1842), *m* F. Schubert, see *Ellen's Hymn! Ave Maria!*
    (1857), *m* V. Gabriel, 71, 118
    (1859), *m* J. S. Bach and C. Gounod, 118
Avenging and Bright (1811), *w* T. Moore, *m* anon., *a* J. Stevenson, 26, 30

Bandit's Life Is the Life for Me, A (1872), *w* & *m* E. Harper, 182
Battle Hymn of the Republic (1862), *w* J. Ward Howe, *m* anon., 113
Bay of Biscay, The (*c.* 1806), *w* A. Cherry, *m* J. Davy, 128
Be a Butterfly Then! (*c.* 1830), *w* (& *m*?) T. Bayly, 37
Bear It Like a Man (*c.* 1865), *w* & *m* H. Clifton (*a* M. Hobson?), 183

General Index

Abel, J., 57
Aberdeen, 123
abolition of the slave trade, 83
Abt, F., 66, 110
Ackerman, R., 52
Act of Proscription (1745), 23
Act of Union (1707), 22
Act of Union (1800), 25
Adams, S. (Michael Maybrick), 119, 130–1, 157–68
Africa, 81, 83–5, 92, 169
African Theatre (NY), 89
agencies, 131–2
Airs Peculiar to the Scottish Highlands, 97
Aladdin, 43
Albani, M., 15
Album of Miss M. Lindsay's Songs, 66
Albyn's Anthology, 97
Alcina, 11
alehouses, 44
Alexander, C., 112, 119, 189
All Hail the Glorious Reign, 203
Allitsen, F., 63
American Missionary Association, 116
American organ, 59
American Tract Society, 112
Americans, The, 8
Amoroso, King of Little Britain, 43
Anacreontic Society, 44
Anderson, L., 69
Anne, Queen, 24
aquadrama, 43
Arab airs, 105–6
Arkwright, R., 3
Armstrong, H., 199
Arne, T., 5–6, 17, 42–3
Arnold, M., 193
Arnold, S., 6, 41, 52
Arnold, S. J., 8, 17
Artaxerxes, 17
Arundel Castle, 87
Ascher, J., 134, 141
Ascherberg, *see* Hopwood & Crew
Associated Board of the Royal Schools of Music, 202
Athalie, 196
Augener, 52, 132
Austen, F., 5
Austen, J., 64
Awakening Conscience, The, front cover, 26, 61

Bach (J.C.) and Abel, 34, 41–2
Bach, J. S., 118, 123
Badarzewska, T., 79
Baillie, J., 93, 101
Balfe, M., 8, 16–22, 67, 92, 101, 122, 127, 138–41, 188
Ballad Concerts (Boosey's), xi–xii, 74, 119, 122–3, 128, 141, 152, 157, 200, 202, 205
ballad concerts (others), 120, 128, 141
Ballads Sung By Mr Dibdin at Ranelagh Gardens, The, 42
Baltimore, 58
banjo (5-string), xv, 82, 86–7, 91–2
Banjo Tutor and Banjo Songs, 92
Banner of St George, The, 203
Barber of Seville, The, 21
Baring-Gould, S., 177, 189
Baritone's Song Folio, 79
Barker, G., 100
Barnard, Lady A., *see* Lindsay, A.

Barnard, C. Alington, *see* Claribel
Barnett, J., 17
Barnett, J. F., 201
Barnum, 88
Barrack-Room Ballads, 172–3, 203
Barri, O., 167
Bath, 36, 123, 130
Battle March of Delhi, The, 177
Battle of Sobraon, The, 177
Bayly, T., 11, 35–8, 52, 54, 60, 86, 94, 108, 202
Beecher Stowe, H., 39
Beethoven, 21, 28–31, 101, 155, 192–3
Beggar's Opera, The, xiv–xv, 1–2, 4–6, 18, 42, 87
Beggar's Wedding, The, 5
Behrend, A., 167
Belfast, 25, 40
Belfast Harp Festival, 25
Belle of New York, The, 203
Bellini, V., 16, 21, 38
Benedict, J., 22, 101
Bennett, W. Sterndale, 62–3
Benson, A., 171
Berlioz, H., 100
Bevan, C., 49
Beverley, Bewick, 177
Bickerstaffe, I., 6, 32
bicycle, 201–2
Bijou Operetta Company, 69
Bingham, C., 203
Bingley and Strange, 54
Birmingham Triennial Festival, 106, 120
Bishop, H., xi, 5, 11–16, 31, 42, 44, 52, 74, 134, 141
Black Dyke Mills Band, 193
black-minstrel troupes, 89
blackface minstrelsy, xi, 60, 82–92, 101, 113–14, 117, 125, 130, 177, 183, 186, 196, 198–9
Blackie, J., 98
Blackwood, H. (Lady Dufferin), 100–1
Blamire, S., 65, 93, 95
Bland, J., 89
Blewitt, J., 62
Bliss, P., 113–15, 117
Blockley, J., 55, 119, 168, 171, 188–9
Bloomsbury, 44
Boer War, 201, 203
Bohee, J., 92
Bohemian Girl, The, 16, 18–21, 122
Bolden, Buddy, 188
Bond Street, 132
Bononcini, G., 1, 5
Boosey & Co. (*see also* ballad concerts), xi, 70–1, 74–5, 112, 118, 122–4, 126–7, 132, 141–2, 148, 151, 155, 157, 160, 169, 202, 204
Booth, General W., 115
Boston, 58, 82, 113, 185
Boswell, A., 93
Boucicault, D., 101
Boyhood of Raleigh, The, 178
Bradford, 120
Braham, D., 199
Braham, J., 8–10, 18, 52, 130–1, 176
Brahms, J., 201
brass bands, 193–4
brass instruments, 49, 110, 123–4
Brecht, B., 5
Bremmer (publisher), 123
Bridal Polka, The, 79